RECREATIONAL LAKES

OF ARIZONA

by: J. Reinhardt & Collaborators

Sunflower Sales
P.O. Box 50328
Phoenix, AZ 85076-0328
(602) 893-6092

Premier Edition

ISBN 0-9639649-0-9

INTRODUCTION

Recreational Lakes of Arizona is intended to aid and facilitate the recreational user of Arizona's inland lakes. This lakes guide describes those lakes (120 plus) which are routinely usable for recreational purposes. Surprisingly, there are in excess of 1250 lakes within Arizona, most of them dry year-to-year or within a given year. The range of lakes extends from the giants of Roosevelt and San Carlos (tens of thousands of acres of water) to the little guys (one and two acres). This book speaks to private and public lakes, "metropolitan" to remote lakes, desert to high-mountain lakes. The **fisherperson, water skier, sailor, picnicker, camper/RVer, hiker/back packer, canoer, equestrian, cycler, hunter/trapper, swimmer, jet skier, power boater,** and **photographer,** will each find value within this publication.

Families, singles, able-bodied, handicapped, young, seniors, residents and **visitor's** interests have been considered. We trust this book serves you well. As any travel or recreational guide is obsolete the moment it is printed; this book is no different. Things change, mostly for the better. We trust you will utilize this guide as it was intended; to enhance your outdoor recreation use of Arizona's superb recreational lakes. There are many other fine publications which will assist you in enjoying Arizona. They are published by both private and public concerns. Please refer to the "Facts, Hints, and Recommendations" section of this book; you are encouraged to acquire them. Many are free. Above all, please remember the most important recreational rule -- **Safety First**. Enjoy, Enjoy!

Information contained herein are presented when the lakes are at full capacity.

Climate/weather conditions must be considered.

All fees and information are subject to change.

Maps are not to scale and should be used in conjunction with current detailed road maps.

Credit/Acknowledgments:

An immeasurable amount of thanks and gratitude are owed to Ginger Reinhardt and Steve Hudnall. This book was possible only due to their skills and determination. Many thanks to my family and friends who encouraged and facilitated this book. Thanks also to the custodians of the lakes who aided in this book's compilation.

Printed by Griffin Printing; Penny Hancock
Sacramento, Ca.

TABLE OF CONTENTS

Page

☐ How to Use This Book------------------------------------ A
☐ Arizona Lake Locator------------------------------------ B
☐ White Mountain Lake Locator --------------------------- C
☐ Lake Index (alphabetical) ------------------------------ D
☐ Lake Index (numerical)) -------------------------------- E
☐ Lake Detail Pages with Maps ------------------------ 1-99
☐ Facts, Hints, Recommendations------------------100-103
☐ San Carlos Apache Reservation -----------------104-105
☐ White Mountain Apache Reservation ---------------- 106
☐ Navajo Nation -- 107
☐ Arizona State Parks ---------------------------------- 108
☐ U.S. National Forests (Forest Service) -----------109-110
☐ Boat Motor Restrictions------------------------------ 111
☐ Where to Fish for What in Arizona------------------ 112
☐ Mileage Index-- 113

Order Form				
	Price	Sales Tax	Quantity	Total Amount
Recreational Lakes of Arizona	$15.95 +	$1.08 x	_____ =	_____

Shipping costs are included in the above price.
Please enclose check or money order.

Name: _____

Address: _____

City, State: _____

Zip: _____

Remit to:

Sunflower Sales
P.O. Box 50328
Phoenix, AZ
85076-0328

Your order will be shipped out the same day your payment is received.

HOW TO USE THIS BOOK

This book is very simple to use. There are a variety of methods by which you can "source" a lake. The simplest method is to know a lake name, look it up in the index alphabetically and then go to the page number specified. Another method is to scan the locator map, choose a lake based on its geographical location, then using the alphabetized index, look up the lake on the corresponding page number. If you're concerned about "boat motor restrictions" or "where to fish for what", review those pages. Obtain the name of the lake, then go to the alphabetized index and look up the page number. Geographical location and the numbered sequence of the lakes in the book are very close. Once you've found a lake you're interested in, review the pages just preceding it or following it and you'll find lakes in the immediate vicinity. Once you've found the lake you're interested in, there is a significant amount of data, facts, and hints for you to ponder. All the written text is self-explanatory. Likely the map will be the only "tricky" part. The shape of the lake is depicted on the page. Relative to itself, the lake **is** to scale. The access roads to the lake are **not** to scale. We have therefore included mile markers and distances between certain points. At the top of each page, there is a paragraph explaining many attributes of the lake. The last portion of each paragraph gives a verbal description on where the lake is located and how to get there. Roads, towns, and distances are specified. It is very important that you use an Arizona highway map in conjunction with this book. Better yet, a regional map such as a forest service map which shows significant detail. The elevation, depth, surface area and shoreline length are specified in a small box in the map section of the page. The symbols on the maps are commonly used by map makers. Parking locations, boat launch ramps, camping areas, stores, marinas, picnic tables, rest rooms, showers, potable water, and first aid stations are routinely identified. Given the smallishness of the map they are not always precisely located, but they are more than adequate. You will find with some frequency the telephone numbers of various private enterprises in the miscellaneous section at the bottom of the page. At the very bottom of the page you'll find the telephone number of the responsible agency if it is a public lake, or owner/concessionaire if private enterprise is involved. These phone numbers at the bottom of the page are the next best source of detailed information about the lake. Generally, the individual at the other end of these phone numbers is very helpful. As you use this book, it will become easier and easier. It has been compiled in a fashion that is relatively simple-minded, primarily because the author is. As you visit these lakes, you may discover something that has been omitted or is in error; please correct us via a note you may drop in the mailbox or a telephone call, collect of course. Please enjoy this book, make good use of it. We would appreciate any ideas on how to enhance this book. Again, just drop us a line. Our intent is to update it routinely. Toward the end of the book you will find sections on the Arizona State Park System, National Forests, the White Mountain Apache Indian Reservation, the San Carlos Apache Indian Reservation, and the Navajo Nation. These pages have both general and specific information about recreational activities on the lands and lakes managed by those agencies. The information presented here is a condensed version of free publications you can obtain from those agencies. And finally, it is suggested that you review the "Facts, Hints, and Recommendations" section in this book. We believe that by closely following these recommendations you will markedly enhance your outdoor recreation.

A special acknowledgment is due to the Arizona Game and Fish Department for their allowing us to print their "Urban Lake" material as they have written it. These lakes are on pages 94 through 99. Game and Fish.... - "Thank you so much."

Arizona Lake Locator

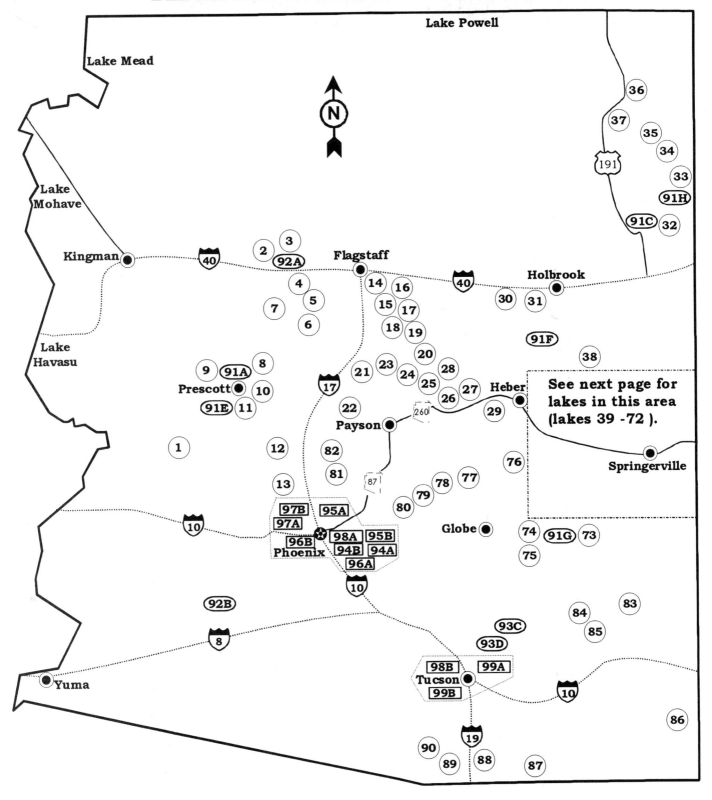

Use this map and the White Mountain map on the following page to locate a lake or set of lakes geographically. The numbers on this map match page numbers for lakes in this book.

B

White Mountain Lake Locator

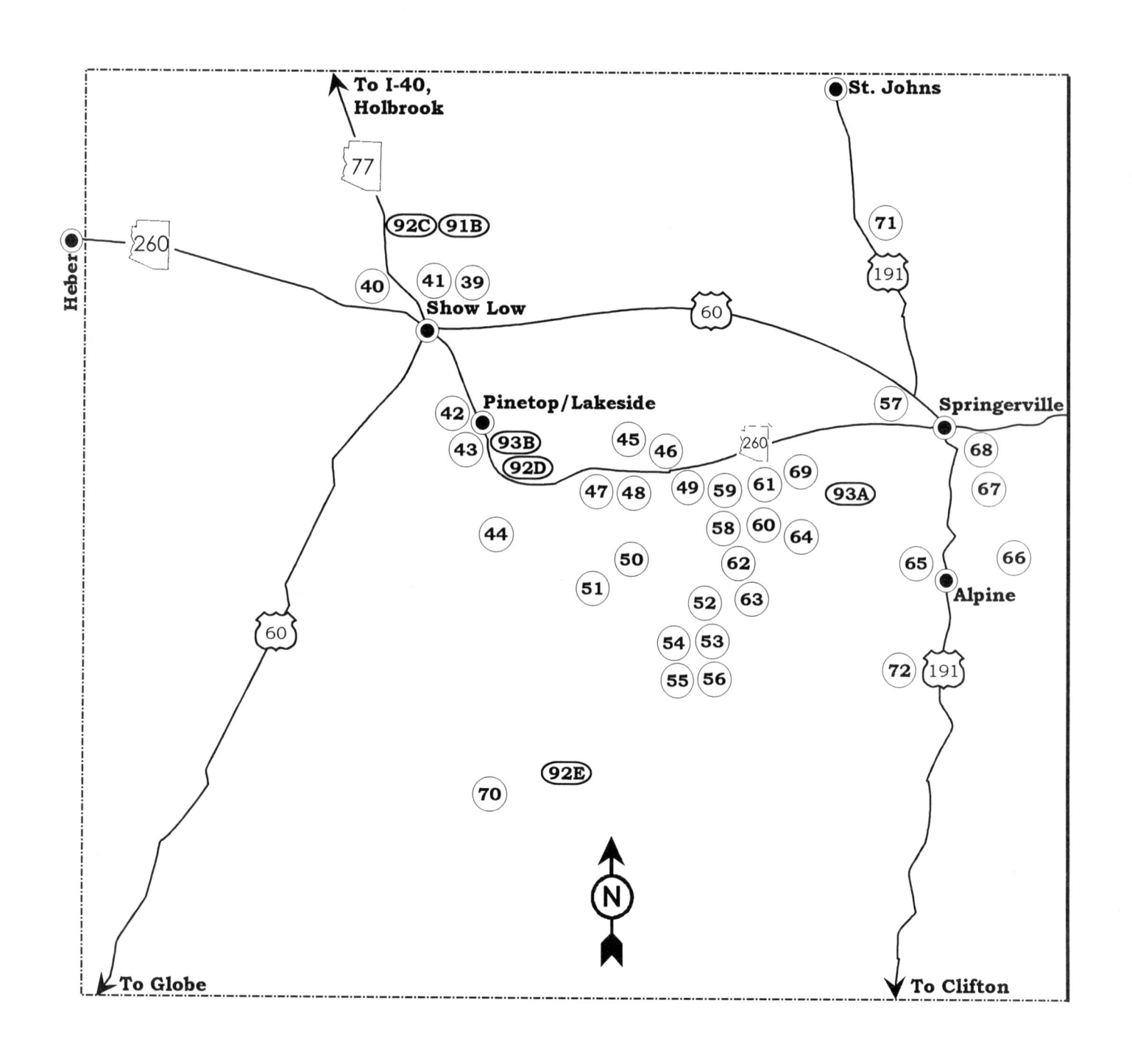

(Insert from previous page)

A

A-1 Lake 48
Ackre Lake 72
Alamo Lake 1
Alvord Lake 96B
Antelope Lake 32
Apache Lake 78
Arivaca Lake 90
Ashurst Lake 17

B

Bartlett Lake 81
Bear Canyon Lake 25
Becker Lake 57
Big Lake 63
Bill's Lake 92C
Black Canyon Lake 29
Blue Ridge Reservoir 23
Boot Leg Lake 64
Bunch Reservoir 61

C

Canal Lake 94B
Canyon Lake 79
Cataract Lake 2
Chaparral Park Lake 94A
Chevelon Canyon Lake 28
Cholla Lake 31
Christmas Tree Lake 51
Clear Creek Reservoir 91D
Concho Lake 38
Cooley Lake 44
Cortez Lake 97A
Colter Reservoir 60
Crescent Lake 62
Cyclone Lake 47

D

Dankworth Pond 83
Desert Breeze Lake 96A
Dog Town Reservoir 4
Drift Fence Lake 54
Dry Lake (#1) 91F
Dry Lake (#2) 91G

E

Earl Park Lake 50
Encanto Lake 97B

F

Fool Hollow Lake 40
Fred's Lake 92D

G

Ganado Lake 91C
George's Lake 70
Granite Basin Lake 9

H

Hawley Lake 50
Horseshoe Cienega Lake 49
Horseshoe Lake 82
Horsethief Basin Lake 12
Hulsey Lake 67
Hurricane Lake 55

J

J.D. Dam Lake 6

K

Kaibab Lake 3
Kennedy Lake 99B
Kinnikinick Lake 19
Kiwanis Lake 95A
Knoll Lake 24

L

Lake of the Woods 93B
Lake Pleasant 13
Lake Sierra Blanca 65
Lakeside Lake 99A
Lee Valley Lake 58
Little Hell's Canyon Lake 7
Little Mormon Lake 39
Long Lake (#1) 39
Long Lake (#2) 20
Lower Goldwater Lake 91E
Lower Lake Mary 14
Luna Lake 66
Lyman Lake 71
Lynx Lake 10

M

Many Farms Lake 37
Marshall Lake 16
Meadows Lake 93A
McHood Park Lake 30
Mexican Hay Lake 69
Mormon Lake 18
Morton Lake 19

N

Nash Tank 92E
Nelson Reservoir 68

P

Pacheta Lake 53
Painted Rock 92B
Papago Pond 98A
Parker Canyon Lake 87
Patagonia Lake 88
Pena Blanca Lake 89
Point of Pines Lake 73

R

Rainbow Lake 42
Red Lake (#1) 33
Red Lake (#2) 92A
Reservation Lake 52
Riggs Flat Lake 84
River Reservoir 61
Riverview Lake 95B
Roosevelt Lake 77
Roper Lake 83
Rose Canyon Lake 93C
Round Rock Reservoir 36
Rucker Canyon Lake 86

S

Sabino Lake 93D
Saguaro Lake 80
San Carlos Lake 75
Seneca Lake 76
Show Low Lake 41
Shush Be Tou Lake 45
Shush Be Zahze Lake 46
Silverbell Lake 98B
Snow Flat Lake 85
Soldier Annex Lake 20
Soldier Lake 20
Stehr Lake 22
Stoneman Lake 21
Sunrise Lake 59

T

Talkalai Lake 74
Tonto Lake 56
Trout Lake 91H
Tsaile Lake 35
Tunnel Reservoir 61

U

Upper Goldwater Lake 11
Upper Lake Mary 15

W

Watson Lake Park 8
Wheatfields Lake 34
Whipple Lake 39
White Horse Lake 5
White Mountain Lake 91B
Willow Lake 91A
Willow Springs Lake 27
Woodland Reservoir 43
Woods Canyon Lake 26

LAKE INDEX (NUMERICAL)

Alamo Lake 1
Cataract Lake 2
Kaibab Lake 3
Dog Town Reservoir 4
White Horse Lake 5
J.D. Dam Lake 6
Little Hell's Canyon Lake 7
Watson Lake Park 8
Granite Basin Lake 9

Lynx Lake 10
Upper Goldwater Lake 11
Horsethief Basin Lake 12
Lake Pleasant 13
Lower Lake Mary 14
Upper Lake Mary 15
Marshall Lake 16
Ashurst Lake 17
Mormon Lake 18
Kinnikinick Lake 19
Morton Lake 19

Long Lake (#2) 20
Soldier Annex Lake 20
Soldier Lake 20
Stoneman Lake 21
Stehr Lake 22
Blue Ridge Reservoir 23
Knoll Lake 24
Bear Canyon Lake 25
Woods Canyon Lake 26
Willow Springs Lake, ... 27
Chevelon Canyon Lake 28
Black Canyon Lake 29

McHood Park Lake 30
Cholla Lake 31
Antelope Lake 32
Red Lake (#1) 33
Wheatfields Lake 34
Tsaile Lake 35
Round Rock Reservoir 36
Many Farms Lake 37
Concho Lake 38
Little Mormon Lake 39
Long Lake (#1) 39
Whipple Lake 39

Fool Hollow Lake 40
Show Low Lake 41
Rainbow Lake 42
Woodland Reservoir 43
Cooley Lake 44
Shush Be Tou Lake 45
Shush Be Zahze Lake 46
Cyclone Lake 47
A-1 Lake 48
Horseshoe Cienega Lake ... 49

Earl Park Lake 50
Hawley Lake 50
Christmas Tree Lake 51
Reservation Lake 52
Pacheta Lake 53
Drift Fence Lake 54
Hurricane Lake 55
Tonto Lake 56
Becker Lake 57
Lee Valley Lake 58
Sunrise Lake 59

Colter Reservoir 60
Bunch Reservoir 61
River Reservoir 61
Tunnel Reservoir 61
Crescent Lake 62
Big Lake 63
Boot Leg Lake 64
Lake Sierra Blanca 65
Luna Lake 66
Hulsey Lake 67
Nelson Reservoir 68
Mexican Hay Lake 69

George's Lake 70
Lyman Lake 71
Ackre Lake 72
Point of Pines Lake 73
Talkalai Lake 74
San Carlos Lake 75
Seneca Lake 76
Roosevelt Lake 77
Apache Lake 78
Canyon Lake 79

Saguaro Lake 80
Bartlett Lake 81
Horseshoe Lake 82
Dankworth Pond 83
Roper Lake 83
Riggs Flat Lake 84
Snow Flat Lake 85
Rucker Canyon Lake 86
Parker Canyon Lake 87
Patagonia Lake 88
Pena Blanca Lake 89

Arivaca Lake 90
Willow Lake 91A
White Mountain Lake, ... 91B
Ganado Lake, ... 91C
Clear Creek Reservoir 91D
Lower Goldwater Lake 91E
Dry Lake (#1) 91F
Dry Lake (#2) 91G
Trout Lake 91H

Red Lake (#2) 92A
Painted Rock 92B
Bill's Lake 92C
Fred's Lake 92D
Nash Tank 92E

Meadows Lake 93A
Lake of the Woods 93B
Rose Canyon Lake 93C
Sabino Lake 93D

Chaparral Park Lake 94A
Canal Lake 94B
Kiwanis Lake 95A
Riverview Lake 95B
Desert Breeze Lake 96A
Alvord Lake 96B
Cortez Lake 97A
Encanto Lake 97B
Papago Pond 98A
Silverbell Lake 98B
Lakeside Lake 99A
Kennedy Lake 99B

At 1150-foot elevation, Alamo Lake is located in west central Arizona, just 35 miles from the California border. Contained within Alamo Lake State Park, this reservoir receives the runoff of over 4700 square miles into the Bill Williams River. Alamo Lake serves a wide variety of recreational users and has some excellent facilities. Alamo Lake is well know throughout the Southwest as an excellent largemouth bass producer. All boating activities are allowed on this 3200-acre beauty, but the "fisher-people" dominate in numbers. Camping facilities are superb ranging from sites with full RV hookups to standard developed sites to primitive camping. Camping/RVing facilities are located away from the shoreline due to fluctuating lake levels. There have been occasions when the level of the lake has risen 11 vertical feet overnight. The hikers and horseback rider have a wide ranging pristine landscape to explore. The summer months at Alamo Lake are hot, hot, hot. There is minimal shade around the lake. Winters offer Arizona's best weather. Desert wildlife abound with fox, coyote, mule deer, wild burros (lots of these guys), desert bighorn sheep, and an eagle or two. Virtually any recreational activity is available to park users. Alamo Lake State Park has a friendly, competent, and helpful staff not surpassed in the State Park System. There is a small store within the park which offers minimal conveniences but does rent boats. Some conveniences are also available at the Wayside Inn located 7.5 miles from the park entrance. The sign is obvious on the way to the park. Access to Alamo Lake is simple. The spring time trip can be particularly enjoyable with the wild flowers in bloom. Access can be from the north coming off I-40 either side of Kingman. This route requires up to 60 miles of dirt road and gets you to the north side of the lake. From the south/east proceed north from Wenden on US Highway 60 for 38 miles on Alamo Lake Road which is adequately marked in town. Wenden resides 50 miles west of Wickenberg. If you're staying at Alamo State Park for a while, there are some great day trips to be had, particularly west along the Colorado River.

See map, next page

CAMPING/RVING	RECREATION	BOATING	MISCELLANEOUS
Tents/Trailers/RVs -18 sites with full RV hookup $12/night -40 sites with water and electricity $12/night -150 developed sites $7/night -tables, grills -ramadas -dump station -drinking water -showers -no reservations accepted -developed campsites are not at shoreline due to fluctuating lake levels -boat camping -primitive camping allowed at various locations around lake -hunt, bring in your firewood -Wayside Inn (RV hookups) located 7.5 miles from lake (propane, cafe, gasoline)	-picnicking -swimming (no beaches) -hiking, rock hounding -horseback riding -sail boarding -sailing, canoeing -jet skiing, water skiing -playground -fishing: largemouth bass (slot limit applies), catfish, bluegill -shore fishing -fish cleaning station -no ATC/ATVs -day-use fee $3/vehicle	-3 improved launch ramps -no motor restrictions -heavy brush in some areas of the lake -lake levels can vary significantly over night -fishing tournaments are common; but no tournaments on the first weekend of each month or on holiday weekends -$3 day-use fee covers boat launch -boat battery charging station (bring your own charger and padlock) -boat/motor rental by the hour or by the day - call 949-7904 for details NOTE: Watercraft are prohibited from entering certain posted areas of Alamo Lake from December 1 until the end of water fowl season	-Convenience store: bait, fishing tackle, licenses, ice, camping supplies, limited groceries, snacks, boat rentals -no gasoline -no propane -no telephone -Ranger Station/first aid at lake -nearest town is Wenden, 38 miles PERMITS AND FEES: SEE SECTION ON ARIZONA STATE PARKS CONTAINED WITHIN THIS BOOK
Information: Alamo Lake State Park (602) 669-2088			

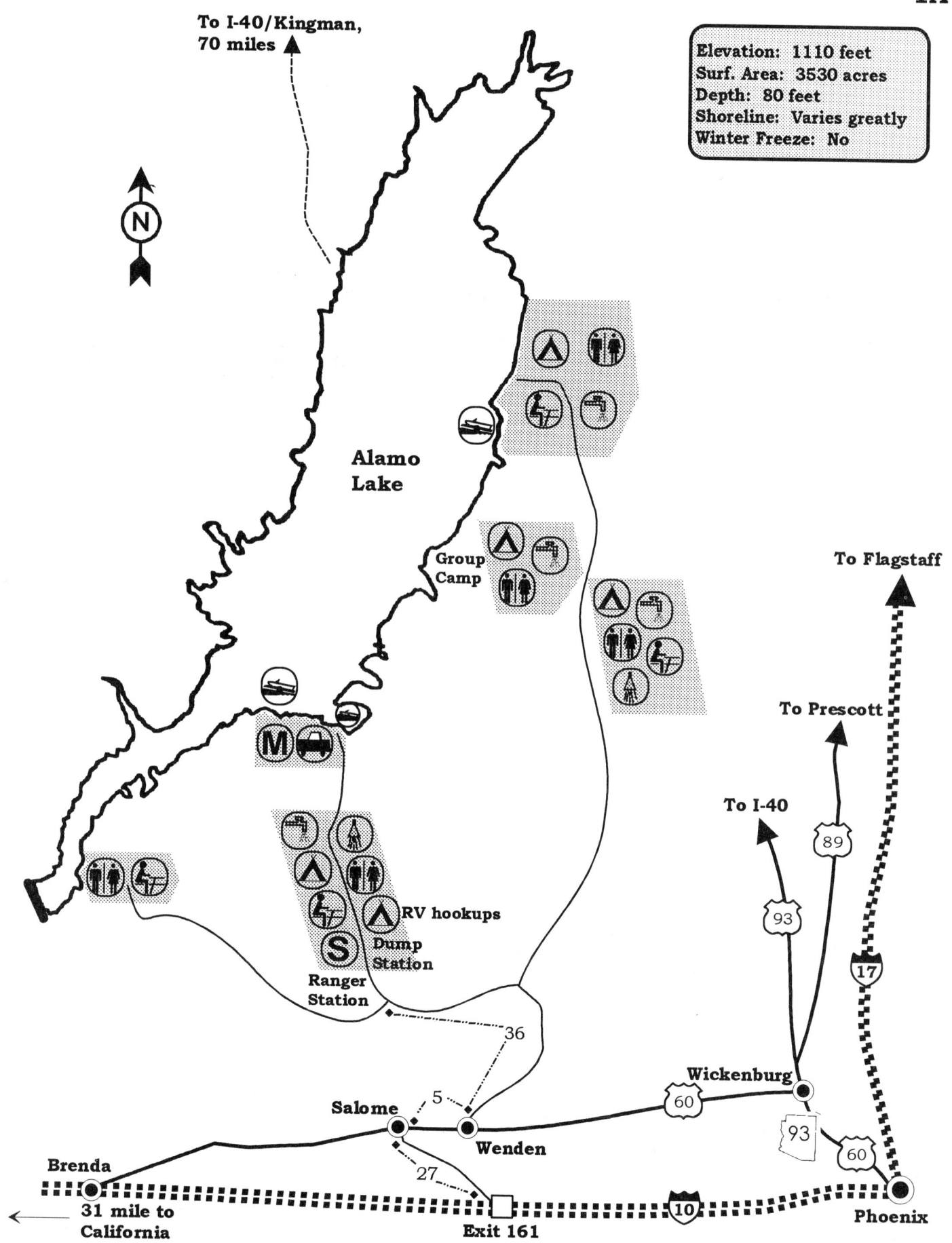

To I-40/Kingman, 70 miles

N

Elevation: 1110 feet
Surf. Area: 3530 acres
Depth: 80 feet
Shoreline: Varies greatly
Winter Freeze: No

Alamo Lake

Group Camp

RV hookups

Dump Station

Ranger Station

To Flagstaff

To Prescott

To I-40

89

93

17

36

5

Wickenburg

60

93

Salome

Wenden

27

Brenda

31 mile to California

Exit 161

10

60

Phoenix

Cataract Lake is surrounded by the town of Williams at a 6800-foot elevation and is managed by the Kaibab National Forest. A small campground sits on the east side of this lake. Williams' town residents are frequently on the shores of the lake with a line in the water. Boat fishermen are also present on this 35-acre pond. As is true with the other recreation sites in the Kaibab National Forest, there are numerous hiking and equestrian trails within a 10-mile radius of Cataract. A vehicle tour up to the top of Bill William's Mountain is certainly worth the trip, especially in the fall when the aspens have changed color. A stop in at the Williams' Ranger District Office will be helpful in information gathering. If the fish aren't biting, try your hand at Elephant Rocks Golf Course just next door. Cataract Lake is too simple to reach, as it sits one mile northwest of Williams, just off Cararact Lake Road. Take Exit 161 from Interstate 40 and go north.

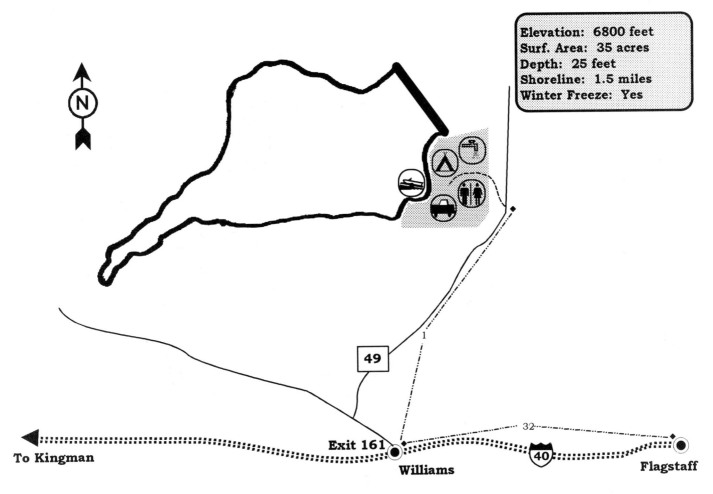

Elevation: 6800 feet
Surf. Area: 35 acres
Depth: 25 feet
Shoreline: 1.5 miles
Winter Freeze: Yes

CAMPING/RVING	RECREATION	BOATING	MISCELLANEOUS
Tents/Trailers/RVs -18 developed sites -$6/night -pit toilets -drinking water -tables -fire rings -no hookups -pets on leash only -private RV parks with full hookups and motels are located one mile east in Williams	-picnicking -hiking -horseback riding -sailing -canoeing -fishing: rainbow trout, brown trout -shore fishing -snoozing	-1 improved launch ramp -8 horse power motor maximum	-open May 15 to Oct 31 -nearest town is Williams, one mile away, all conveniences and facilities available -campground host available -lake freezes in winter but a short hike would yield some reasonable ice fishing just before the ice goes off
Information:	Kaibab National Forest (602) 635-2633		

2

KAIBAB LAKE

As the name indicates, Kaibab Lake is contained within the Kaibab National Forest and sits at a 6800-foot elevation. Camping is easy and convenient and two handicapped campsites are available as well as two group campsites. All facilities and conveniences are at hand in Williams, just four miles away. The hiking and equestrian trails on the Kaibab National Forest are excellent. Please check with the ranger station in Williams. Kaibab Lake can be fished from either a boat or from shore with the latter the favorite. The lake is stocked with trout frequently. Paved or well maintained gravel roads make the access easy. From Williams, take I-40 east two miles to exit 165, turn north on to Arizona Highway 64 and go about 2 miles to the campground entrance on the left (west) side of the road. The facilities here are very nice and given the easy access and proximity to the Grand Canyon, it can be very busy. Plan ahead with reservations.

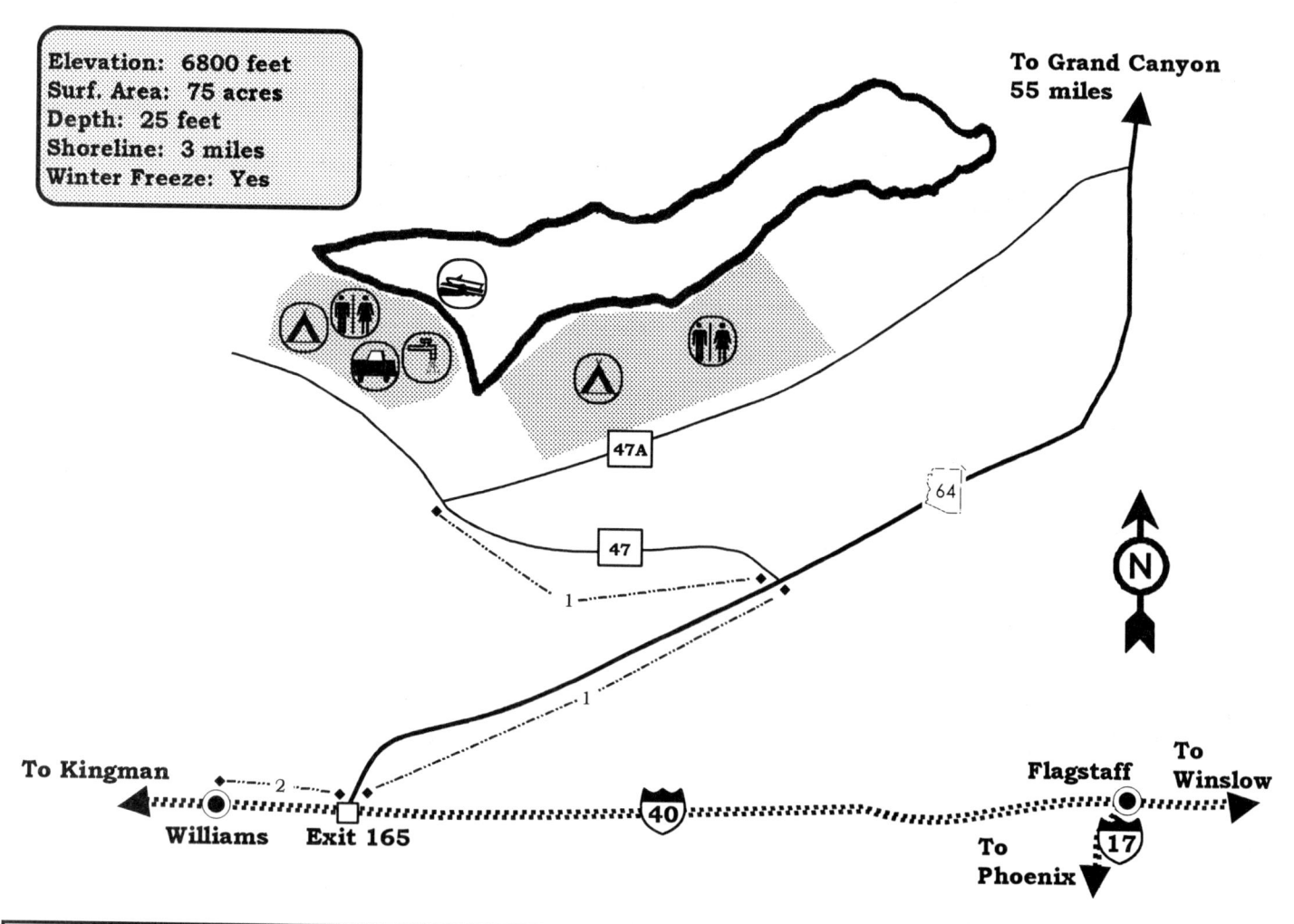

Elevation: 6800 feet
Surf. Area: 75 acres
Depth: 25 feet
Shoreline: 3 miles
Winter Freeze: Yes

To Grand Canyon 55 miles

47A

64

47

1

N

1

To Kingman

Flagstaff

To Winslow

2

Williams   Exit 165

40

17

To Phoenix

CAMPING/RVING	RECREATION	BOATING	MISCELLANEOUS
Tents/Trailers/RVs -72 developed sites -2 handicapped sites -no hookups -$8/night -pit toilets -garbage bins -tables -fire rings -drinking water (no water November - April) -dump station (fee)	-picnicking -horseback riding -canoeing, sailing -hiking NOTE: many and varied established hiking trails within 10-mile radius of lake - obtain documentation at ranger station in Williams -fishing: rainbow trout, brown trout, green sunfish -shore fishing -no swimming	-1 boat ramp -8 horse power motor maximum	-open May 15 to Oct 31 -nearest town is Williams, 4 miles southeast - all conveniences and facilities available in Williams -campground host available -many and varied large and small wildlife in surrounding forests -naturalist programs offered by Forest Service personnel
Information:	Kaibab National Forest (602) 635-2633		

Dog Town Reservoir is a 50-acre lake which sits just east of Bill Williams Mountain in the Kaibab National Forest. There is a sizable national forest campground which can serve well for a jumping off point of one of the many excellent hiking or equestrian trails contained within this national forest. During non-winter months, a drive up the Bill Williams Road (Forest Road 111) to the top of the mountain can give you excellent views of the San Francisco Peaks, the Prescott/Chino Valley area, and the Grand Canyon to the north. The road is gravel and prefers a high clearance vehicle. Anglers can work from a boat or the shore with equal success for the stocked trout. Access is easy going south from Williams on Forest Road 173 (Perkinsville Road) for 4 miles, turn left (east) onto Forest Road 140 for 3 miles to Forest Road 132; turn left onto 132 to campground. The roads are reasonably well maintained but are closed in winter by snow cover.

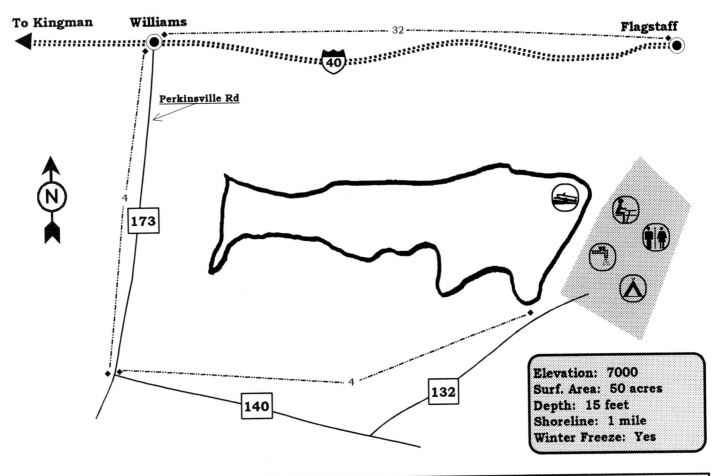

Elevation: 7000
Surf. Area: 50 acres
Depth: 15 feet
Shoreline: 1 mile
Winter Freeze: Yes

CAMPING/RVING	RECREATION	BOATING	MISCELLANEOUS
Tents/Trailers/RVs -60 developed sites -$7/night -pit toilets -drinking water -dump station (fee) -tables -fire rings -group camp sites available (reservations only)	-picnicking -sailing -canoeing -nature trail -hiking -horseback riding NOTE: the hiking and equestrian trails in the Kaibab National Forest are excellent - see ranger station in Williams for details -fishing: rainbow trout, brook trout, brown trout -shore fishing	-1 improved launch ramp -electric motors only	-open May 15 to Oct 31 -nearest town is Williams, 8 miles to the northwest -campground host available -road closed in winter months due to snow
Information:	Kaibab National Forest (602) 635-2676		

4

WHITE HORSE LAKE

White Horse Lake sits at a 7000-foot elevation adjacent to the Sycamore Canyon wilderness and is managed by the Kaibab National Forest. The conveniences and facilities at the lake are excellent for camping. Cabins and campsites at the convenience store/lodge. Boat rental and other conveniences are available at the store. This 35-acre lake can be fished from the shore or a boat with either bringing success. The Kaibab National Forest has many excellent hiking and equestrian trails which serves the outdoors person. Douglas fir and ponderosa pine dominate the terrain which contains significant amounts of small game and large wildlife. A trip to the Sycamore Canyon area just to the east of the lake is a must. The panoramic view is exceptional. Access is easy taking Forest Road 173 (Perkinsville Road) south out of Williams for 9 miles to Forest Road 110. Turn left onto 110 and go 7 miles and turn left onto Forest Road 109. Follow 109 east three miles to the lake. The roads are paved or well maintained gravel, suitable for sedans.

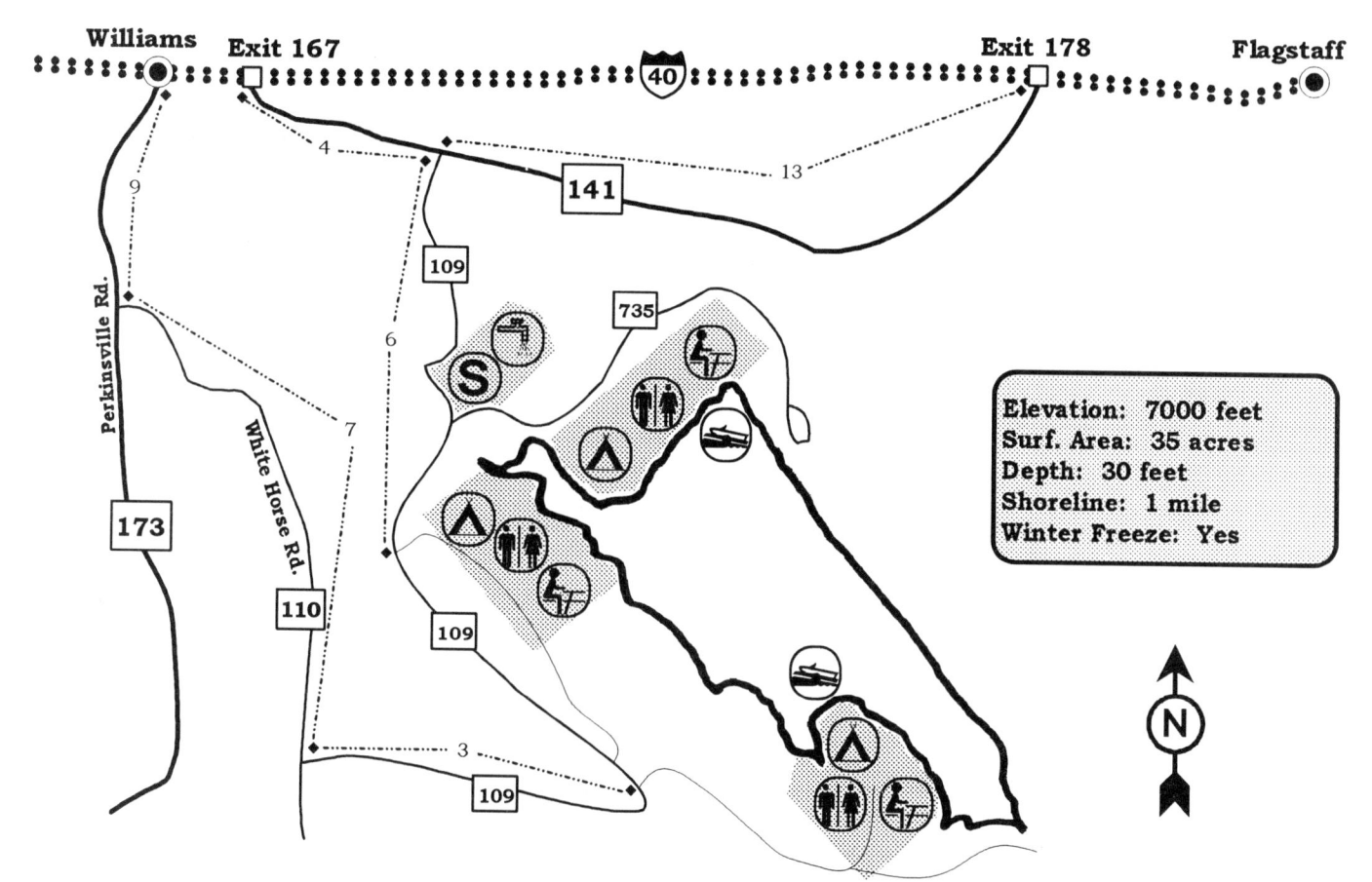

Elevation: 7000 feet
Surf. Area: 35 acres
Depth: 30 feet
Shoreline: 1 mile
Winter Freeze: Yes

CAMPING/RVING	RECREATION	BOATING	MISCELLANEOUS
Tents/Trailers/RVs -85 sites -$6/night -2 campsites fitted for handicapped -no hookups -drinking water (no water November - April) -pit toilets -dogs on leash only -tables -fire pits	-canoeing, sailing -picnicking -hiking NOTE: the hiking and equestrian trails in the Kaibab National Forest are excellent - see ranger station in Williams for details -fishing: brown trout, rainbow trout -shore fishing -ice fishing in winter and road is plowed -no swimming	-electric motors only -boat rentals at convenience store: canoes, row boats, paddle boats (no motors for rent) -2 improved ramps	-telephone number of store at lake is: 1-800-439-9757 -convenience store at lake: boat rentals, food, drinks, ice, tackle, bait, license, supplies -season of use is May 15 to Oct 31
Information:	Kaibab National Forest (602) 635-2633		

J.D. DAM LAKE

Located on the southern tip of the Kaibab National Forest, at 7000-foot elevation, J.D. Dam Lake sits midway between Round Mountain and the Sycamore Canyon Wilderness. This is a shallow lake which frequently freezes solid. This lake poses special requirements on the angler as it is "artificial lures and flies only." Before fishing this lake, make sure you understand these special requirements. There are no facilities at all at J.D. Dam Lake so open, primitive camping is the best you'll have. At 15 acres you can shore fish the entire lake or drag in a small inflatable or canoe. While you're in the area, don't forget to cruise south on Forest Road 110, 4 miles to Sycamore Point Vista. This offers a breath-taking view of lower Sycamore Canyon with Mingus Mountain on the distant horizon. The red rocks of the lower canyon make a stark contrast with the white formation on the canyon sides. Access to J.D. Dam Lake can be tough, rough and bumpy on a dirt road. Take Forest Road 173 (Perkinsville Road) south from Williams for 9 miles to Forest Road 110, follow 110 for 10 miles to Forest Road 105, turn right (west) here and the lake is right there.

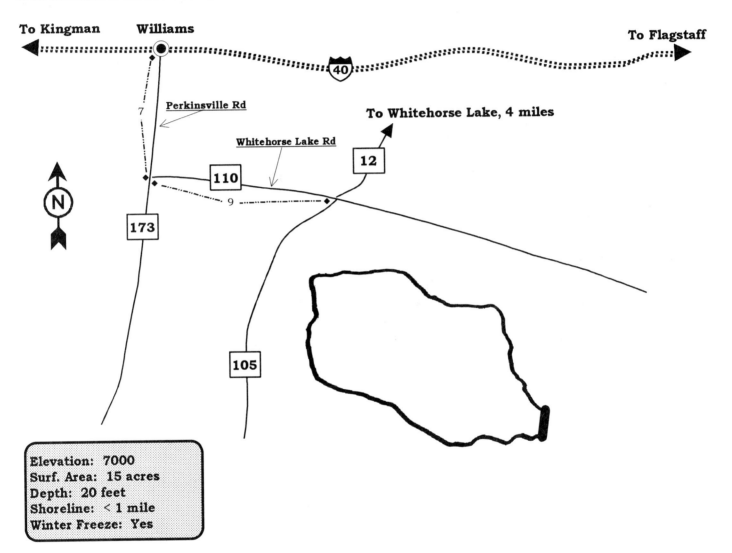

Elevation: 7000
Surf. Area: 15 acres
Depth: 20 feet
Shoreline: < 1 mile
Winter Freeze: Yes

CAMPING/RVING	RECREATION	BOATING	MISCELLANEOUS
-no developed camping facilities at lake -nearest campground is 5 miles north at White Horse Lake	-hiking -horseback riding -no facilities at lake -fishing: brown trout, rainbow trout -shore fishing NOTE: artificial lures and flies only - no live bait	-electric motors only -no launch area -bring in a boat or canoe you can carry by hand	-roads not cleared of snow in winter -nearest town is Williams, 16 miles northwest -season of use is May to Oct 31
Information:	Kaibab National Forest (602) 635-2633		

LITTLE HELL'S CANYON LAKE

A 15-acre pond adjacent to US Highway 89, just south of Ashfork, Little Hell's Canyon Lake is managed by the Kaibab National Forest. There are no conveniences or facilities at the lake. If you fish from a boat, plan to carry it in a distance. The lake sits at a 6200-foot elevation and has 10 acres of surface area. The lake sits right on the east side of US Highway 89, 10 miles south of the I-40 and US Highway 89 Junction at Ashfork. There's not much at the lake or in the area.

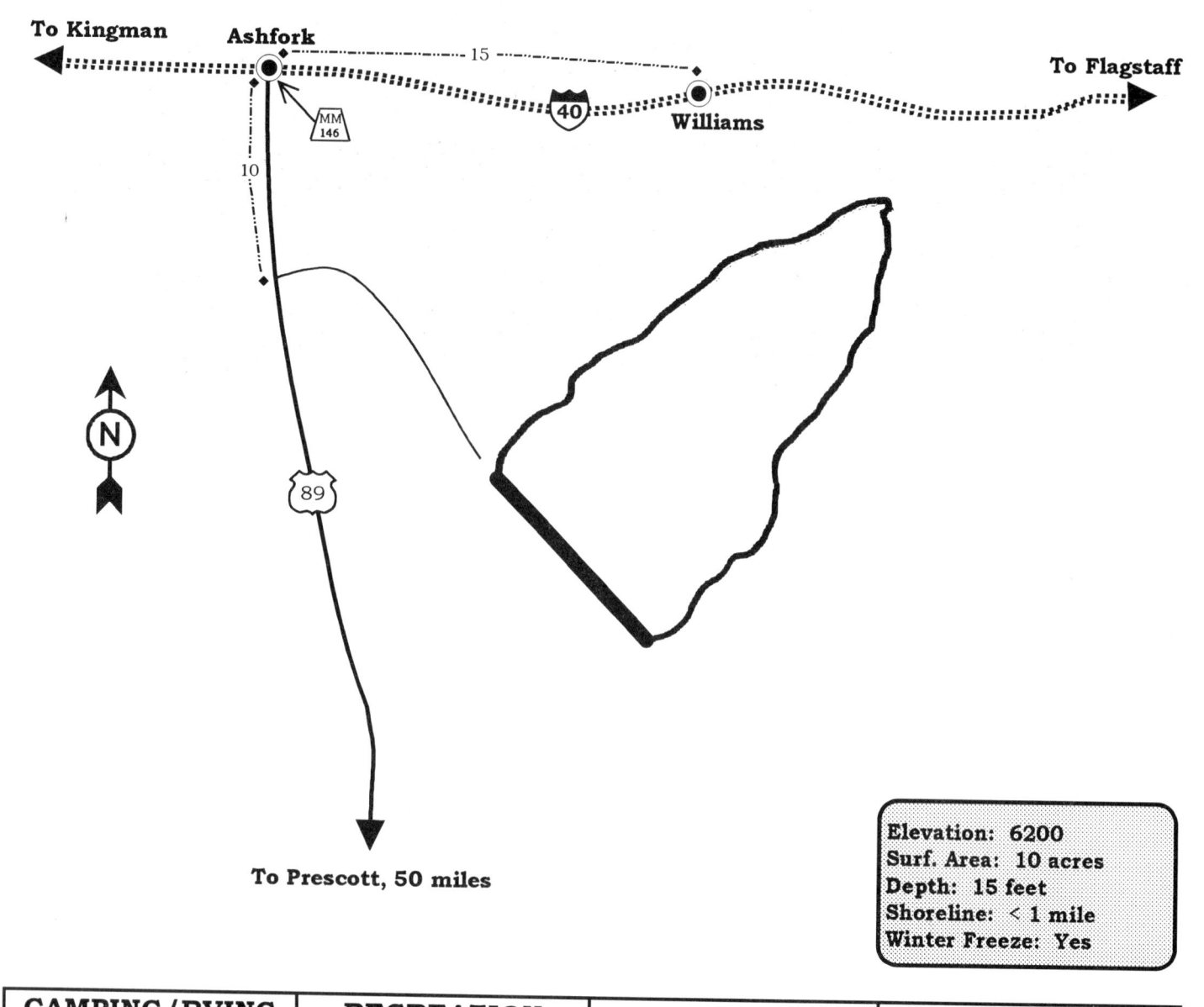

To Prescott, 50 miles

Elevation: 6200
Surf. Area: 10 acres
Depth: 15 feet
Shoreline: < 1 mile
Winter Freeze: Yes

CAMPING/RVING	RECREATION	BOATING	MISCELLANEOUS
-no camping facilities at lake -no national forest campgrounds within a 25-mile radius	-hiking -canoeing -picnicking: there is a small state-operated picnic area just south of the lake along US Highway 89 in the Prescott National Forest - there are 12 picnic sites (open year round) -fishing: trout -shore fishing	-no launch area -carry in access only for canoes or inflatables -electric motor only	-nearest town is Ashfork, 10 miles north on US Highway 89
Information:	Kaibab National Forest (602) 635-2633		

Watson Lake waters are managed by the Chino Valley Irrigation District, with the park located on the west side of the lake managed by the Prescott Parks and Recreation Department. Sitting at 5100 foot elevation, just northeast of Prescott, Watson Lake's Campgrounds exceeds minimum requirements with their flush toilets, hot showers, and handicapped facilities. This camping location gives access to the sites and workings of the town of Prescott as well as the Prescott National Forest. Fishermen will have a mixed bag catch, mostly from a boat, as the 3.5 miles of shoreline is generally tough to reach. There is 150 acres for boating with no restrictions. There is a playground at the lake. Access to Watson Lake is very easy. Proceed north from Prescott on Highway 89 for 3 miles; the lake is visible from the road on the right hand (east) side of the highway.

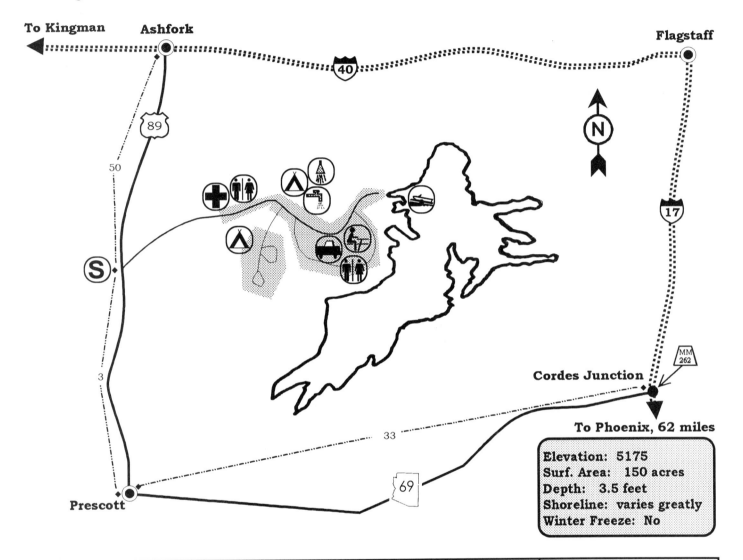

Elevation: 5175
Surf. Area: 150 acres
Depth: 3.5 feet
Shoreline: varies greatly
Winter Freeze: No

CAMPING/RVING	RECREATION	BOATING	MISCELLANEOUS

Tents/Trailers/RVs
-49 campsites
-$8/night
-2 with electricity
  $11/night
-tables, grills
-flush toilets
-handicapped toilets
-showers
-group camping spaces
  available
	-canoeing
	-hiking
	-picnicking
	-horseback riding
	-horseshoe pits
	-racket ball court
	-fishing: catfish, largemouth
	  bass, bluegill, crappie
	NOTE: shore fishing difficult
	-$1.50/vehicle day-use fee
		-no motor restrictions
		-1 ramp
			-park ranger on station
			-all facilities and
			  conveniences available in
			  Prescott, 3 miles southwest
			  on Arizona 89

Information:	Prescott Park and Recreation Department (602) 776-6213		

GRANITE BASIN LAKE

At a 5600-foot elevation, Granite Basin Lake sits on the edge of Granite Mountain wilderness within the 1.2 million acre Prescott National Forest. There are both individual and group campgrounds adjacent to the lake plus picnic areas next to the shoreline. The lake has been recently drained and refilled which took the fishing prospects to zero. Fear not, the lake was restocked in the fall of 1992. At four acres, a boat is useless. Shore fishing is just fine. There are numerous trails, thus the hiker probably has the best time of it now with the abundant wildlife and flora. The same goes for the equestrian. The weather is consistent with the altitude. Summer days are warmish with cool evenings. Thunderstorms in the late summer afternoons are usual. Access is simple. Go west on Arizona 255 from Prescott for 4 miles, turn north (right) on 374 for 5 miles. You have pavement or reasonably well maintained gravel roads all the way.

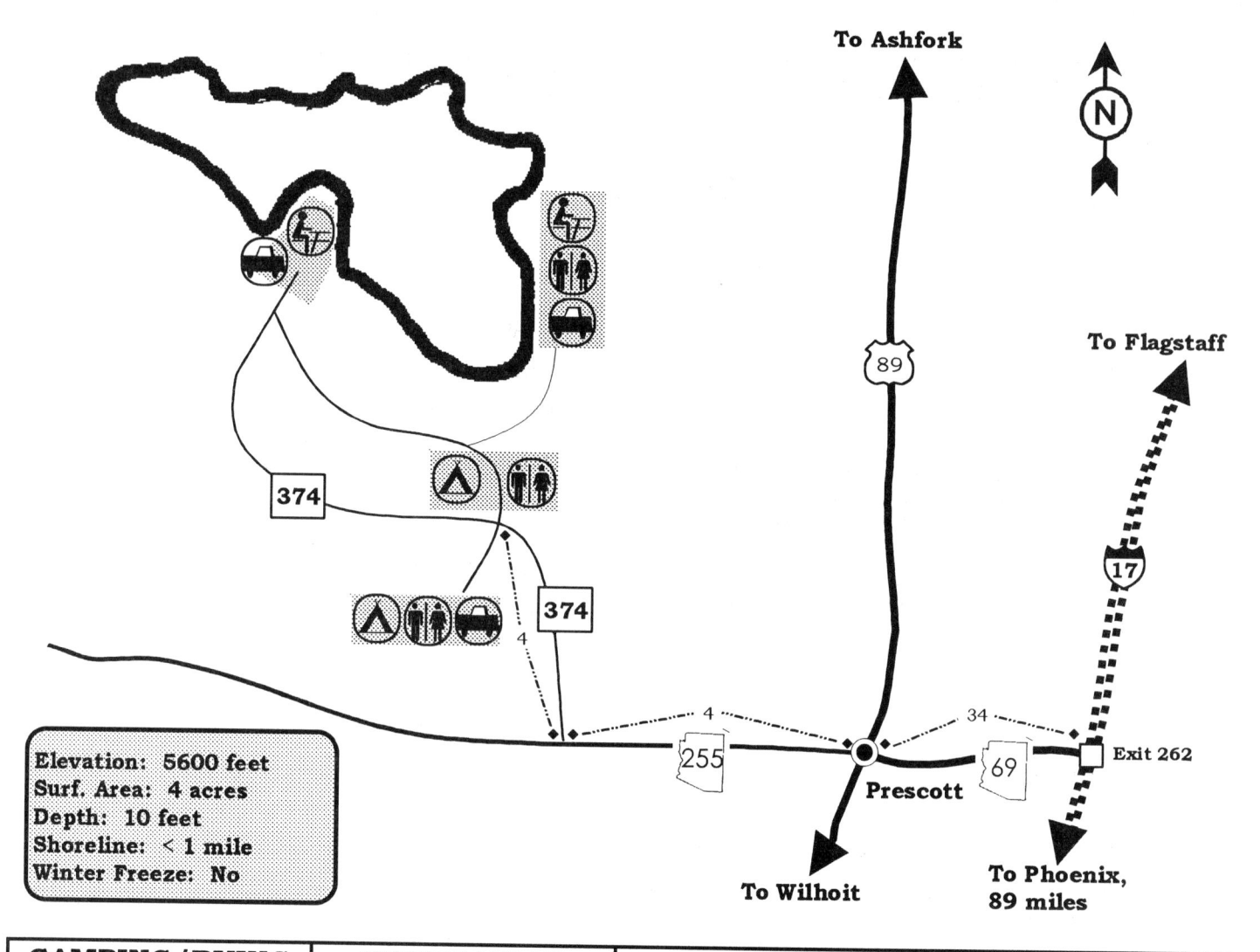

Elevation: 5600 feet
Surf. Area: 4 acres
Depth: 10 feet
Shoreline: < 1 mile
Winter Freeze: No

CAMPING/RVING	RECREATION	BOATING	MISCELLANEOUS
Tents/Trailers/RVs -18 sites -pit toilets -tables -grills -no showers -no drinking water -group campground: 100 maximum - fee and reservations required	-hiking -horseback riding -canoeing -picnic area with tables and grills at lake shore -fishing: mixed bag, warm water species -shore fishing -no swimming	-electric motor only -no launch area -at 4 surface acres, anything other than a small inflatable or canoe is not worth the effort	-nearest town is Prescott, 8 miles to the east -open year round -for documentation on Prescott National Forest facilities, stop at the Bradshaw Ranger Station on Highway 69, just east of Prescott, or call (602) 445-7253
Information:	Prescott National Forest (602) 445-7253		

Managed by the Prescott National Forest, Lynx Lake sits at a 5600-foot elevation. Given its climatic conditions and proximity to the Phoenix area, the lake is very busy in summer months. Two campgrounds surround the lake with adequate facilities. A lakeside store is well equipped with the necessary camping supplies, groceries, fishing tackle, and bait. Boat rentals are also available. At 55 acres, the lake is not long and thus seems more crowded than it really is. The forests surrounding the lake are pristine. The hikers, picnickers, and equestrians will enjoy the wildlife and flora. If the fish aren't biting, try your hand at panning for gold. Lynx

Creek was once the most productive gold bearing creek in the state. If you like to drive, there are two Bradshaw Mountain motor tours which will guide you to historical mining-related sites in Yavapai County. The tour maps are available free from the local (Bradshaw) forest service office. You can't go to Lynx Lake without a visit to downtown Prescott, just seven miles west. It is a "big little" town. Access to Lynx Lake is paved almost entirely. From a point 4 miles east of Prescott on Arizona Highway 69, turn south onto Walker Road (Forest Road 197) and go 3 miles. You'll be there.

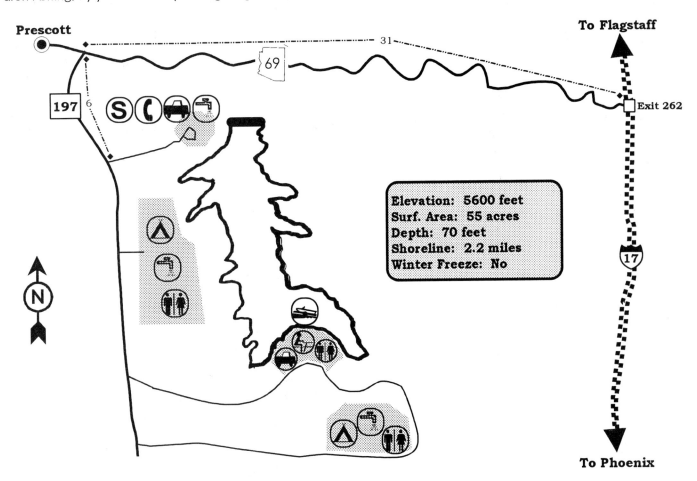

Elevation: 5600 feet
Surf. Area: 55 acres
Depth: 70 feet
Shoreline: 2.2 miles
Winter Freeze: No

CAMPING/RVING	RECREATION	BOATING	MISCELLANEOUS
Tents/Trailers/RVs -2 campgrounds adjacent to lake -77 total sites -$6/night -tables, grills, drinking water -pit toilets -no showers -various other forest service campgrounds within a 20-mile radius of lake	-picnicking -sailing, sail boarding, canoeing -hiking -horseback riding -gold panning -group picnic area managed by store, 50 people max - call the store at 1(602)778-0720 -shore fishing -no swimming	-electric motor only -boat ramp -boat/motor rental at lake store	-nearest town is Prescott with full conveniences and services, 7 miles away -Convenience store at lake: boat and motor rentals, ice, tackle, bait, snacks, groceries, camping supplies -store telephone number is: (602) 778-0720
Information:	Prescott National Forest (602) 445-7253		

UPPER GOLDWATER LAKE

Upper Goldwater Lake sits at a 6000-foot elevation and is managed by the city of Prescott Parks and Recreation Department. The lake itself is within the Prescott National Forest boundaries. Upper Goldwater Lake is a day-use facility only and no camping is allowed. A nominal day-use fee is charged per vehicle. National forest campgrounds and private campgrounds abound within a 10-mile radius of the lake. There are 24 established picnic areas with ramadas, tables, and grills. A mixed bag of fish can be caught but rarely any trout. This lake is generally not stocked. Special bait rules apply. There is reasonable access for shore fishing. Given its proximity to the city of Prescott, a visit to this historical town is a must if you're in the area. The surrounding Prescott National Forest has many outdoor activities which can augment an afternoon at Upper Goldwater Lake. By the way, Lower Goldwater Lake does exist but is not for public access. To reach Upper Goldwater Lake, go south from Arizona Highway 69 within the city limits of Prescott onto Senator Highway, continue south for 4 miles and turn west (right), continue 1/2 mile to the lake.

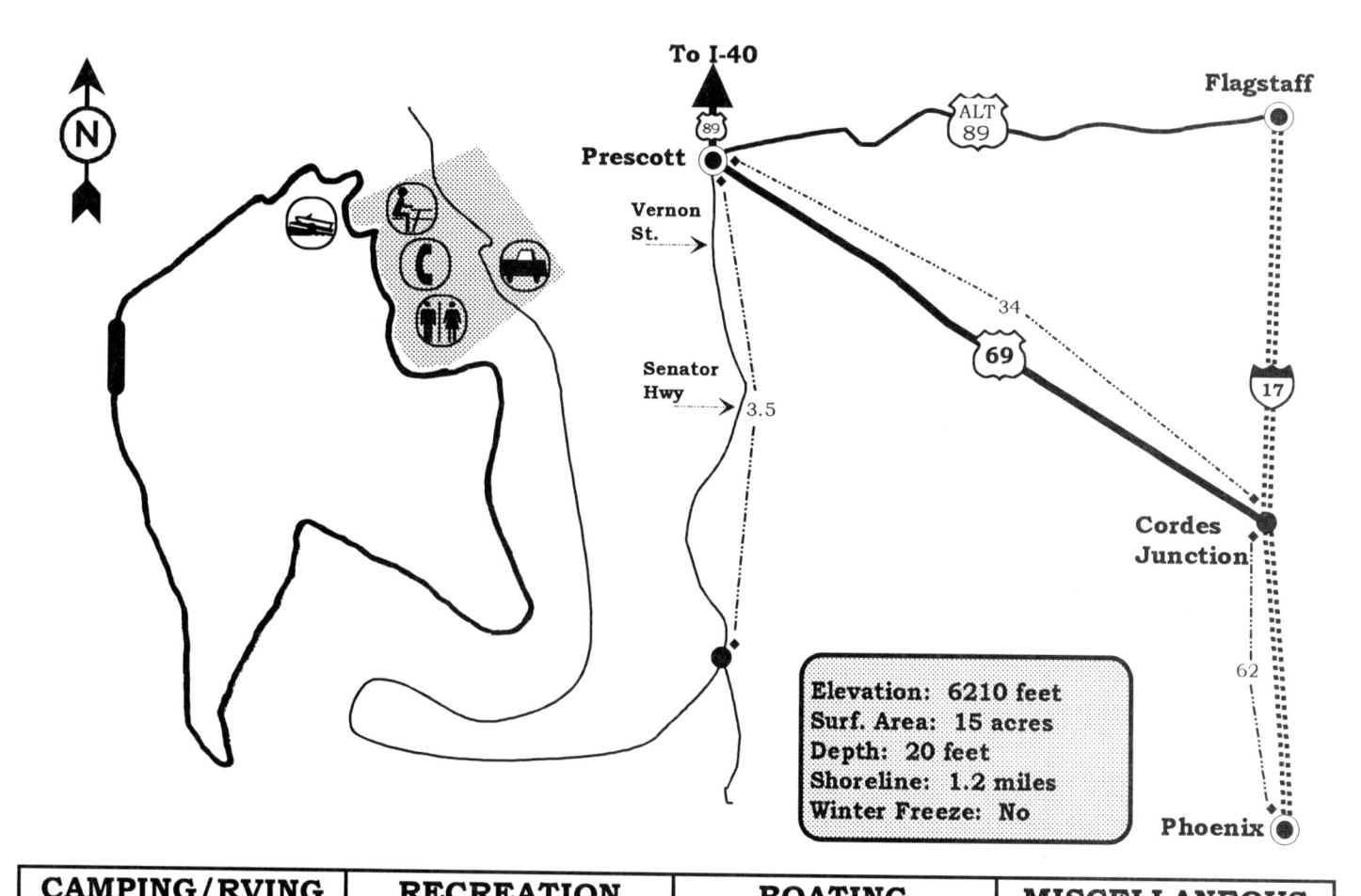

Elevation: 6210 feet
Surf. Area: 15 acres
Depth: 20 feet
Shoreline: 1.2 miles
Winter Freeze: No

CAMPING/RVING	RECREATION	BOATING	MISCELLANEOUS
-no camping at lake, day-use only -pit toilets (handicapped) -2 Prescott National Forest campgrounds (Upper Wolf Creek and Lower Wolf Creek) located 5 miles south of the lake on Senator Highway - other national forest campgrounds located west of the lake on Highway 89, south of Prescott	-canoeing -hiking -sailing -picnicking: 24 established picnic sites with tables and grills -fishing: largemouth bass, catfish, crappie, bluegill (no live bait allowed) -shore fishing	-electric motor only -1 improved launch	-all conveniences and facilities are available in Prescott which is 4 miles north on Senator Highway -park ranger lives on site -open year round -day-use fee is $1.50/vehicle
Information:	Prescott Parks and Recreation Department (602) 776-6213		

At 7000 feet, surrounded by "Castle Creek Wilderness," resides Horsethief Lake (a.k.a. Horsethief Basin Lake). This lake and its surrounding forest facilities are managed by the Prescott National Forest. Two national forest campgrounds are within three miles of the lake. The closest has water and therefore there is a fee. The angler could use a boat on the 3-acre pond but shore fishing is just fine for the warm water catch. Hiking or horseback riding can be pleasurable in the high forested pine. The

weather is consistent with the high altitude and is sometimes busy during summer months given its proximity to the Phoenix metropolitan area. Access to Horsethief Lake is a bit tough with 35 miles of dirt road. Exit from Highway 17 and head towards Cordes on Forest Road 259; continue on 259 for 19 miles to Crown King, from Crown King it is another 7 miles to the lake on Forest Road 52. Going is slow - just take your time.

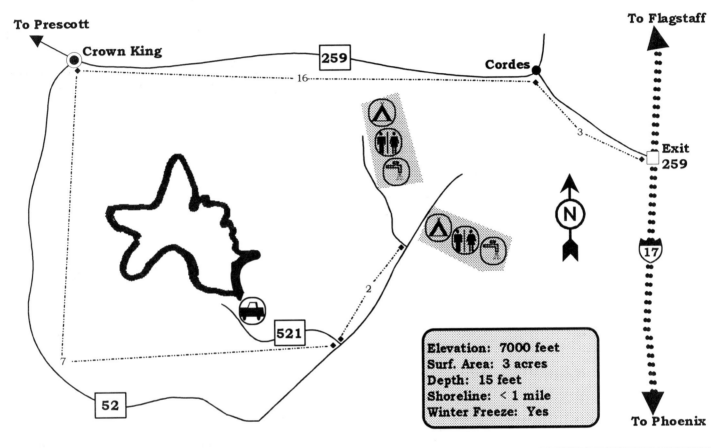

Elevation: 7000 feet
Surf. Area: 3 acres
Depth: 15 feet
Shoreline: < 1 mile
Winter Freeze: Yes

CAMPING/RVING	RECREATION	BOATING	MISCELLANEOUS
-no camping at or adjacent to lake Tents/Trailers/RVs -2 national forest campgrounds nearby: Hazlett Hollow - 1 mile away -16 developed sites -$6.00/night -tables, grills, ramadas -pit toilets -drinking water Kentuck Campgrounds 3 miles from lake -20 sites -tables, pit toilets -no fee, no water	-picnicking -hiking -canoeing -horseback riding -fishing: largemouth bass, catfish, sunfish -shore fishing -no swimming -snoozing	-electric motor only -no launch ramp -recommend small inflatable or canoe with electric trolling motor - the size of this lake (3 acres) requires no more	-nearest town is Crown King, 7 miles northwest on dirt road (1/2 hour) -Crown King has small store, restaurant, gasoline, and telephone -no facilities or services at lake -Recommendation: bring in everything you need
Information:	Prescott National Forest (602) 445-7253		

12

LAKE PLEASANT

Lake Pleasant, or maybe it should be called the "new" Lake Pleasant, sits at 1700-foot elevation within the Lake Pleasant Regional Park, managed by Maricopa County Park and Recreation. The park and lake are open year round for camping, recreation, and water sports and resides just 30 miles northwest of Phoenix. The September 1992 completion of the "new" Waddel Dam on the Aqua Fria River has the lake now capable of 10,400 surface acres, nearly triple the previous size. The new dam is greater than 1 mile long and holds 22 million cubic yards of earth, which rises 331 feet from ground level and holds back up to 830,000 acre feet of water. With the heavy rains of Spring 1993, the lake level has risen to nearly 2/3rds of capacity, resulting in the disappearance of all previously existing facilities. They are now all under water. Fear not, plans are set and construction is underway on a variety of enhanced facilities. Currently there is a 4-lane concrete launch ramp on the east side of the lake, near the dam. This launch is on private land managed by the Maricopa Water District. Currently under construction, adjacent to the launch ramp is a full-service marina (Pleasant Harbor Marina). Boat slips are in with significant construction activity going on. On the west side of the lake, within the Lake Pleasant Regional Park, construction of a 10-lane boat ramp is ongoing, with completion scheduledfor spring 1994. Until complete, primitive launching anywhere along the west side is allowed. Initial marina and developed campsite construction is generally the only other construction you'll see in 1994. But, there is still no limit to what Lake Pleasant has to offer. The fisherman will be served well by any of the six predominant species in the lake. There are reports that 16 different species inhabit the lake. Water skiers, jet skiers, horseback riders, swimmers, hikers, canoers, houseboaters, pleasure boaters and hunters still have all the natural facilities required. Sailing and sailboating can be superb here, given the open terrain and northwesterly winds. Jet skiers are restricted to a bay on the northwest side of the dam which segregates them form the general boating public. Just below the dam you see a small lake called Hank Raymond Lake. It appears very inviting but stay away. This small pond is on private land and serves as a reservoir on the Beardsley Canal. The weather at Lake Pleasant will be similar to Phoenix on any given day. The shoreline is barren with minimal shade. Be prepared for the hot sun of summer. Truly, Lake Pleasant is a four-season lake with moderate winter weather. The rolling desert hills surrounding the lake are of a particular desert beauty, stunning at both morning and evening. While boating on Lake Pleasant, be aware of the "bald eagle and wild life closure" area. A pair of bald eagles have recently hatched an eaglet and they are being well protected by a variety of agencies. Lake Pleasant, whether it has full facilities or not is/will continue to be a very busy lake. In fact, during the summer months it is recommended that you arrive early on weekend days to avoid being shut out due to over crowding. Another work of caution, be mindful of the construction equipment and workers on the road. Obey the signs; remember safety first. Access to Lake Pleasant is very simple. Proceed west on Arizona Highway 74 from Interstate I-17 at exit 223. Ten mile later you'll be at the lake. There are very good signs. The road(s) are paved all the way. There are three road to the lake; one to the east side boat launch (Pleasant Harbor Marina), the second to the visitors' center above the dam, the third or most westerly leads to the park and up the west side. Excellent access; you'll enjoy Lake Pleasant.

See map, next page

CAMPING/RVING	RECREATION	BOATING	MISCELLANEOUS
Tents/Trailers/RVs -no developed sites -primitive camping only -porta-johns -$6/vehicle/day -no water -boat camping around lake shore -if you want a camp fire, bring in your wood **Planned Expansion** -full RV facilities -developed campgrounds -developed group campgrounds -hotel, restaurant	-hiking, picnicking -hunting/trapping -canoeing -sailing, sail boarding -water skiing, jet skiing -fishing: largemouth bass, crappie, channel catfish, bluegill, talapia, white bass -visitor center at dam -$6 park entrance fee **Planned Expansion** -outdoor education center -fishing bridge -picnic areas -beach	-no motor restrictions -Pleasant Harbor Marina on east side of lake -4-lane concrete launch -fees: $6/day, $85/season -wet/dry storage -Primitive launching on west side of lake -jet skiers limited to one particular bay just northeast of new dam -stobe light warning system for winds above 18 knots **Planned Expansion** -2 full-service marinas -wet/dry storage -navigational aid system -10-lane ramp to be complete in spring of 1994	-Ranger/first aid station at park entrance -nearest towns: Wickenberg, 25 miles northwest or Phoenix, 20 miles southeast -visitor center at dam -nearest conveniences or gasoline at I-17 and Arizona 74, 8 miles from lake -Ben Avery shooting range just four miles east of lake -Pleasant Harbor Marina: phone number is 465-1000 -no public telephones -bass tournament on Wednesday nights **Planned Expansion** -general store -restaurant
Information:	Maricopa County Parks (602) 566-1969		

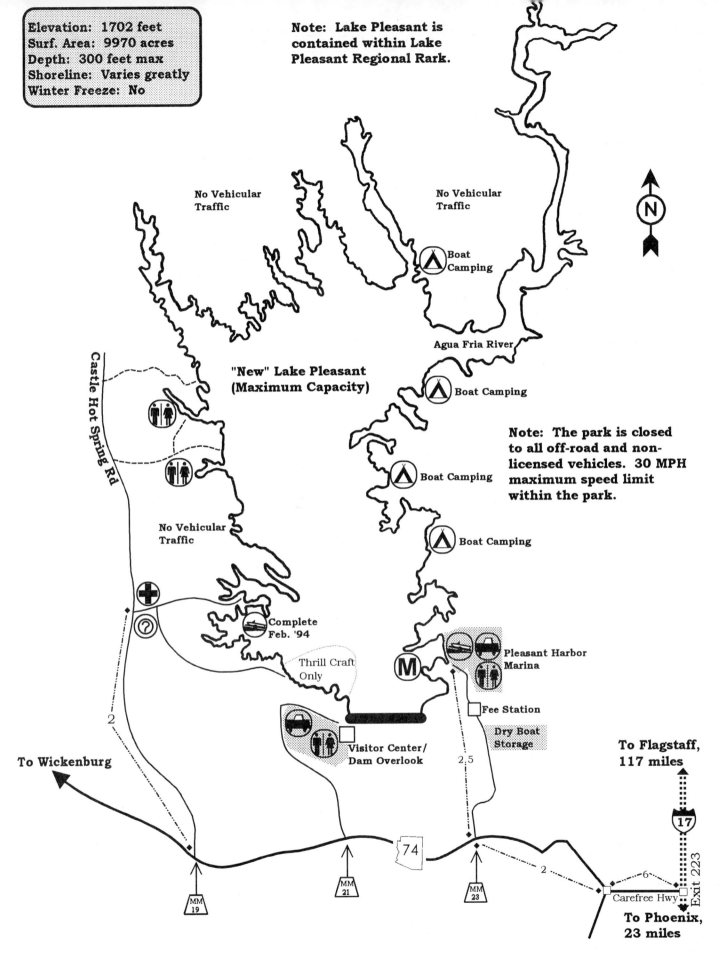

Elevation: 1702 feet
Surf. Area: 9970 acres
Depth: 300 feet max
Shoreline: Varies greatly
Winter Freeze: No

Note: Lake Pleasant is contained within Lake Pleasant Regional Rark.

No Vehicular Traffic

No Vehicular Traffic

Boat Camping

Agua Fria River

Boat Camping

"New" Lake Pleasant (Maximum Capacity)

Boat Camping

Note: The park is closed to all off-road and non-licensed vehicles. 30 MPH maximum speed limit within the park.

Boat Camping

No Vehicular Traffic

Castle Hot Spring Rd

Complete Feb. '94

Thrill Craft Only

Pleasant Harbor Marina

M

Fee Station

Dry Boat Storage

Visitor Center/ Dam Overlook

N

2

To Wickenburg

2.5

To Flagstaff, 117 miles

74

MM 19

MM 21

MM 23

2

17

Exit 223

6

Carefree Hwy

To Phoenix, 23 miles

13A

LOWER LAKE MARY

Lower Lake Mary is just northwest of Upper Lake Mary at 6900 feet in the Coconino National Forest. The lake is 100 acres, long, skinny, and relatively shallow. Late summer months find it rather weedy. There are no camping facilities at the lake but you may launch a boat and shore camp on the side opposite the highway. Various national forest campgrounds are located within 15 miles of the lake with the closest at Upper Lake Mary. Fishermen will find that the catch is similar to Upper Lake Mary, 2 miles southeast. The water level can fluctuate year to year or within a year depending on drought conditions or irrigation water demands. This lake has

been known to go dry. The surrounding forests are spectacular. The hiker certainly must carry a camera. Both large and small wildlife about It would be a rare day or evening that you wouldn't see either an elk or mule deer more specifically a herd. They come to the lake for their water needs. Weather in the summer months is perfect; sunny, warm afternoons in the sun with cool nights. Lower Lake Mary is located 9 miles southeast of Flagstaff on the Lake Mary/Mormon Lake Road (Forest Highway 3). For other information, please refer to Upper Lake Mary or Mormon Lake.

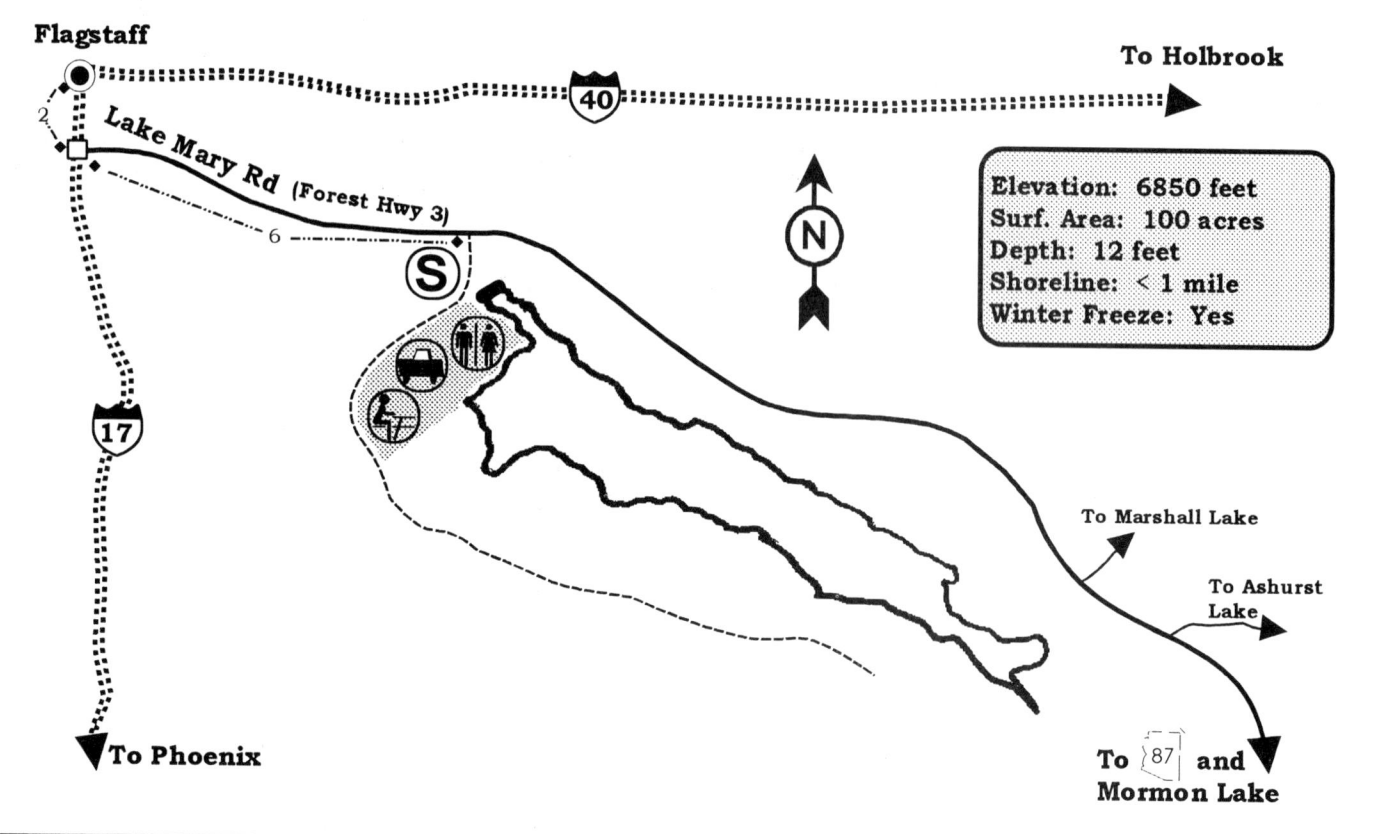

Elevation: 6850 feet
Surf. Area: 100 acres
Depth: 12 feet
Shoreline: < 1 mile
Winter Freeze: Yes

CAMPING/RVING	RECREATION	BOATING	MISCELLANEOUS
-Tent camping at the lake via boat access only (no facilities) Tents/Trailers/RVs -camp at various national forest campgrounds located south and east of the lake -closest is Lake View about 4 miles from lake -no drinking water at lake -composting toilets -campgrounds open from Memorial Day to mid-September	-picnicking (ramadas) -swimming -canoeing -water skiing -hiking -fishing: northern pike, walleye trout, bluegill -shore fishing -hunting	-no vehicular boat launch; carry-in boats only -no motor restrictions	-nearest town is Flagstaff, 9 miles northwest - full conveniences and facilities there -lake freezes in winter -dead and downed wood may be collected for use
Information:	Coconino National Forest (602) 774-1147		

Contained within the Coconino National Forest, Upper Lake Mary sit at 6800 foot elevation within a fine pristine woodland. The lake is long and skinny at 600 acres and has no boating restrictions. There is a national forest campground adjacent to the lake with another just a mile or two south of the lake. The angler will catch a mixed bag here be it from a boat or the accessible shoreline. Hey - the local campgrounds even claims a fish cleaning station; that ought to tell you something. Various day trips are within immediate range of Upper Lake Mary, be they to small quaint towns, the big city Flagstaff, or a hike through the surrounding wildernesses. Try a trip to the Walnut Canyon National Monument just east of Flagstaff. Access is paved entirely. Upper Lake Mary is 16 miles south of Flagstaff on Lake Mary-Mormon Lake Road. You can see the lake from the highway. If you're traveling through the area at night, please be cautious of both the large and small wildlife possibly crossing the roadways.

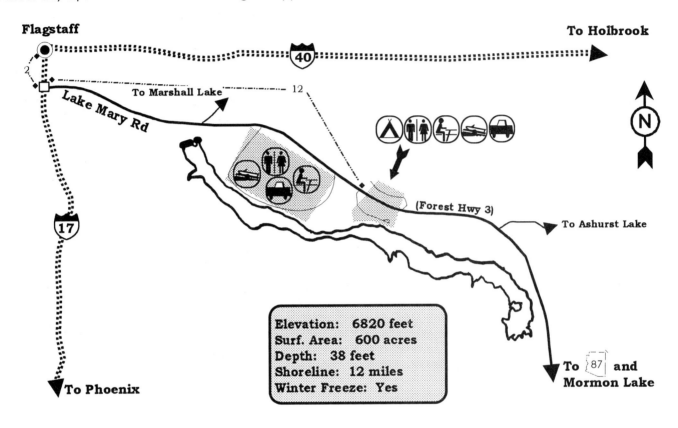

Elevation: 6820 feet
Surf. Area: 600 acres
Depth: 38 feet
Shoreline: 12 miles
Winter Freeze: Yes

CAMPING/RVING	RECREATION	BOATING	MISCELLANEOUS
Tents Only Lake View National Forest Campgrounds -campgrounds open from Memorial Day to mid-September -30 sites -tables, grills -pit toilets, drinking water Tents/Trailers/RVs Pine Grove National Forest Campground -46 sites -$7/night -flush toilets, drinking water -tables, grills	-swimming -horseback riding -canoeing -water skiing -picnicking: (picnic area on northwest corner of lake) -hiking -fishing: northern pike, walleye catfish, rainbow trout -shore fishing -visits to surrounding lakes such as Ashurst, Marshall, or Mormon Lake might be fun	-no motor restrictions -3 launch ramps -the lake is long and skinny, don't be surprised that the water skiers interfere with the canoes and small boat guys	-nearest town is Flagstaff - full conveniences and facilities 16 miles northwest on Lake Mary-Mormon Lake Road -Various private campgrounds with full hookups along Lake Mary-Mormon Lake Road
Information:	Coconino National Forest (602) 774-1147		

MARSHALL LAKE

Sitting at 6900 foot elevation in the Coconino National Forest is beautiful Marshall Lake. The word beautiful cannot be overused here. If there was scenic forested mountain beauty with wildlife and vegetation it would be embodied in Marshall Lake and its surroundings. The horseback rider and hiker certainly have the best of it here. There are no facilities or conveniences at this lake. Primitive camping is allowed if you pack it in/pack it out. Trout fishing is doable from a boat or shore. If this isn't the place to stay, then it is the place to visit. The big game and ground wildlife is at maximum concentration. Just about better than a zoo. If you're in the area, remember to visit the cliff dwellings at the Walnut Canyon National Monument, just 3 miles north as the crow flies or 24 miles over the roadways. Access to Marshall Lake is over a rough road (Forest Road 128) north from the Lake Mary-Mormon Lake Road about 9 miles south of Flagstaff.

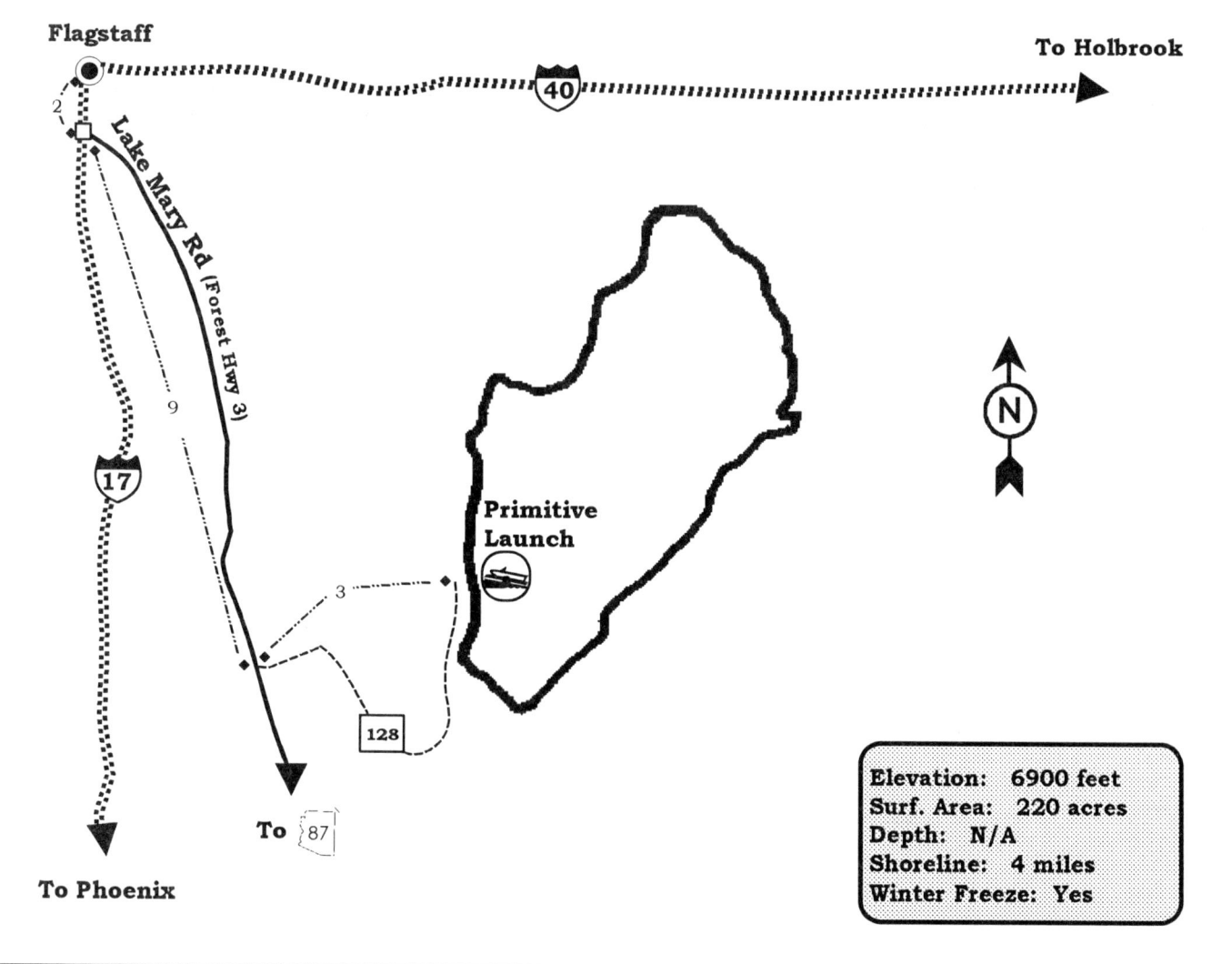

Elevation: 6900 feet
Surf. Area: 220 acres
Depth: N/A
Shoreline: 4 miles
Winter Freeze: Yes

CAMPING/RVING	RECREATION	BOATING	MISCELLANEOUS
-no developed campsites at or adjacent to the lake -full RV hookups and campgrounds 10 miles northwest in Flagstaff -National forest campgrounds located 5 miles southeast adjacent to Upper Lake Mary	-canoeing -hiking -picnicking -horseback riding -fishing: rainbow trout -shore fishing -no facilities at the lake	-electric motor only -primitive launch ramp on east side -recommend a small canoe or inflatable with electric trolling motor	-no conveniences or facilities at lake -nearest town is Flagstaff, 10 miles northwest -northwest side of lake is closed to vehicular traffic
Information:	Coconino National Forest (602) 774-1147		

Ashurst Lake is in north central Arizona's Coconino National Forest. At 7100 feet it frequently freezes over. Its proximity to Flagstaff (80 miles) and its shore fishing ease of access, makes this a very popular and sometimes busy lake. Ashurst Lake can generally be counted on to have water in it even if there are prolonged periods of low precipitation. Camping is allowed but conveniences are scarce. Trout are the name of the game at Ashurst. Troll deep during summer months on this 160 acre beauty. Mountain bikers enjoy the area given the roads, trails, and paths. The wildlife in the surrounding forests is plentiful. Large game as well as small roam freely. Access is east of the Lake Mary-Mormon Lake Road (Forest Highway 3) 17 miles south of Flagstaff. Then 4 miles on Forest Road 82E. A road nearly circles the lake with adequate trails all around.

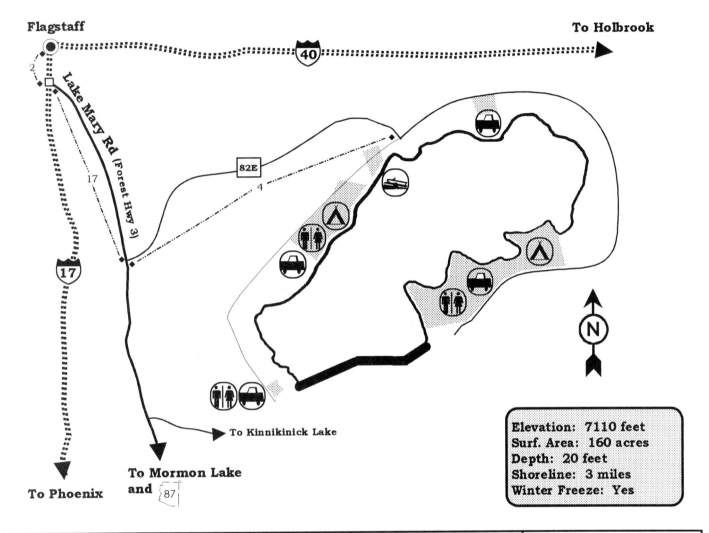

Elevation: 7110 feet
Surf. Area: 160 acres
Depth: 20 feet
Shoreline: 3 miles
Winter Freeze: Yes

CAMPING/RVING	RECREATION	BOATING	MISCELLANEOUS
Tents/Trailers/RVs -2 campgrounds at lake -51 sites -tables, grills -vault toilet -drinking water	-swimming -canoeing, sailing, wind surfing -hiking, picnicking, photography -horseback riding -mountain biking -fishing: rainbow trout, brook trout -shore fishing -ice fishing NOTE: in hot summer months, troll deep	-boat launch -8 horse power motor maximum	-nearest town is Flagstaff, 20 miles northeast -many conveniences along Lake Mary-Mormon Lake Road -no services at lake
Information:	Coconino National Forest (602) 774-1147		

MORMON LAKE

Mormon Lake is a mirage in that sometimes it's there and sometimes it's not. Same with the fish, sometimes they're there, sometimes not. This is all a result of inconsistent water supply and inconsistent usage. Mormon Lake is located in a beautiful section of Coconino National Forest just 25 miles southeast of Flagstaff. There are two national forest campgrounds on the west side of the lake but not directly on the lake. Private RV campgrounds are on the south end of the lake in a town of the same name "Mormon Lake." The lake sits at 7100 foot elevation, thus freezes over in winter if there is any water in it. When there is water in the lake, the size of the lake will vary greatly. Even if it's full, it is shallow and weedy. If you want to fish, try nearby Upper Lake Mary, Ashurst, or Kinnikinick Lakes; they are all close by. The hiker has the best of all worlds in this bountiful woodland. Wildlife abounds in these forested hills. Access is entirely paved to and around the lake. Take the Lake Mary-Mormon Lake Road southeast from Flagstaff for 25 miles and you'll hit it. Again, you can circle the lake if you please. When traveling in the region at night, be aware of the big game coming down out of the hills for a drink. It's tough to see them most of the time.

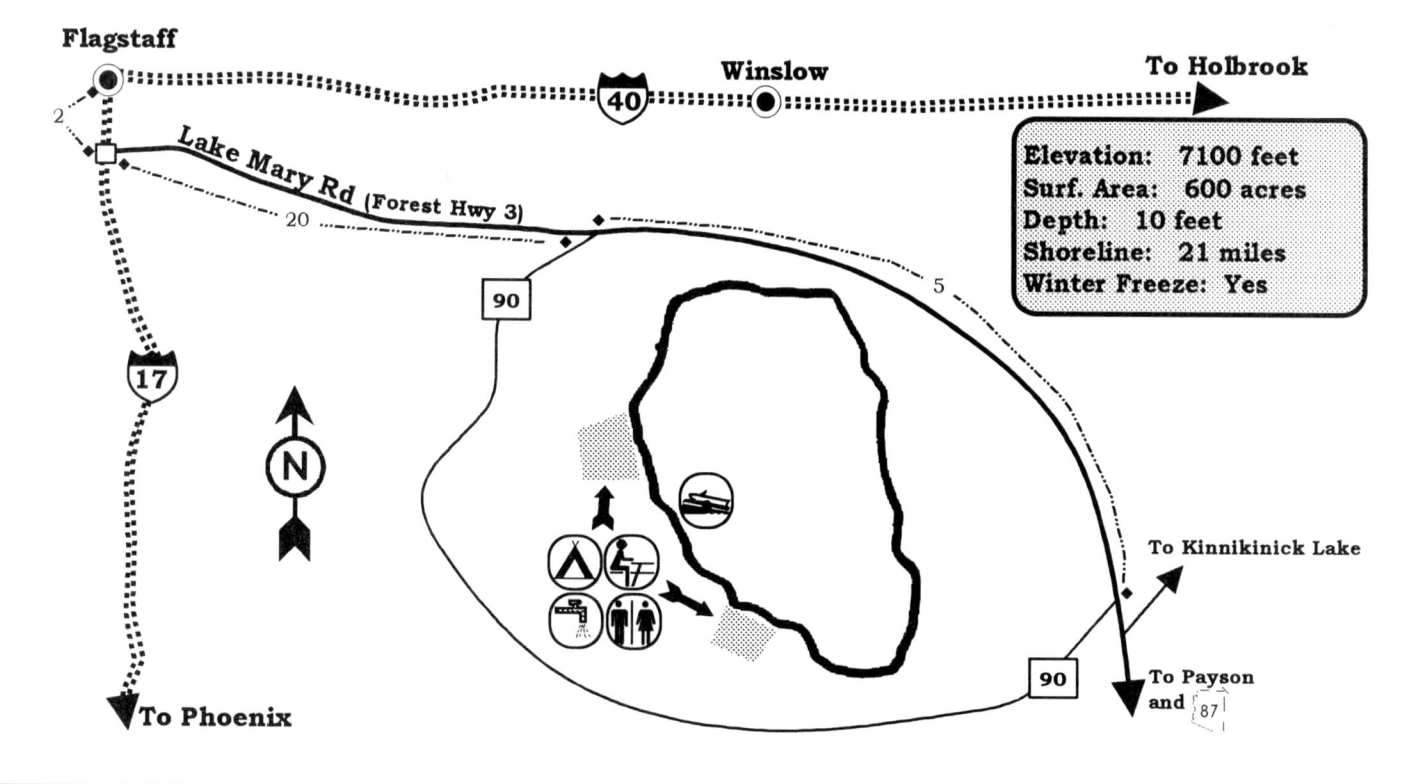

Elevation: 7100 feet
Surf. Area: 600 acres
Depth: 10 feet
Shoreline: 21 miles
Winter Freeze: Yes

CAMPING/RVING	RECREATION	BOATING	MISCELLANEOUS
Tents/Trailers/RVs -2 national forest campgrounds on west side of lake Dairy Springs Campground -30 sites - $7/night -tables, fire rings -pit toilets, drinking water Double Springs Campground(preferably for tents) -15 sites - $6/night -tables, grills -vault toilets, drinking water -campgrounds open from Memorial Day to mid- September	-swimming -canoeing -hiking -picnicking -horseback riding -water skiing -wind surfing -biking -fishing: (there are no fish in Mormon Lake as of this printing) -shore fishing	-primitive boat launch -no motor restrictions -lake is shallow and weedy - canoes, row boats, and inflatables are best	-nearest facilities or conveniences are at south end of lake in the town of Mormon Lake -the lake may be drained or may freeze over in winter -full RV hookups at private campgrounds in town of Mormon Lake - south end of lake

Information:	Coconino National Forest (602) 774-1147

Kinnikinick Lake and the adjacent Morton Lake are located in north central Arizona's Coconino National Forest. At 7000 feet, the lake freezes over in winter and may well supply some good ice fishing. Summer months offer a variety of stocked trout on this 120-acre lake that can be fished by boat or from shore. The pinon and juniper surrounding this lake make it a picturesque location to enjoy your favorite outdoor activity. Elk are particularly common with some antelope scattered in. Camping facilities are limited and sparse. Conveniences are minimal also. Access is east from the Lake Mary-Mormon Lake Road, 29 miles south of Flagstaff, then 9 miles on Forest Roads 125 and 82. This location can be pleasantly remote for those self-contained outdoorsy types.

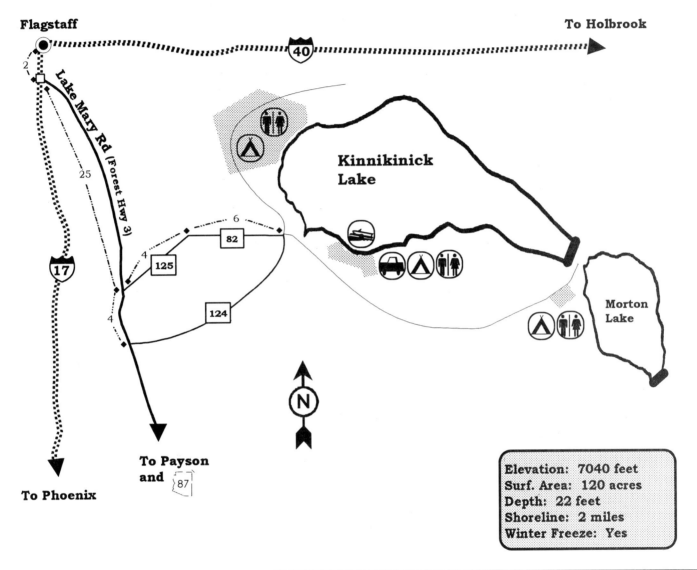

Elevation: 7040 feet
Surf. Area: 120 acres
Depth: 22 feet
Shoreline: 2 miles
Winter Freeze: Yes

CAMPING/RVING	RECREATION	BOATING	MISCELLANEOUS

Tents/Trailers/RVs
-13 sites
-no hookups
-rest rooms
-tables, grills
-fire pits
-no drinking water
	-swimming
	-picnicking
	-hiking
	-horseback riding
	-canoeing, sailing
	-fishing: rainbow trout,
	  brown trout, cutthroat
	  trout
	-shore fishing
		-launch ramp
		-8 horse power motor
		  maximum
		-relatively shallow with
		22-foot average depth
			-closest town is Flagstaff, 37
			  miles northwest
			-conveniences located
			  along Lake Mary-Mormon
			  Lake Road, 10 miles west of
			  lake
			-open year round

Information:	Coconino National Forest (602) 774-1147		

SOLDIER / SOLDIER ANNEX / LONG LAKE (#2)

This three-lake combo sits at a 6700-foot elevation on the eastern side of the Coconino National Forest. These three lakes are all within 1 mile of one another and are connected, thus whatever fish species are in one are in the others. In spite of the elevation, these lakes are managed as warm water fisheries but there is an occasional rainbow caught. Long Lake is by far the largest at 270 acres with Soldier Lake and Soldier Annex 30 and 60 acres respectively. The only motor restriction is on Soldier Lake, electric trolling motor only. There are no facilities at these lakes whatsoever and boat launching is primitive. if you're "self-contained" this is an excellent spot to get away from it all. But be cautious, the roads

linking the lakes are very rough with a high clearance vehicle recommended. The closest developed campsites are at Blue Ridge, Kinnikinick or Rock Crossing National Forest Campgrounds. The surrounding area has all the pristine beauty of the Coconino National Forest. The hiker will relish the flora and. fauna on any of the six major trails contained within the Blue Ridge Ranger District. Summer weather is what you might expect at this elevation; moderate summer days, cool evenings. Access is not the easiest, but these lakes can be reached from either the south via Highway 87 or from the west off of Forest Highway 3 (Mormon/Lake Mary Road). The route from Highway 87 keeps you on the pavement a bit more.

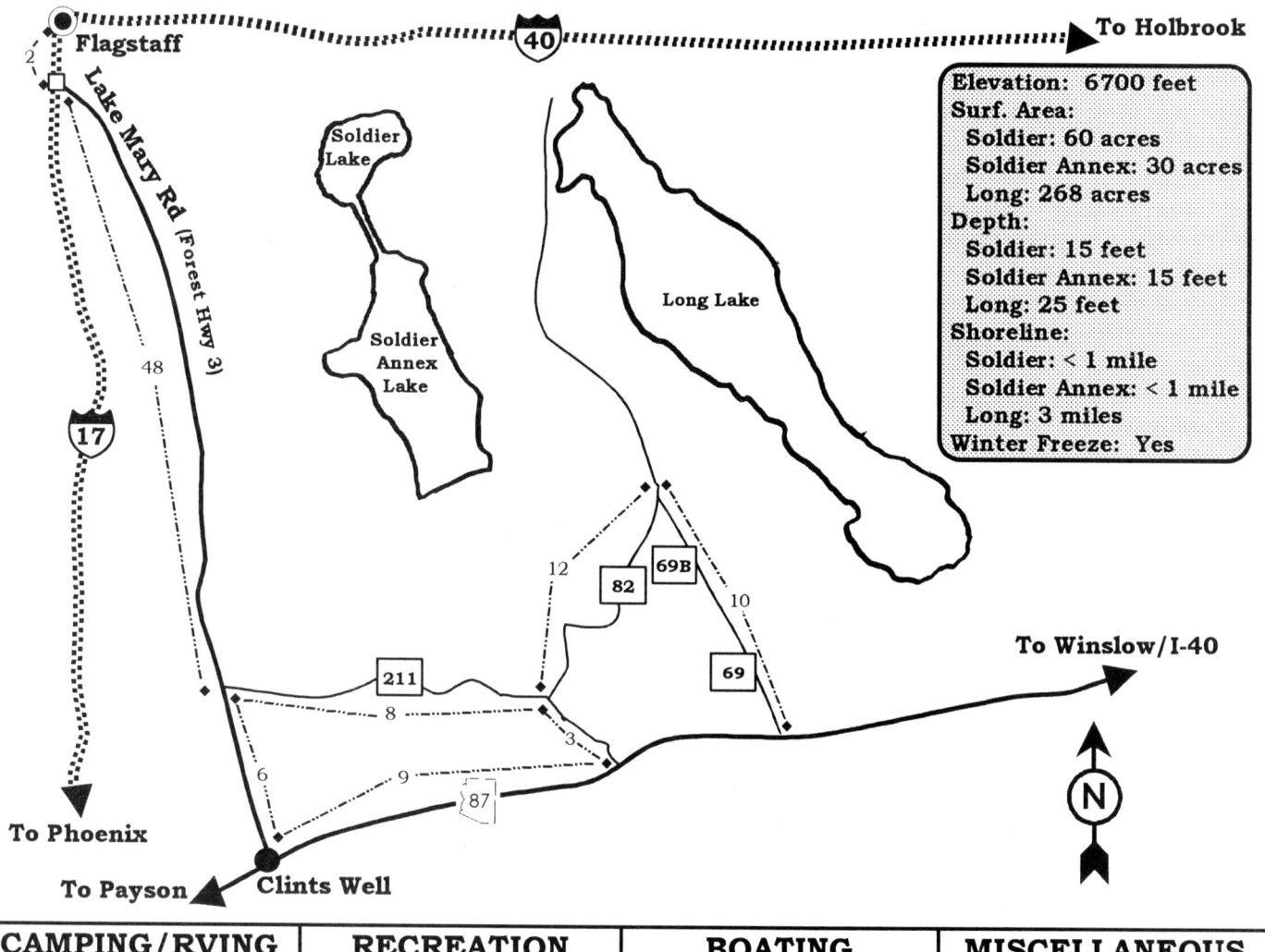

Elevation: 6700 feet
Surf. Area:
    Soldier: 60 acres
    Soldier Annex: 30 acres
    Long: 268 acres
Depth:
    Soldier: 15 feet
    Soldier Annex: 15 feet
    Long: 25 feet
Shoreline:
    Soldier: < 1 mile
    Soldier Annex: < 1 mile
    Long: 3 miles
Winter Freeze: Yes

CAMPING/RVING	RECREATION	BOATING	MISCELLANEOUS
Tents/Trailers/RVs -camping allowed but no developed sites or facilities -closest developed campgrounds are at Kinnikinick Lake or Blue Ridge or Rock Crossing -dead and downed wood may be collected for use	-swimming -canoeing -picnicking -hiking -hunting -fishing: northern pike, walleye largemouth bass, channel catfish, trout -shore fishing	-Soldier Lake has restriction of electric motor only -Soldier Annex and Long Lake have no motor restrictions -boat launching is primitive -Long Lake - 268 acres -Soldier Lake - 30 acres -Soldier Annex Lake - 60 acres	-access between Long Lake and Soldier/Soldier Annex Lakes is difficult - high-clearance vehicle recommended -closest conveniences are on Highway 87 at Clint's Well, 24 miles southwest
Information:	Coconino National Forest (602) 774-1147		

Stoneman Lake, at 6200 foot elevation, resides within the 1.8 million acre Coconino National Forest. It has the distinction of being the only permanent lake in Arizona which is not manmade. The lake resides within a volcanic crater. There are no facilities or conveniences at the lake other than a launch ramp. No developed camping exists at or near the lake. One is left with primitive camping. The lake is best fished from a boat due to the weeds which ring the lake's perimeter. Access to Stoneman Lake is east of I-17, north of Camp Verde. Take the "Stoneman Lake Interchange" Forest Road 213, east 9 miles to the lake.

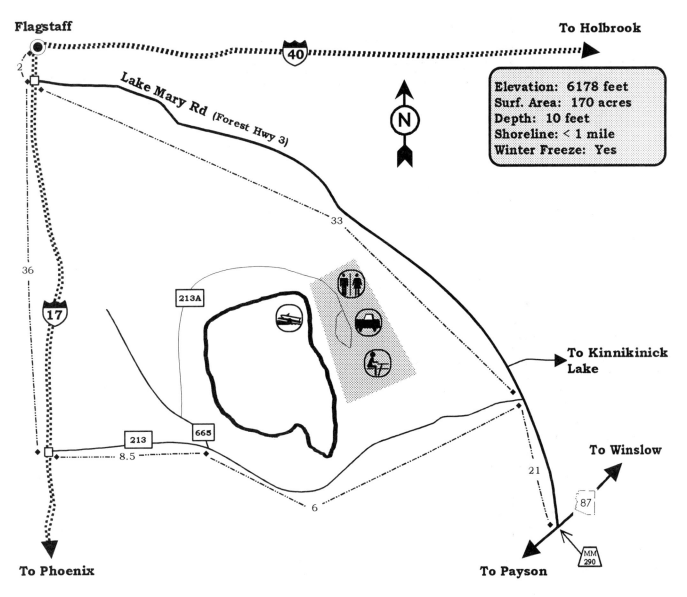

Elevation: 6178 feet
Surf. Area: 170 acres
Depth: 10 feet
Shoreline: < 1 mile
Winter Freeze: Yes

CAMPING/RVING	RECREATION	BOATING	MISCELLANEOUS
-no camping at the lake site -various campgrounds located in the Coconino National Forest - the closest are Mormon Lake to the north and Beaver Creek to the south	-hiking, vault toilets -picnicking (tables) -horseback riding -fishing: northern pike, yellow perch NOTE: fishing is best from a small boat/canoe due to weeds which grow near the perimeter of the lake	-electric motor only -gravel launch area	-nearest conveniences at Happy Jack, 9 miles to the southeast -nearest town is Camp Verde, 30 miles west

Information:	Coconino National Forest (602) 774-1147

STEHR LAKE

Stehr Lake is a nondescript, not very useful lake which sits at 3500 foot elevation on the southern tip of the Coconino National Forest. This shallow and weedy lake is only a few acres. This lake contains a warm water variety of fish. There are no facilities whatsoever at the lake. Primitive camping is allowed. The surrounding environment could be called "low shrub." There is really nothing to draw one to Stehr Lake except solitude.

Access is from either the west Camp Verde or the east Pine/Strawberry off of Forest Road 708. From Pine/Strawberry the distance is shorter, 13 miles from the highway. At any rate, go south from Forest Road 708 on Forest Road 502 for 3 miles. Continuing past the lake would bring you to the Childs Power Plant which sits on the Verde River. The lake is on the east side of Forest Road 502.

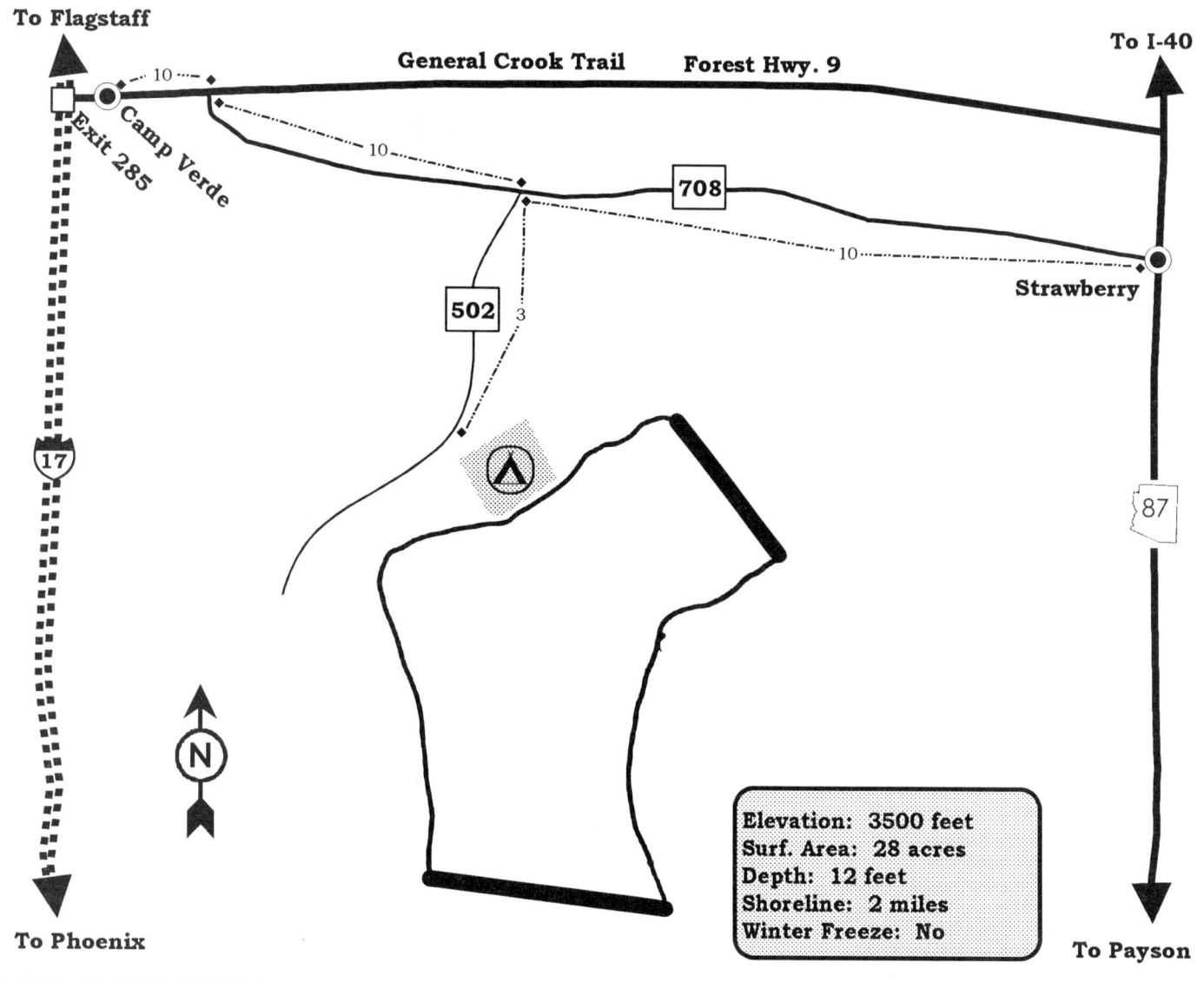

Elevation: 3500 feet
Surf. Area: 28 acres
Depth: 12 feet
Shoreline: 2 miles
Winter Freeze: No

CAMPING/RVING	RECREATION	BOATING	MISCELLANEOUS
-no developed campsites at or near the lake -nearest national forest campgrounds is Clear Creek, 6 miles east of Camp Verde, 20 miles from the lake	-canoeing -picnicking -hiking -horseback riding -fishing: largemouth bass, catfish, sunfish NOTE: shore fishing difficult -snoozing -no swimming	-electric motors only -lake is shallow, weedy, and less than 5 acres -boating is not recommended, but a small canoe or inflatable is OK	-nearest town is Camp Verde, 25 miles -Childs Power Plant is located on the Verde River, just 3 miles southwest

Information:	Coconino National Forest (602) 567-4501

At a 6700-foot elevation, Blue Ridge Reservoir is within the Coconino National Forest. A long, slender U-shaped lake, it belongs to anglers. Set in a deep steep walled canyon, this lake is best fished by boat. Some spots on this 70-acre lake approach 800-feet deep thus a 150-foot average depth exists. Shore fishing is a bit difficult. One of the more scenic lakes up in the coolness of the Rim, there is some excellent hiking in the surrounding acreage. Significant amounts of wildlife abound. Access is very easy. Take 87 north from Payson and turn east at a point 4 1/2 miles north (mile marker 295) of the town of Clint's Wells on Forest Road 751, another 6 miles on is a very good road and you are there.

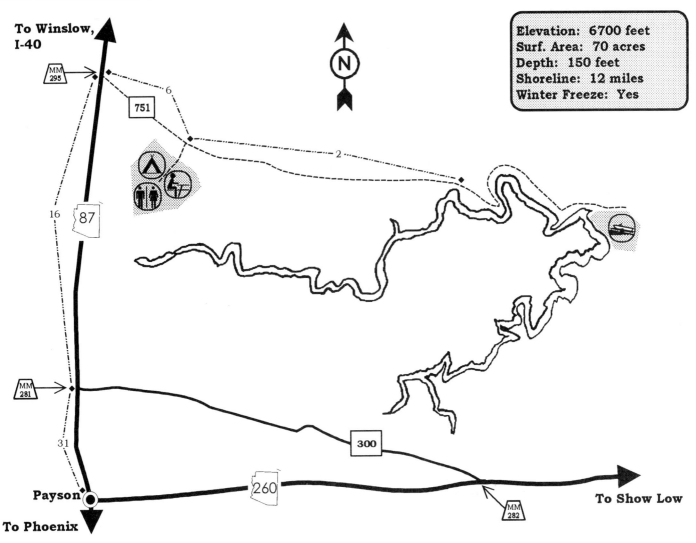

Elevation: 6700 feet
Surf. Area: 70 acres
Depth: 150 feet
Shoreline: 12 miles
Winter Freeze: Yes

CAMPING/RVING	RECREATION	BOATING	MISCELLANEOUS
Trailers/Tents/RVs -no camping at or very near this lake -Blue Ridge and Rock Crossing Campgrounds are within a few miles of lake -tables -drinking water -rest rooms -no showers -user fee	-canoeing -hiking -fishing: rainbow trout, brown trout, book trout, cutthroat trout -shore fishing limited -picnicking -ice fishing (access roads not cleared in winter)	-launch ramp -8 horse power motor maximum NOTE: cavernous underwater terrain - depth/fish finder might be useful	-nearest town is Clint's Well, 10-1/2 miles away -varied and plentiful services along Highway 87 near lake -seasonal use April to October

Information:	Coconino National Forest (602) 477-2255

23

KNOLL LAKE

Knoll Lake, at 7400-foot elevation, sits at the east edge of the Coconino National Forest. One of the "Rim Lakes" it has many of the same attributes. Knoll Lake is best known for its quiet fishing and solitude. The location and access to this lake keeps the summer Phoenix crowds down. It is a simple enough road to the lake that requires patience and time but well worth it. Fishing is the order of the day at Knoll Lake with plenty of shoreline access for those without boats. The two sprawling arms of this 75-acre beauty makes trolling both effective and pleasurable. Be sure to circle the island with your boat - more than a few big ones have been landed here. Spring and fall provide the best times for the angler.

Camping is allowed at this lake which has moderate facilities. A day trip to Knoll is certainly doable even if it is for a quiet picnic or a hike. Weather is perfect in summer, warmish days, cool nights. Certainly the wild raspberries growing in Leonard Canyon will be a treat for the Knoll Lake hiker or even the casual wanderer. Access is northeast from Arizona Highway 260 past Woods Canyon Lake on the Rim Road (Forest Road 300) to 295B (also a forest service road). As long as you're on top of the rim, you might as well cruise the entire Rim Road to view its splendor and beauty. A word of caution: the Rim Road is not the best maintained, care should be taken but any vehicle can make the tour. Be patient.

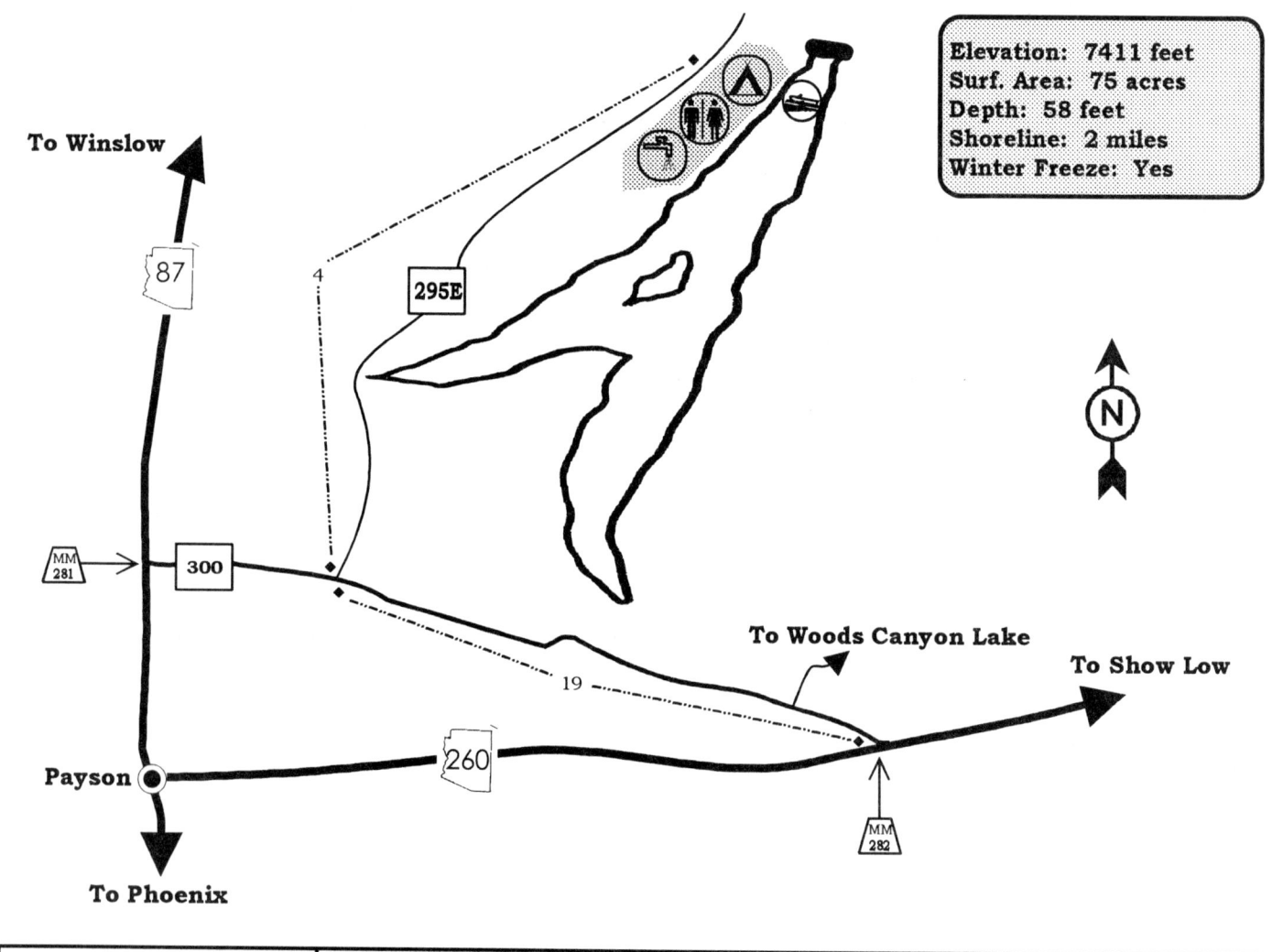

Elevation: 7411 feet
Surf. Area: 75 acres
Depth: 58 feet
Shoreline: 2 miles
Winter Freeze: Yes

CAMPING/RVING	RECREATION	BOATING	MISCELLANEOUS
Tent/Trailers/RVs -42 campsites -user fee -open May to September -drinking water -rest rooms -no showers	-picnicking -hiking -canoeing -fishing: rainbow trout, brown trout -shore fishing -ice fishing (access roads not cleared in winter)	-electric motors only -boat launch	-nearest town is Clint's Well, 32 miles away -nearest conveniences at Woods Canyon Lake store -season is May to September -wild raspberry picking in season just north in Leonard Canyon
Information:	Coconino National Forest (602) 477-2255		

Bear Canyon Lake is contained within the Apache-Sitgreaves National Forest. This is one lovely lake with its surrounding marshy meadows and aspen groves. Ponderosa pine and Douglas fir are the predominant vegetation around most of the lake. This lake seems untouched as its usage is low resulting directly from two facts: First, there is a steep walk of one-quarter mile to the lake (no car access) and, secondly, the angler is restricted to artificial lures only. At a 7500-foot elevation, it is plenty cool in the summer. Thus, the camper who is willing to pack in what they need will find solitude, comfort, and beauty. The lake is 65 acres in a canyon with three miles of shoreline. A small boat/raft or canoe serves the angler best. The capable hiker will certainly enjoy the variety of trails at the lake itself or in the general area. Wildlife abounds in this most natural setting. Access is north from Highway 260 for 12 miles on the "Rim Road" (Forest Service Road 300), then 3 more miles north on Forest Service Road 89 to a paved lake entrance. The access roads can be difficult. Be patient.

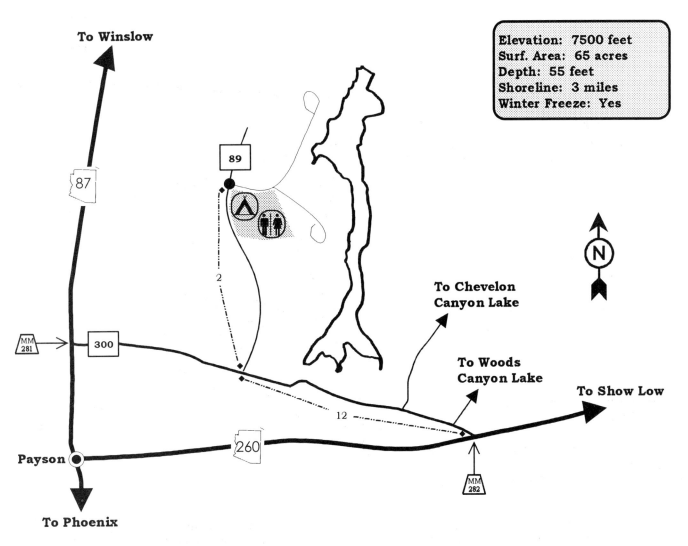

Elevation: 7500 feet
Surf. Area: 65 acres
Depth: 55 feet
Shoreline: 3 miles
Winter Freeze: Yes

To Winslow

To Chevelon Canyon Lake

To Woods Canyon Lake

To Show Low

Payson

To Phoenix

CAMPING / RVING	RECREATION	BOATING	MISCELLANEOUS
-no developed sites at lake -open camping -primitive toilets -pack it in - pack it out -no water	-hiking, canoeing, picnicking -fishing: rainbow trout, brook trout, cutthroat trout -artificial lures only (no live bait) -shore fishing is difficult with trees up to waters edge	-electric motor only -no launch ramp -no vehicle access to lake -all boats/motor equipment must be carried 1/4 mile down a steep but excellent trail	-closest town is Heber -closest convenience is the Woods Canyon Lake store -access roads not cleared in winter
Information:	Apache Sitgreaves National Forest (602) 289-2471		

WOODS CANYON LAKE

Woods Canyon Lake is located within the two-million acre Apache-Sitgreaves National Forest. Sitting on the top of the Mogollon Rim at 7500 feet, this "Rim Lake" is one of the busiest due to its easy access, cool summer days, and fine facilities. The lake itself is primarily an angler's pond at 55 acres with plenty of stocked rainbow to catch in the summer months. Ice fishing can be excellent also. The lake is best fished from a boat but there is plenty of shore fishing access on its three miles of shoreline. Camping in the cool pines and aspen can be very relaxing at any of the five very-close-to-the-lake campgrounds. The immediate area will have plenty of people in it so solitude is not a strong point. But there is not so many people as to scare away the abundant wildlife roaming in the forest. The hiker will want for nothing in the beautiful surrounding forests, nor will the horseback rider. Day-use and group-use facilities are more than adequate. Remember to work your way up Leonard Canyon in late summer - the raspberry picking can be superb. Access is 22 miles east of Payson on Highway 260 then 4 miles north on Forest Route 105 which is paved to the lake. Just follow the signs. It is very very easy to reach. Highway 260 has services and conveniences east or west of the turn off.

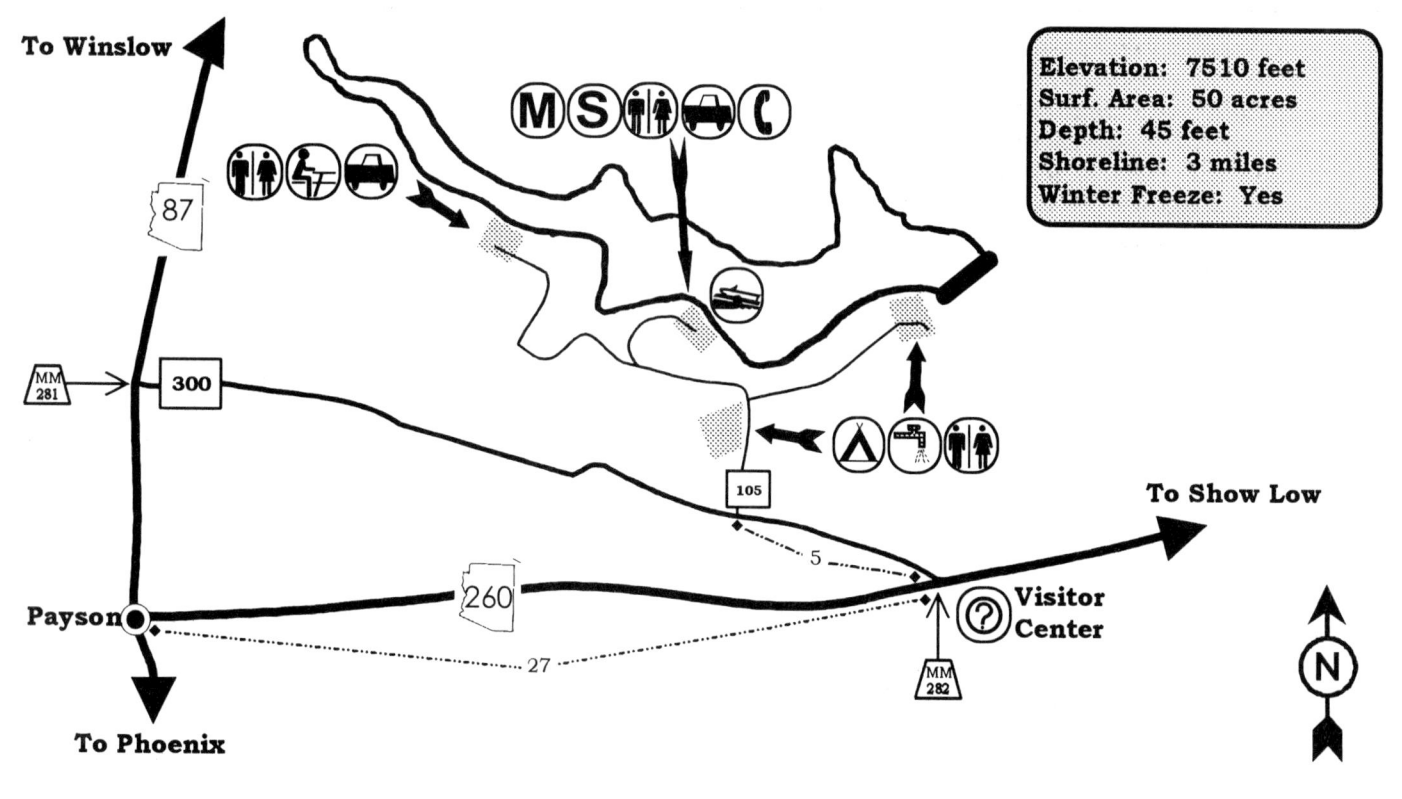

Elevation: 7510 feet
Surf. Area: 50 acres
Depth: 45 feet
Shoreline: 3 miles
Winter Freeze: Yes

CAMPING/RVING	RECREATION	BOATING	MISCELLANEOUS
Tents/Trailers/RVs Five Forest Service campgrounds (240 total sites) adjacent to or within four miles of the lake -drinking water -dump station -rest rooms -no RV hookups -recommend early arrival on summer weekends -reservation: 1-800-283-0267 (recommend but not required)	-picnicking, hiking -group picnic area -canoeing, horseback riding -fishing: rainbow, brown trout -shore fishing, ice fishing -no swimming NOTE: recent concern for public safety has resulted in the disallowing of hunting, indiscriminate discharge of firearms, air rifles or gas guns - contact ranger district for specifics at (602) 333-4372 or (602) 289-2471	-electric motor only -improved ramp - no fee -courtesy dock -boat/motor rental at lake store	-season: May to October -convenience store at lake: boat/motor rental, bait, groceries, drinks, camping supplies, tackle, license, fuel/oil -plenty of campfire wood lying around surrounding forest -raspberries in season to the northwest in Leonard Canyon -nearest town is Heber, 26 miles east

Information: Apache-Sitgreaves National Forest (602) 289-2471

Willow Springs Lake is typical of the high mountain Mogollon Rim lakes with its cool weather and scenic atmosphere. This 150-acre lake is managed by the Apache-Sitgreaves National Forest. A national forest campground is located one miles from lake. At 7500 foot elevation, fishing and picnicking or just enjoying the cool summer days seems adequate to draw summer crowds.

The 8 horsepower motor restriction cancels the water skiing, thus the angler, be they from boat or shore, can rely on a quiet day. Canoer's and hikers love Willow Springs Lake. Willow Springs Lake has all the high mountain beauty Arizona has to offer. Access is easy on a 1-mile paved road (Forest Route 149) north of Arizona 260, 32 miles from Payson.

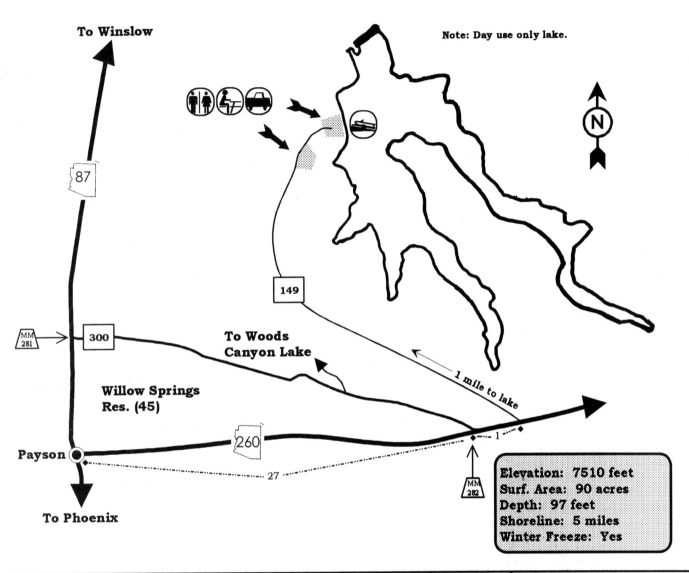

Note: Day use only lake.

To Winslow

To Woods Canyon Lake

Willow Springs Res. (45)

Payson

To Phoenix

1 mile to lake

Elevation: 7510 feet
Surf. Area: 90 acres
Depth: 97 feet
Shoreline: 5 miles
Winter Freeze: Yes

CAMPING/RVING	RECREATION	BOATING	MISCELLANEOUS
Tents/Trailers/RVs Sinkhole Campground 1 mile from lake -26 sites -$5/night -water, fire ring -primitive toilets -campground host on site -recommend early arrivals on weekends	-hiking -sailing, canoeing -picnicking -fishing: rainbow, brown, brook and cutthroat trout -shore fishing -no facilities at lake shore other than primitive toilets	-1 improved ramp -8 horse power motor maximum -small boat dock	-closest convenience at Woods Canyon Lake store -closest town is Heber -firewood may be picked up for use -raspberries in season to the northwest in Leonard's Canyon
Information:	Apache-Sitgreaves National Forest (602) 535-4481		

CHEVELON CANYON LAKE

Chevelon Canyon Lake is one of the "Rim Lakes" on the Apache-Sitgreaves National Forest which serves the greater Phoenix area as a cool summer weekend retreat. It is at 6400 feet and set in a deep canyon well off the main roads. Chevelon Canyon Lake offers solitude and some excellent fishing for those who will brave the three-quarter mile incline to and from the lake. There are no camping conveniences at or near the lake with essentially no conveniences at all for recreation. This is relatively remote with only the serious campers and anglers in attendance. With 200 acres, a boat works well here but the three-quarter mile trek up and down the canyon walls is tough to say the least. Shore fishing is just fine and accessible on the six miles of shoreline. Some locals keep a boat hidden nearby or chained to a tree. Not a bad idea. Hikers will revel here as elsewhere on the rim, wildlife abounds. Remember, Chevelon Canyon Lake is "remote" so the rules are "pack it in/pack it out." Access can be from the north through Winslow, 44 miles south of town. Take Highway 99 south to Forest Road 504, then 169, then 169B. These are reasonably well maintained gravel roads. From the south, take the Woods Canyon Lake turn off from Highway 260 to 169 north and you'll arrive 23 miles later on gravel and dirt roads. Highway 260 has many services and conveniences either side of the Woods Canyon turn off.

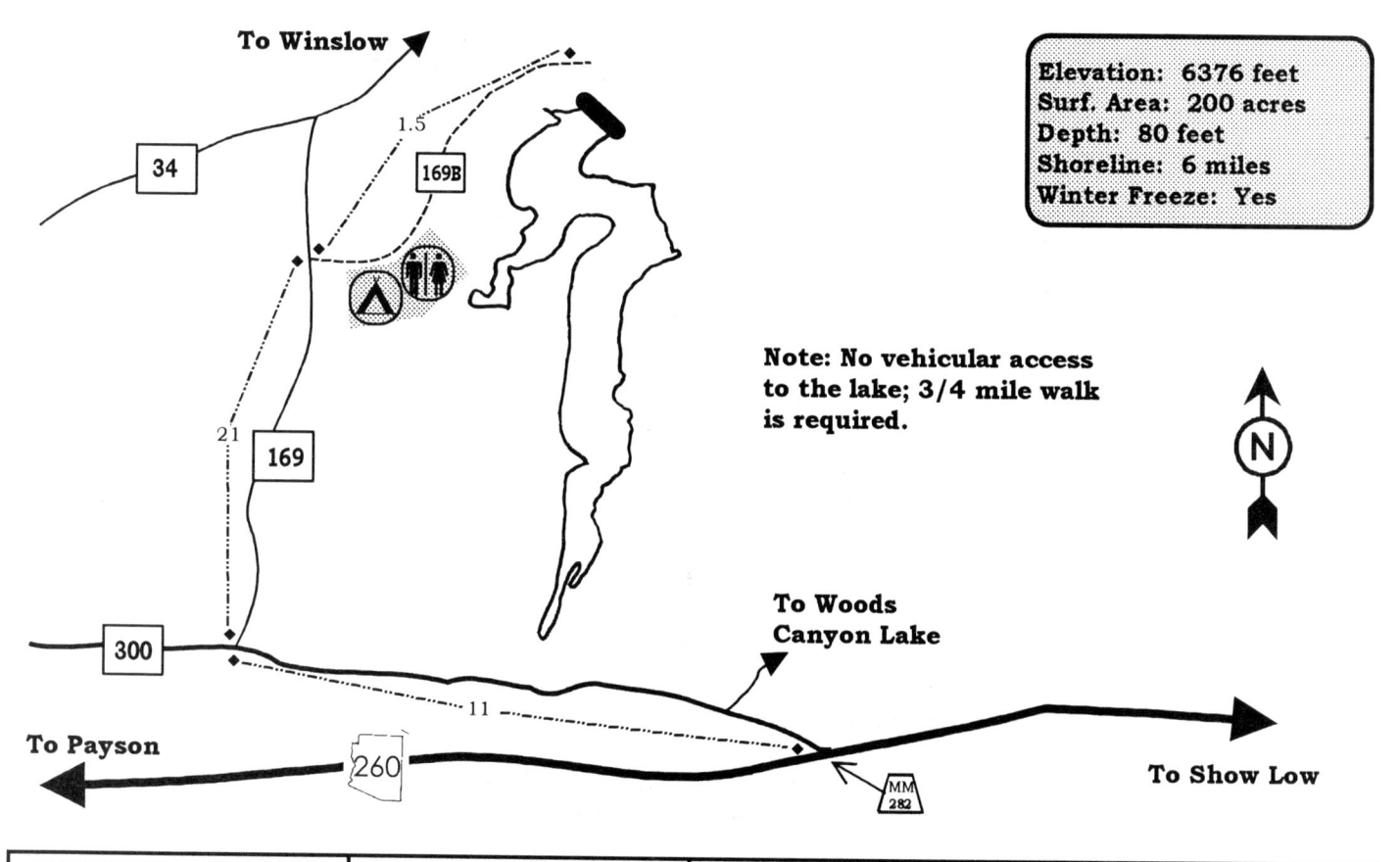

Elevation: 6376 feet
Surf. Area: 200 acres
Depth: 80 feet
Shoreline: 6 miles
Winter Freeze: Yes

Note: No vehicular access to the lake; 3/4 mile walk is required.

CAMPING/RVING	RECREATION	BOATING	MISCELLANEOUS
Tents/Trailers/RVs -campground up hill 3/4 mile from lake -no developed sites, primitive camping only -no hookups -no drinking water -pit toilets only -essentially there are no camping facilities at or near the lake -pack it in - pack it out	-hiking -canoeing -horseback riding -fishing: rainbow trout, brown trout -shore fishing -no day-use facilities	-8 horse power motor maximum -no ramp -recommend small or inflatable boat or canoe -some locals keep a boat at the lake chained to a tree	-open year round -closest conveniences are located at Woods Canyon Lake store -closest town is Heber, 50 miles -raspberries in season to the northwest in Leonard Canyon (pick to your hearts content) -plenty of campfire wood lying around -access roads not cleared in winter

| Information: | Apache-Sitgreaves National Forest (602) 289-2471 |

Black Canyon Lake is typical of the many Mogollon Rim lakes in its beauty and usage. Managed by the Apache-Sitgreaves National Forest, it sits at a 7100-foot elevation and is approximately 78 acres. The primary activity in this forest-surrounded beauty is trout fishing. Shore fishing and trolling, from a small boat are both popular. Ice fishing is available in winter although the access roads are not cleared of snow. Crowds are moderate due to the six miles of dirt/gravel roads which are not particularly well maintained. Open camping is available along most of this six-mile trek. There is one campground three miles from the lake with minimal facilities. Quiet is the order of the day at Black Canyon Lake and its surrounding forests of ponderosa pine and mixed conifer. Access is south of Arizona Highway 260 at mile marker 291. There is six miles of dirt/gravel road, the lake is easy to find by just following the signs. The last one-quarter mile just before the lake is paved with ample parking at lakeside.

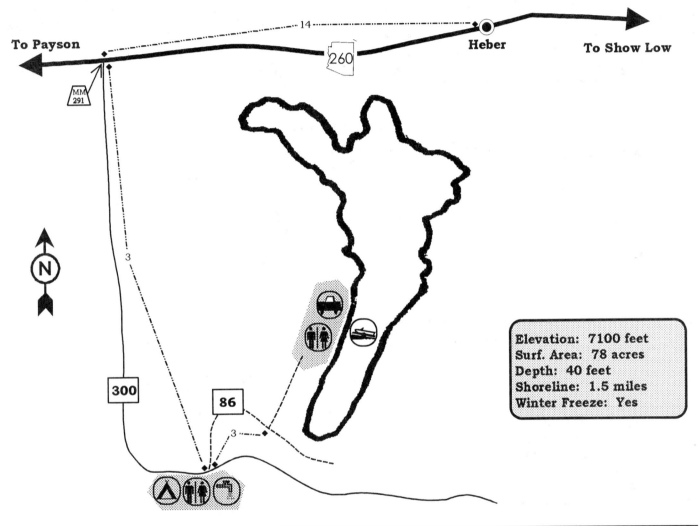

To Payson

Heber

To Show Low

14

260

MM 291

N

3

300

86

3

Elevation: 7100 feet
Surf. Area: 78 acres
Depth: 40 feet
Shoreline: 1.5 miles
Winter Freeze: Yes

CAMPING/RVING	RECREATION	BOATING	MISCELLANEOUS
-camping not allowed within 1/4 mile of lake -Black Canyon Rim campground is three miles from lake: 20 sites, $4/night -water, tables, fire pits, grills -rest rooms primitive -dogs on a leash only -open camping along access roads to lake: no utilities, no services	-picnicking -canoeing -hiking -horseback riding -fishing: brown trout, rainbow trout -shore fishing -ice fishing (access roads not cleared in winter though) -no ATVs/ATCs	-improved launch ramp -electric motor only	-nearest town is Heber, 13 miles away -nearest conveniences 7.5 miles at Forest Lakes -variety of services within five miles east or west on Highway 260 -plenty of firewood lying around the forest for campfires
Information:	Apache Sitgreaves National Forest (602) 535-4481		

MCHOOD PARK LAKE

Known previously as Clear Creek Reservoir, McHood Lake is now managed by the city of Winslow. Its services are built around meeting the needs of the city's inhabitants. Camping is allowed but only a minimal number of sites are constructed. Day-use-facilities are excellent to include a group pavilion for picnicking. Jet ski course in summer, horseshoe pits, defined swimming area, and small playground are within the park. The lake's

surroundings are relatively barren so bring your own shade. The angler will have an easier time of it midweek when things are quieter and may catch some of the stocked rainbows, bass or a catfish guy. Access is simple, 6 miles south of Winslow on State Highway 99. From the south, come up State Highway 87 from Payson (90 miles) and turn right on to Highway 99. Paved roads all the way make this lake very accessible.

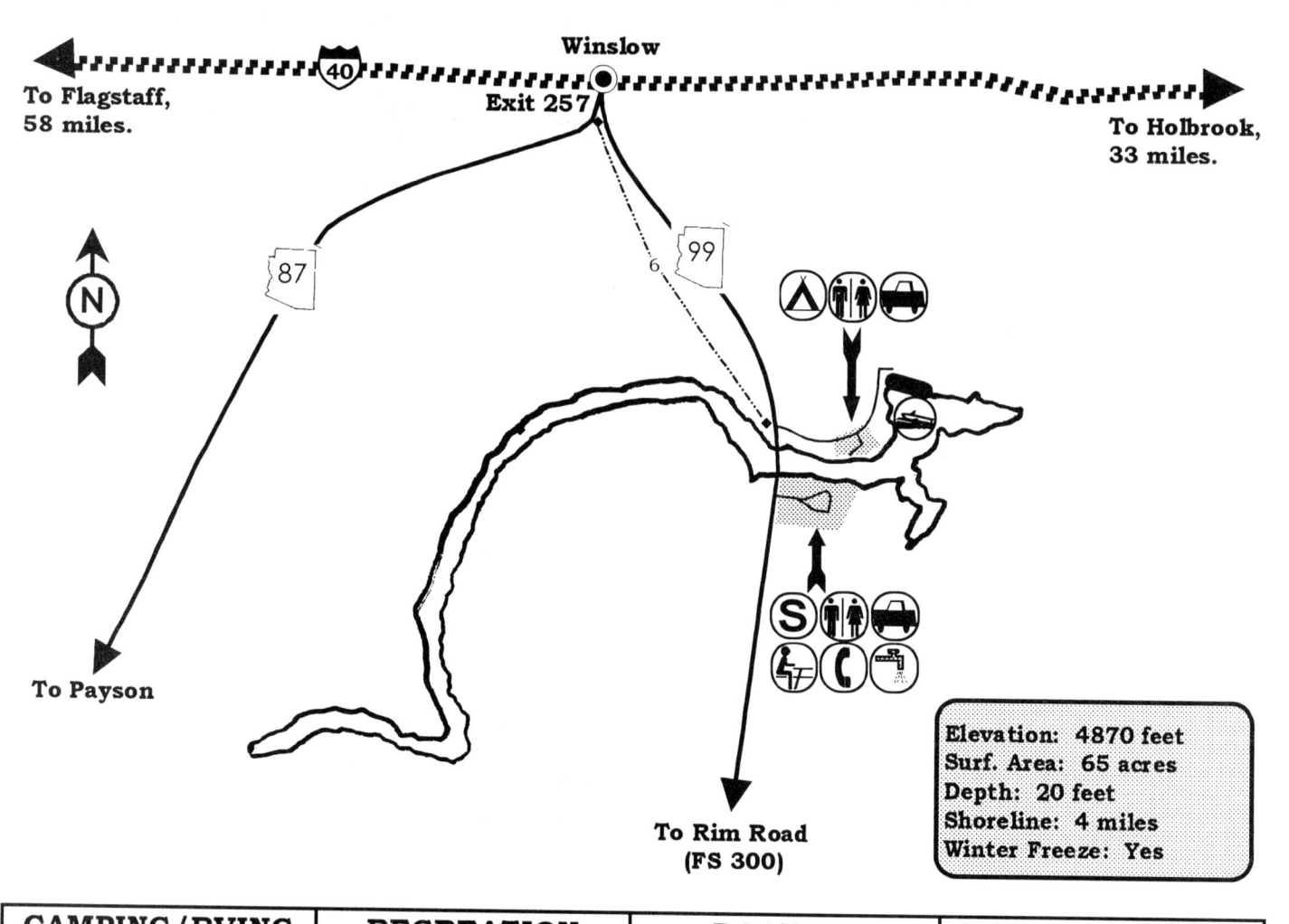

Elevation: 4870 feet
Surf. Area: 65 acres
Depth: 20 feet
Shoreline: 4 miles
Winter Freeze: Yes

CAMPING/RVING	RECREATION	BOATING	MISCELLANEOUS
Tents/Trailers/RVs -3 RV sites with electricity/water at $7/night -7 developed sites at $6/night -ramadas -tables -grills -drinking water -hot showers -rest rooms	-picnicking: ramadas, tables, grills -swimming -canoeing, sailing -fishing: rainbow trout, bass, catfish -recreational use fees: Winslow resident $2/vehicle, nonresident $3/vehicle, $20/yearly pass, group use pavilion $30/day -horseshoe pits -playgrounds	-improved ramp -no motor restrictions -jet ski course constructed in summer -convenience dock	-nearest town is Winslow -no conveniences or service at lake -public telephone
Information:	Winslow Park and Recreation Department (602) 289-5714		

Cholla Lake is managed by the Navajo County Park and Recreation Department. At 5000 foot elevation, it is a rare lake on this high desert mesa. The lake's primary purpose is water storage for the adjacent Cholla Power Plant (steam/electric). The primary activity on this 360-acre lake is water skiing. Day-use facilities are abundant for picnicking and swimming. RVers and tent campers will find a nice home here in a small group of trees adjacent to the lake. The angler will find catfish and bass in the shallow, warm, and weedy water. The summer months are warm and generally windy. Boaters need to be aware of the recommended boating patterns posted at the launch ramp. Access to Cholla Lake is on a paved road 1 mile south of Interstate 40, 11 miles west of Holbrook (exit 277).

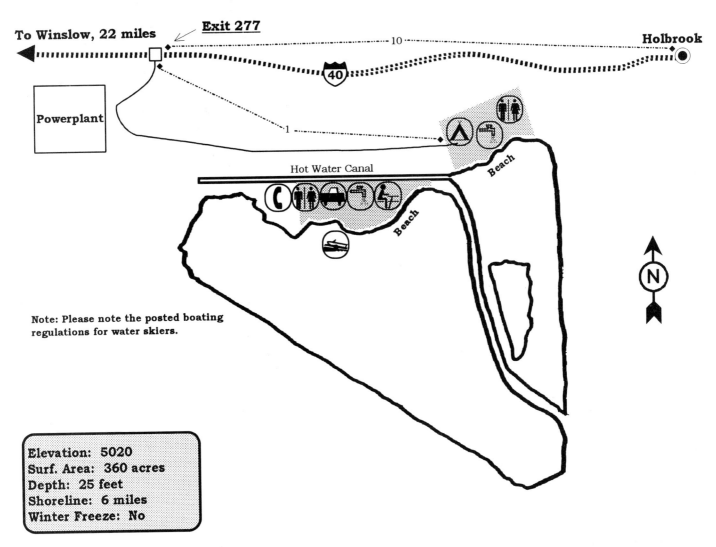

Note: Please note the posted boating regulations for water skiers.

Elevation: 5020
Surf. Area: 360 acres
Depth: 25 feet
Shoreline: 6 miles
Winter Freeze: No

CAMPING/RVING	RECREATION	BOATING	MISCELLANEOUS
-15 camping sites (no reservations) 10 RV sites; water and power only, no sewer camping fees: $7 basic site, $10 water and electricity -rest rooms, no showers -drinking water -no glass in the park -no dump station	-picnicking: ramadas, grills, and tables -swimming: small sandy beach, no swimming in hot canal -water skiing, sail boarding -sailing -fishing: catfish, bass -shore fishing -volleyball pit in picnic area	-1 improved ramp -no motor restrictions -some sections of lake closed to boating -beware of posted boating regulations -heavy weed growth in summer	-public telephone in park -nearest town is Holbrook -no conveniences at the lake -no glass containers in park -handicap rest rooms -day-use fees: $2 county resident, $3 non-county, $25 annual permit -minimal shade at the lake
Information:	Navajo County Park and Recreation Department (602) 288-3717		

ANTELOPE LAKE

Antelope Lake resides in the southern end of the Chuska Mountains, on the Navajo Nation. At 7300 feet, it is strictly a trout lake, but receives little pressure. Again, spring and fall are the best fishing times, with the summer bringing weeds, weeds, and more weeds in this 10-foot deep, 3-acre pond. Camping is allowed but there are no facilities at the lake. Special permits and fees are required for fishing, boating, back country use, hunting and trapping. This is one place to go if you're looking to avoid crowds. the Chuska Mountains offer spectacular scenery for the hiker or equestrian. Remember to take along a camera. The Navajo Nation offers significant opportunities for sight seeing and experiencing the local culture. Be sure to get a local map of this 16-million acre reservation, there is much to see. The woven basketry and silver work made locally is unparalleled. To get to Antelope Lake, from I-40 go north at Exit 343 and head towards Pine Springs. The distance from I-40 to the lake is 22 miles. The last few miles are a bit rough. Please, before you enter the Navajo Nation, make sure you are aware of any and all special requirements for camping, hunting, fishing or boating.

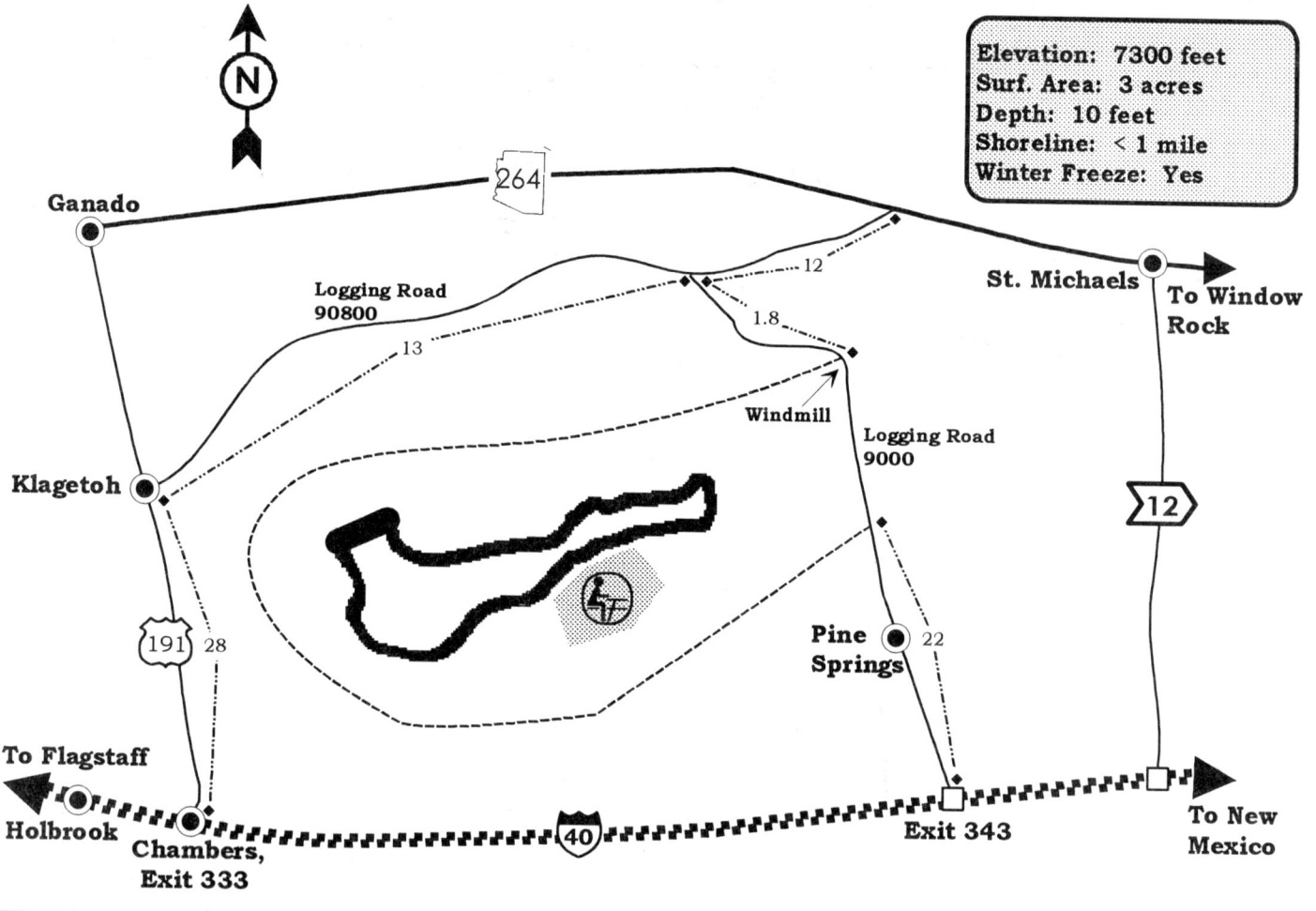

Elevation: 7300 feet
Surf. Area: 3 acres
Depth: 10 feet
Shoreline: < 1 mile
Winter Freeze: Yes

CAMPING/RVING	RECREATION	BOATING	MISCELLANEOUS
Tents/Trailers/RVs -no developed campsites -open primitive camping is allowed -pets on leash only -use of firearms prohibited	-picnicking, horseback riding -canoeing -hiking (back country permit required) -fishing: rainbow trout -shore fishing -no swimming -no ATVs/ATCs -hunting/trapping (permit and fee required) -napping	-electric motor only -no launch -boating permit and fee required	-nearest conveniences in Pine Springs, 9 miles south -nearest town is Window Rock (18 miles northwest) PERMITS AND FEES: camping, boating, fishing, and other recreational activities require a permit and fee - see section on the Navajo Nation contained within this book
Information:	Navajo Nation Park and Recreation (602) 871-6647 - Tourism Dept. (602) 871-6673		

Red Lake (#1) sits at 5500 foot elevation and resides on the Navajo Nation. This Red Lake should not be confused with another Red Lake (#2), which is dry and is located 8 miles northeast of Williams, Arizona, approximately 200 miles to the west. Oddly enough, the Arizona/New Mexico border cuts right through this lake but has no impact on permits or fees for the lakes use. The lake is usually muddy, which has resulted in the appropriate name. Camping is permitted, but no facilities are available. Red Lake is a large lake at over 900 acres, but a motor restriction of electric motor only still applies to this very shallow lake. While on the reservation, you should take advantage of the remarkable scenery. A day trip north or west is well worth the drive. Local artistry of silver work and woven basketry is unparalleled. Access to Red Lake is simple. Proceed north from I-40 at mile marker 358 and pass through Fort Defiance. The lake is a bit less than 50 miles from I-40 on Indian Highway 12. Please, Before you enter the Navajo Nation, make sure you are aware of any special requirements relative to camping, hiking, fishing, hunting or boating. Again, they are available from the number listed below.

Elevation: 7100 feet
Surf. Area: 908 acres
Depth: 6 feet
Shoreline: Varies greatly
Winter Freeze: Yes

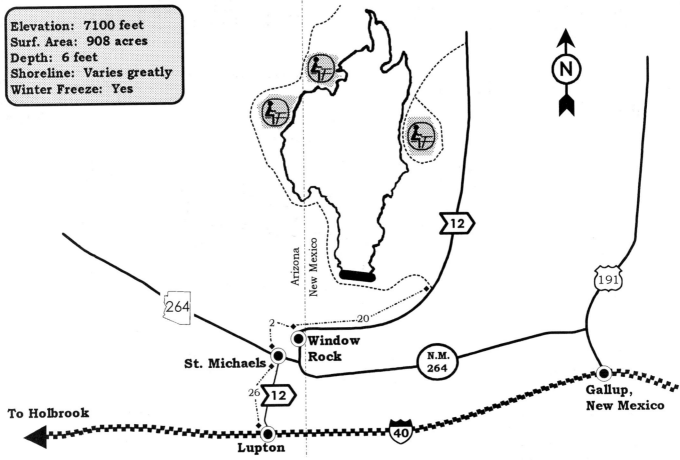

CAMPING/RVING	RECREATION	BOATING	MISCELLANEOUS
Tents/Trailers/RVs -no developed campsites -open primitive camping is allowed -pets on leash only -use of firearms prohibited -closest lodging in Navajo, New Mexico	-picnicking, horseback riding -sailing, sail boarding, canoeing -hiking (back country permit required) -fishing: channel catfish, large mouth bas, bullhead (special permits and limits apply) -shore fishing -no swimming -no ATVs/ATCs -hunting/trapping (permit and fee required)	-electric motor only -no launch -boating permit and fee required	-nearest conveniences are in the town of Navajo, New Mexico, just 2 and 1/2 miles south of the lake PERMITS AND FEES: camping, boating, fishing, and other recreational activities require a permit and fee - see section on the Navajo Nation contained within this book
Information:	Navajo Nation Park and Recreation (602) 871-6647 - Tourism Dept. (602) 871-6673		

WHEATFIELDS LAKE

At a 7300-foot elevation, Wheatfields Lake is located on the 16-million acre Navajo Nation in northeastern Arizona. The Navajo Nation is the largest Indian reservation in North America and is host to a wonderful people, culture, and much scenic beauty. There are a dozen or so major lakes in this rugged country and the surrounding Chuska Mountains provide some spectacular scenery and landscape. Wheatfields Lake is the most popular of the Navajo Nation's lakes due to its ease of access combined with excellent spring and fall trout fishing. The lake covers 270 acres and has an adjacent campground and small store. Hiking the surrounding hills and forests will yield some memorable scenery with an occasional deer or turkey among the abundant small game. While on the Navajo Nation, be certain to take in the local sites and events. Canyon de Chelley National Monument is immediately west of the lake with easy access. The reservation's silver work and woven basketry are unparalleled. Wheatfields Lake has easy access. Proceed north from I-40 at Exit 357 just a few miles from the New Mexico border. You'll pass through Window Rock (reservation headquarters) on this 70-mile journey. Please, before you enter the Navajo Nation, make sure you are aware of any and all special requirements for camping, hunting, fishing or boating.

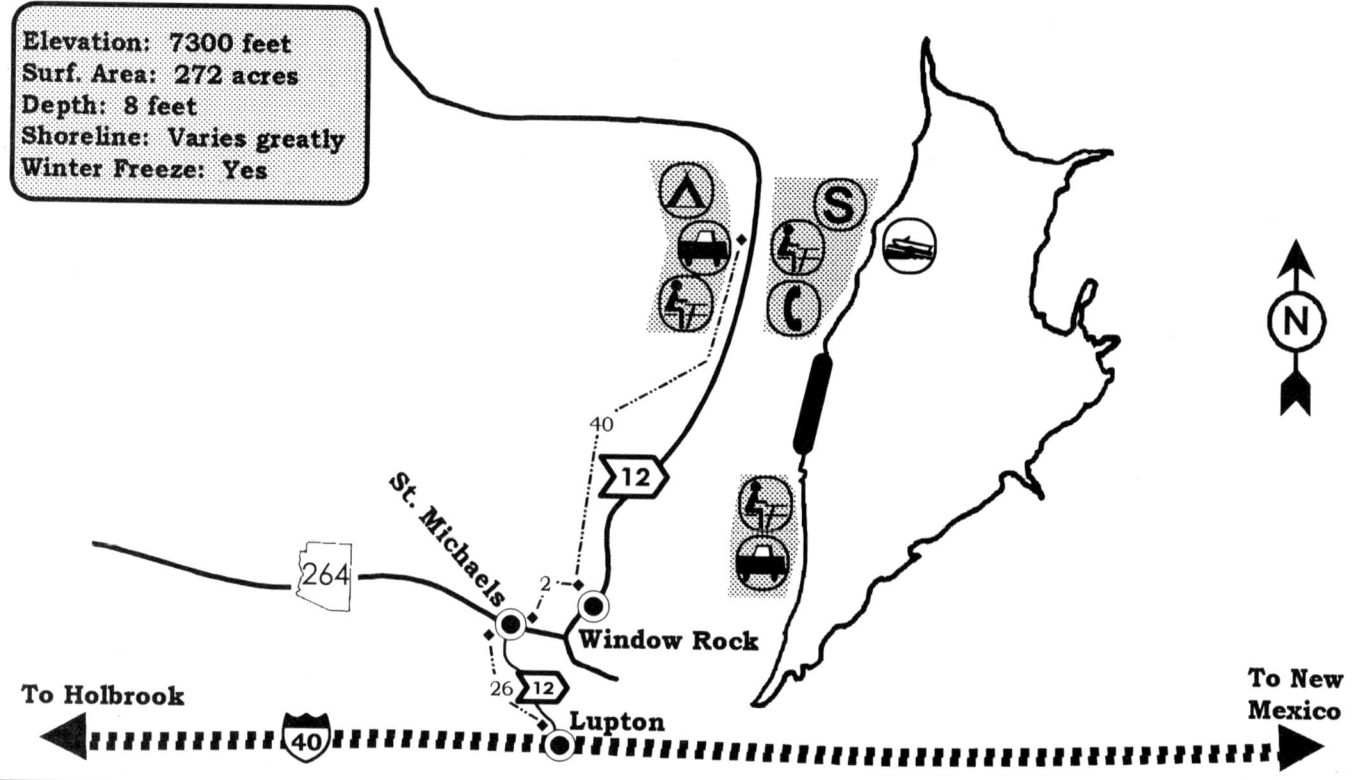

Elevation: 7300 feet
Surf. Area: 272 acres
Depth: 8 feet
Shoreline: Varies greatly
Winter Freeze: Yes

St. Michaels
264
40
12
2
Window Rock
26 12
Lupton
40
To Holbrook
To New Mexico
N

CAMPING/RVING	RECREATION	BOATING	MISCELLANEOUS
Tents/Trailers/RVs -tables, grills -$2/person/night -pets on leash only -use of firearms prohibited on reservation -closest motels are in Chinle just west	-picnicking, horseback riding -sailing, sail boarding, -canoeing -hiking (back country permit required) -fishing: (special permit and fee required, special limits) rainbow trout, brook trout, brown trout, cutthroat trout -shore fishing, ice fishing -no swimming -no ATVs/ATCs -hunting/trapping (permit and fee required)	-electric motor only -boating permit and fee required -1 unimproved launch	-seasonal convenience store: bait tackle, groceries, pay phone -closest town is Window Rock, 43 miles south PERMITS AND FEES: camping, boating, fishing, and other recreational activities require a permit and fee - see section on the Navajo Nation contained within this book
Information:	Navajo Nation Park and Recreation (602) 871-6647 - Tourism Dept. (602) 871-6673		

Tsaile Lake (Say'Lee) sits at 7010 foot elevation and is just a few miles northwest of Wheatfields Lake on the Navajo Nation. At 260 acres, it is a fine cold water fishery and receives 20 thousand rainbows and browns annually. Spring and fall fishing are the best, but ice fishing can be excellent. The quality of the fishing and ease of access combine to make it one of the "busier" lakes on the reservation. The surrounding hills and forest will yield some memorable scenery for the hiker or equestrian.

While on the Navajo Nation, be certain to take in the local sites and events. Canyon de Chelley National Monument is just west of the lake with easy access. The reservation's silver work and woven basketry are unparalleled. Tsaile Lake has an easy access. Proceed north from I-40 at the Exit 357, just a few miles from the New Mexico border. You'll pass through Window Rock (reservation headquarters) on this 73-mile journey. Tsaile Lake is just a few miles north of Wheatfields Lake.

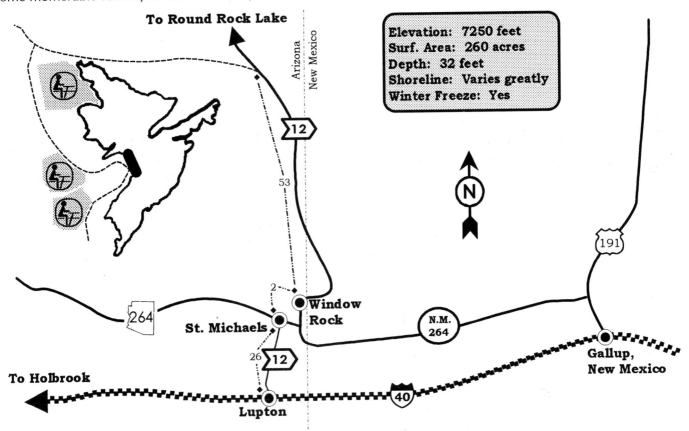

Elevation: 7250 feet
Surf. Area: 260 acres
Depth: 32 feet
Shoreline: Varies greatly
Winter Freeze: Yes

CAMPING/RVING	RECREATION	BOATING	MISCELLANEOUS
Tents/Trailers -no developed campsites -permit and fee required $2/head/night -RVs not recommended -pets on leash only -use of firearms prohibited	-picnicking: ramadas, tables, grills -hiking (back country permit required) -horseback riding -sailing, sail boarding, canoeing -fishing: (special permit and fee required - special limits) rainbow trout, cutthroat trout, brown trout, channel catfish -ice fishing -no swimming, no ATVs/ATCs -hunting/trapping (permit and fee required)	-electric motor only -unimproved launch ramp -boating permit and fee required	-convenience store at Wheatfields Lake, just a few miles on Indian Route 12 -closest town is Chinle, 25 miles west on Indian Route 64 -Navajo Community College less than one mile away PERMITS AND FEES: camping, boating, fishing, and other recreational activities require a permit and fee - see section on the Navajo Nation contained within this book
Information:	Navajo Nation Park and Recreation (602) 871-6647 - Tourism Dept. (602) 871-6673		

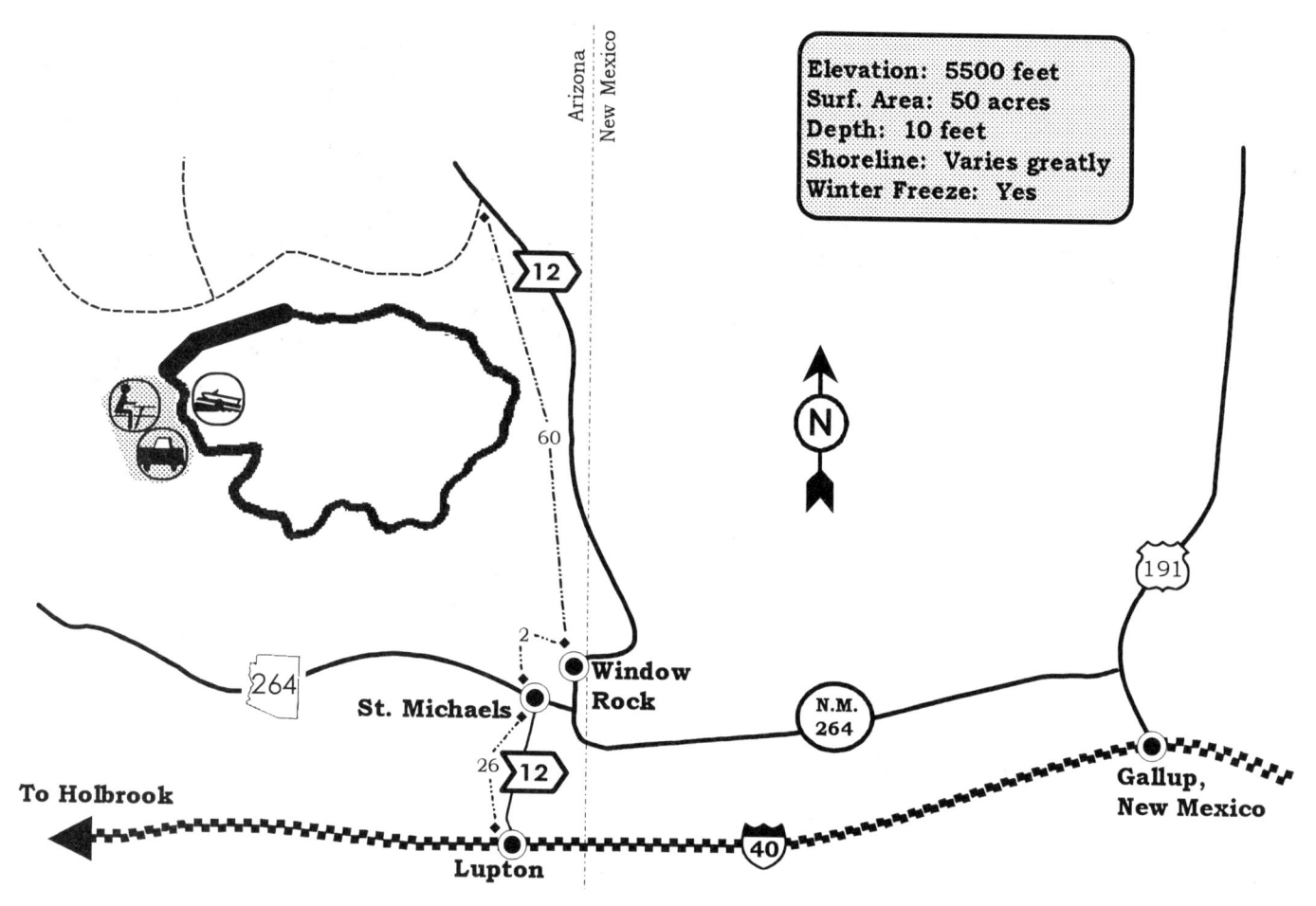

ROUND ROCK RESERVOIR

Round Rock Reservoir sits in the red rock country of the 16-million acre Navajo Nation. At a 5500-foot elevation, the lake has been down sized in recent years. Fishing for channel catfish is the primary activity. Camping is allowed but there are no facilities. For the fisherman, it would not be a wise choice to pass up the excellent lakes within a 50-mile radius south of Round Rock. The Navajo Nation has much to offer in the way of scenic beauty and fine culture. Canyon de Chelley is just south of Round Rock Reservoir, be sure to visit it. The lake itself is just 1 mile south of the town of Red Rock, which is less than 40 miles south of the Utah border. Access can be via US Highway 160 out of Flagstaff or north from I-40 at Chambers on US Highway 191. Either way, you're on major roads but the passage north from I-40 is considerably more scenic. Prior to your recreation on the Navajo Nation, please assure that you are aware of any special requirements for camping, hunting, fishing or boating.

Elevation: 5500 feet
Surf. Area: 50 acres
Depth: 10 feet
Shoreline: Varies greatly
Winter Freeze: Yes

CAMPING/RVING	RECREATION	BOATING	MISCELLANEOUS
Tents/Trailers/RVs -no developed campsites -pets on leash only -use of firearms prohibited	-picnicking -sailing, sail boarding, canoeing -hiking (back country permit required) -horseback riding -fishing: (permit and fee required) channel catfish -shore fishing -no swimming -no ATVs/ATCs -hunting/trapping (permit and fee required)	-electric motor only -boating permit and fee required -1 unimproved launch	-closest town is Red Rock, 1 mile north on Indian Highway 12 -Chinle, 32 miles south has all services PERMITS AND FEES: camping, boating, fishing, and other recreational activities require a permit and fee - see section on the Navajo Nation contained within this book
Information:	Navajo Nation Park and Recreation (602) 871-6647 - Tourism Dept. (602) 871-6673		

Many Farms Lake is located on the Navajo Nation in northeastern Arizona, just a few miles northwest of the Canyon de Chelley National Monument. At greater than 1000 acres, it is the largest of the area lakes. With no motor restrictions, it is available for all water sports. The surrounding mountains provide unique and spectacular landscape the hiker and equestrian will never forget. The lake sits at 5300 feet elevation, thus fishing yields warm water species. While near the center of the Navajo Nation, don't pass on the opportunity to see the abundant natural wonders. Artistry of woven basketry and silver work by the locals are unparalleled. Access to Many Farms Lake is simple as it lies just 1 mile east of US Highway 191, approximately 100 miles north of Interstate 40.

Elevation: 5300 feet
Surf. Area: 1000 acres
Depth: 6 feet
Shoreline: 6.5 miles
Winter Freeze: Yes

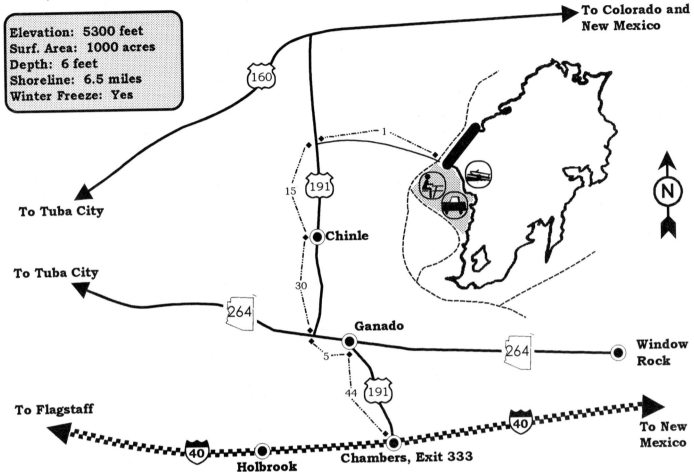

CAMPING/RVING	RECREATION	BOATING	MISCELLANEOUS
Tents/Trailers/RVs -no developed sties -permit and fee required $2/head/night -pets on leash only -use of fire arms prohibited	-picnicking, horseback riding -sailing, sail boarding, canoeing -hiking (back country permit required) -water skiing -fishing: (special permit and fee required - special limits) channel catfish, largemouth bass, bluegill -shore fishing, ice fishing -no swimming -no ATVs/ATCs -hunting/trapping (special permit and fees required)	-no motor restrictions (any size motor allowed) -boating permit and fee required -1 unimproved launch	-nearest town is Chinle, 15 miles south -closest conveniences are in settlement of Many Farms, two miles from lake PERMITS AND FEES: camping, boating, fishing, and other recreational activities require a permit and fee - see section on the Navajo Nation contained within this book
Information:	Navajo Nation Park and Recreation (602) 871-6647 - Tourism Dept. (602) 871-6673		

CONCHO LAKE

At a 6300-foot elevation, Concho Lake is managed by Arizona Game & Fish. This lake is located in the small town of Concho Valley and is just a "locals" fishing hole, quiet and peaceful. There are minimal camping facilities and they are not well maintained. Trolling will be your best bet but shore fishing is popular in this shallow/weedy 60-acre pond. This lake is certainly easy to find. It sits right on Arizona Highway 61 at mile-marker 369, 17 miles west of St. Johns, 3-1/2 miles west of the intersection of Highways 180A and 61.

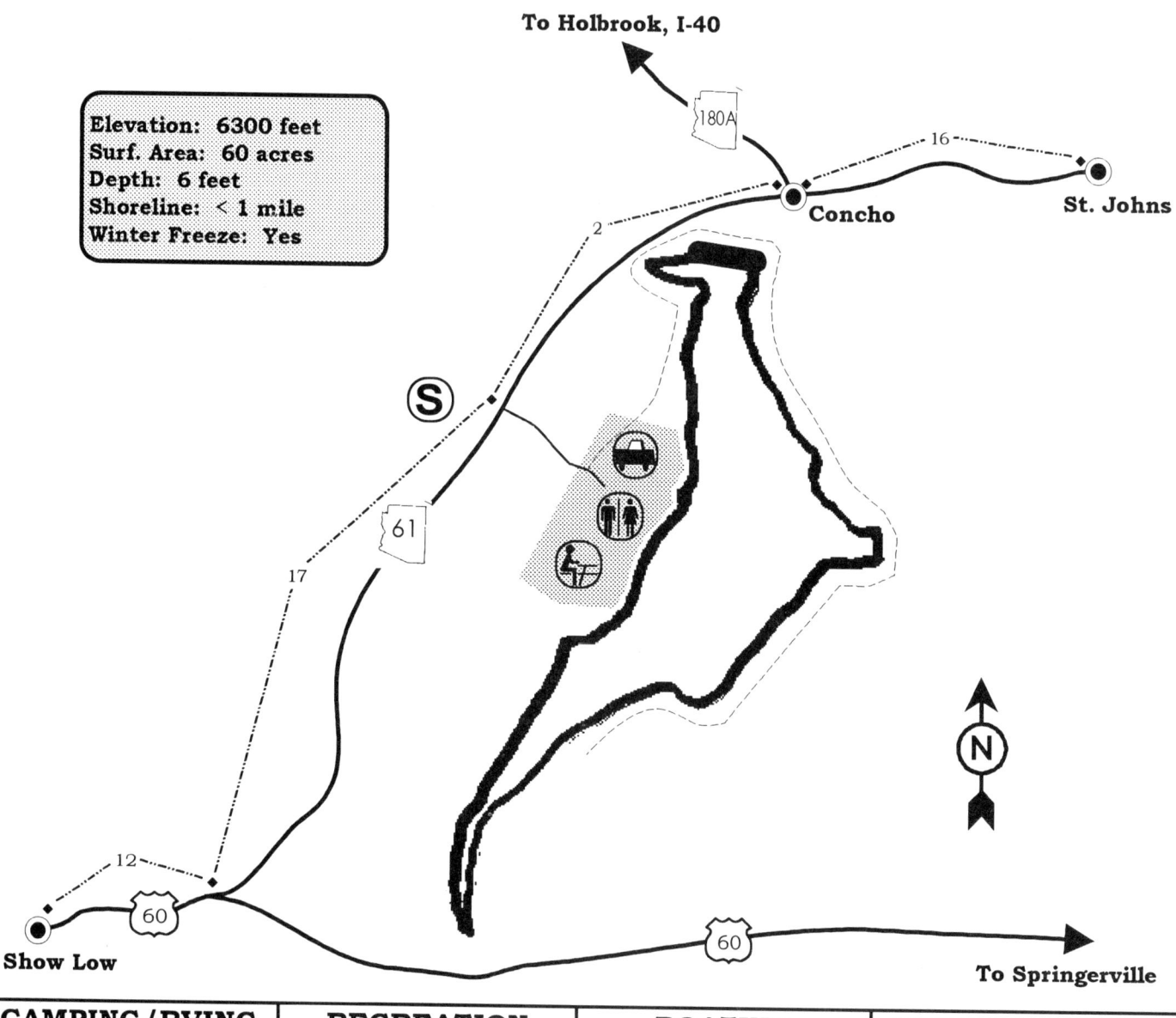

Elevation: 6300 feet
Surf. Area: 60 acres
Depth: 6 feet
Shoreline: < 1 mile
Winter Freeze: Yes

CAMPING/RVING	RECREATION	BOATING	MISCELLANEOUS
Tents/Trailers/RVs -7 sites - no fee -ramadas, tables, grills (this camping area is poorly maintained) -open camping around lake -pit toilets -no water	-fishing: rainbow trout, brook trout -shore fishing (dirt road circles the lake) -trolling with a cowbell or lure is the best bet	-electric motor only -improved launch -shallow and weedy lake	-nearest conveniences just across street from lake at small store: gasoline, food, bait -public telephone -nearest town is St. Johns, 17 miles away -golf course located next to lake which provides entertainment if the fish are not biting
Information:	Arizona Game and Fish Department (602) 367-4281		

Little Mormon, Whipple, and Long Lake are a threesome located five miles west of Show Low on the Apache-Sitgreaves National Forest. At 6900 feet elevation, Long Lake, which only sometimes has water in it, and Whipple Lake are on the west side of the access road while Little Mormon Lake is on the east. There are precisely 0 (zero) facilities or conveniences at these lakes and other than fishing, the recreational joys are limited. The land surrounding the lakes is barren save the high desert brush.

The water is murky with a warm water catch. Whipple is marked by seven small islands when the water level is low enough. Driving around or down to the lake shore prudently calls for a high-riding, 4-wheel drive vehicle. Actually, horseback riding in the area can be quite enjoyable. Access to these three lakes is on a well maintained gravel road (Forest Road 251), north at mile marker 345 from US Highway 60. These guys are just four miles west-northwest of Show Low.

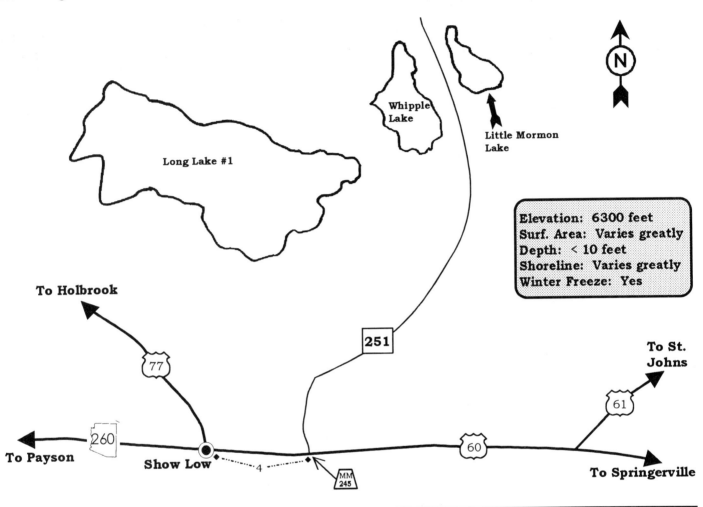

Whipple Lake

Little Mormon Lake

Long Lake #1

To Holbrook

Elevation: 6300 feet
Surf. Area: Varies greatly
Depth: < 10 feet
Shoreline: Varies greatly
Winter Freeze: Yes

251

77

To St. Johns

61

260

60

To Payson

Show Low

4

MM 245

To Springerville

CAMPING/RVING	RECREATION	BOATING	MISCELLANEOUS
-no developed campsites -no facilities whatsoever -primitive camping allowed -private campgrounds and RV parks located 5 miles west on Arizona Highway 60 -nearest national forest campgrounds located 8 miles west at Fool Hollow Lake	-canoeing -hiking -horseback riding -fishing: largemouth bass, sunfish, catfish -shore fishing	-primitive launching only -these lakes are shallow and weedy with various wood obstructions under the surface, it is recommended that a small inflatable or canoe be used with an electric trolling motor	-no facilities or conveniences at the lake whatsoever -all facilities and conveniences located 5 miles west of lake in Show Low

Information:	Apache-Sitgreaves National Forest (602) 33-4301

FOOL HOLLOW LAKE

At 6500-foot elevation, Fool Hollow Lake is managed by the Arizona State Park System. This is a recent change. There are significant upgrades to the facilities currently under construction and scheduled for completion in the spring of '94. Further construction of a visitor's (educational) center and road work are now in the planning stages and scheduled for construction over the next several years. Fool Hollow Lake is an easy access, "close-in" lake/recreation area within the city limits of Show Low. Currently there is primitive camping on the lake's west side. The boater will find launch facilities on both the east and west sides of the lake. The 5.2 miles of shoreline is a favorite with the local anglers. Future fishing will likely be good, with 70,000 trout planted in 1992. Fool Hollow is a 149 acre beauty with all services and conveniences located within a few miles. Access is simple by proceeding north on 32nd Ave. from Old Linden Road, just off Arizona Hwy 260 at mile marker 338.

Note: This lake is within the city limits of Show Low.

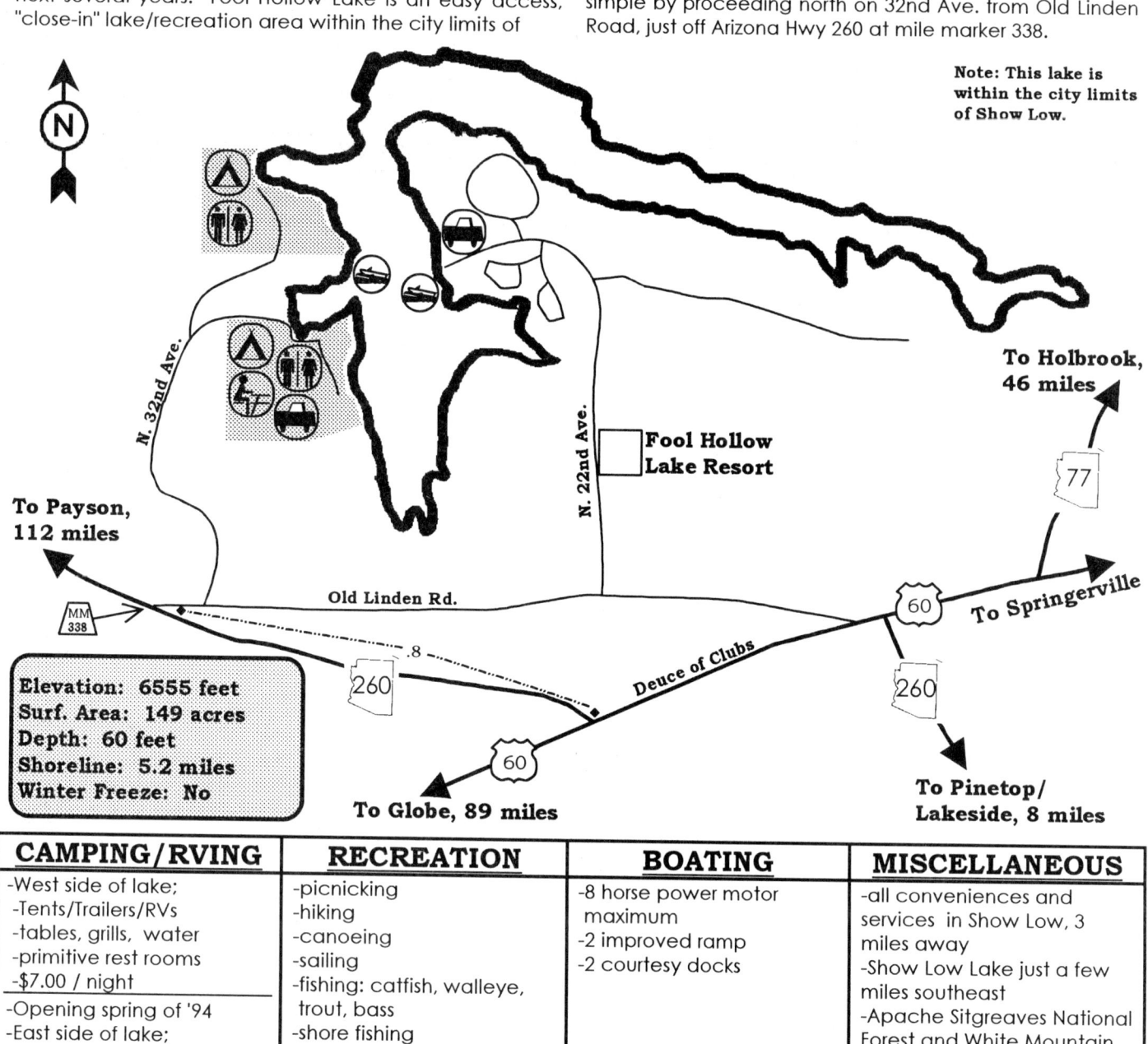

Elevation: 6555 feet
Surf. Area: 149 acres
Depth: 60 feet
Shoreline: 5.2 miles
Winter Freeze: No

CAMPING/RVING	RECREATION	BOATING	MISCELLANEOUS
-West side of lake; -Tents/Trailers/RVs -tables, grills, water -primitive rest rooms -$7.00 / night -Opening spring of '94 -East side of lake; -92 developed sites (52 full RV hookups, 40 with water and electricity, $12.00 / night) -hot showers, flush toilets (handicapped) -group camping -tables and grills	-picnicking -hiking -canoeing -sailing -fishing: catfish, walleye, trout, bass -shore fishing -$3.00/vehicle day-use fee -Opening spring of '94 -handicapped trail and fishing pier	-8 horse power motor maximum -2 improved ramp -2 courtesy docks	-all conveniences and services in Show Low, 3 miles away -Show Low Lake just a few miles southeast -Apache Sitgreaves National Forest and White Mountain Apache Reservation nearby; they offer numerous outdoor opportunities PERMITS AND FEES: SEE SECTION ON ARIZONA STATE PARKS CONTAINED WITHIN THIS BOOK
Information:	Arizona State Park (602) 537-3680		

SHOW LOW LAKE

The 100-acre Show Low Lake sits at 6350-foot elevation and is perfect for those who don't want to be to far from the action. Show Low Lake is just 4 minutes from all the conveniences of Show Low Arizona. The Navajo County Park Department manages a 145-acre park at the lake, which includes camping, a store, boat rental, boat dock and an improved launch. Some camp sites are very picturesque, located on a knoll adjacent to the lake. RVs, trailers, and tenters are welcome, but there are no hookups. Weather at Show Low Lake is perfect in the summer, with pleasant, sunny days and cool evenings. Winter brings some snow and cold but moderately. Fishing on Show Low Lake take up most users time and a variety of species can be caught. This lake can lay claim to the state record walleye of 12 pounds, 12 ounces and nearly 30 inches long. Boat use and shore fishing are both popular. Motors only to 8 horse power are allowed. The surrounding forests and hills of the Apache-Sitgreaves National Forest and the adjacent White Mountain Indian Reservation offer much to the hiker, equestrian, stream/lake fisherman, any naturalist really. Swimming is allowed, but at this elevation the water doesn't warm up much. The park is open year round and there is a campground host on site. The small concession is open only April through October. Access to Show Low Lake couldn't be easier. Four miles east of Show Low on Arizona 260, turn north for 1 mile and you're there. It is paved all the way.

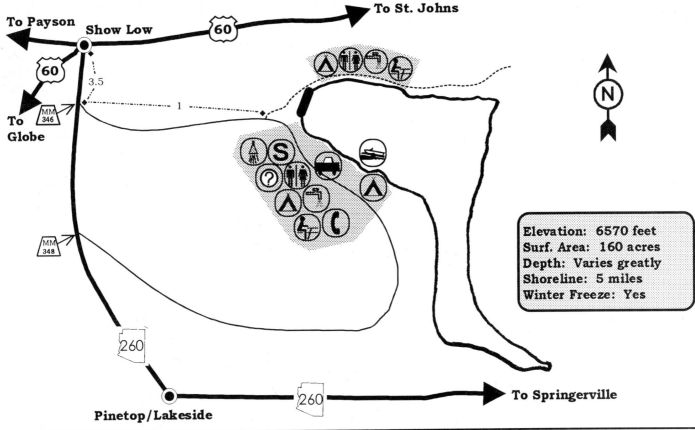

Elevation: 6570 feet
Surf. Area: 160 acres
Depth: Varies greatly
Shoreline: 5 miles
Winter Freeze: Yes

CAMPING/RVING	RECREATION	BOATING	MISCELLANEOUS
Tent/Trailers/RVs -68 campsites -tables, fire rings, grills -$7/night at waters edge -$6/night regular -no hookups -flush toilets -drinking water -showers -open year round, reservations available ($5 non-refundable, (602) 537-4126)	-sailing, canoeing -hiking, swimming -horseback riding -fishing: rainbow trout, brown trout, walleye, catfish, largemouth bass -shore fishing -no ATVs/ATCs -children's playground	-8 horse power motor maximum -launch -boat rentals at store	-public telephones -dogs on leash only -store open 6am - 6pm, bait snacks -many and varied facilities within Show Low and Pinetop/ Lakeside (5 minutes 1 way, 10 minutes the other) -Show Low Lake County Park (602) 537-4126
Information:	Navajo County Park Department (602) 524-6161		

RAINBOW LAKE

Rainbow Lake at 80 acres is a busy "in town" lake located essentially within the city limits of Lakeside, Arizona. Given its ease of access, it receives significant fishing pressure. A national forest campground (Lakeside) is located adjacent to the lake. Most of the shoreline is privately owned, so be aware of property owner's rights. There is an improved launch ramp on Game and Fish property, located at the west end of the dam. The lake is particularly shallow with an average depth of six feet.

The Game and Fish Department frequently clears the weeds in summer and stocks the lake routinely. The lake is best fished from a boat. At 6700 feet, the weather during the summer months is pleasant to say the least. This lake is a good choice for those who desire conveniences close by. Everything you need is within a couple of miles. Rainbow Lake is located 1 block off of Arizona Highway 260 at Neils-Hanson Street in Lakeside.

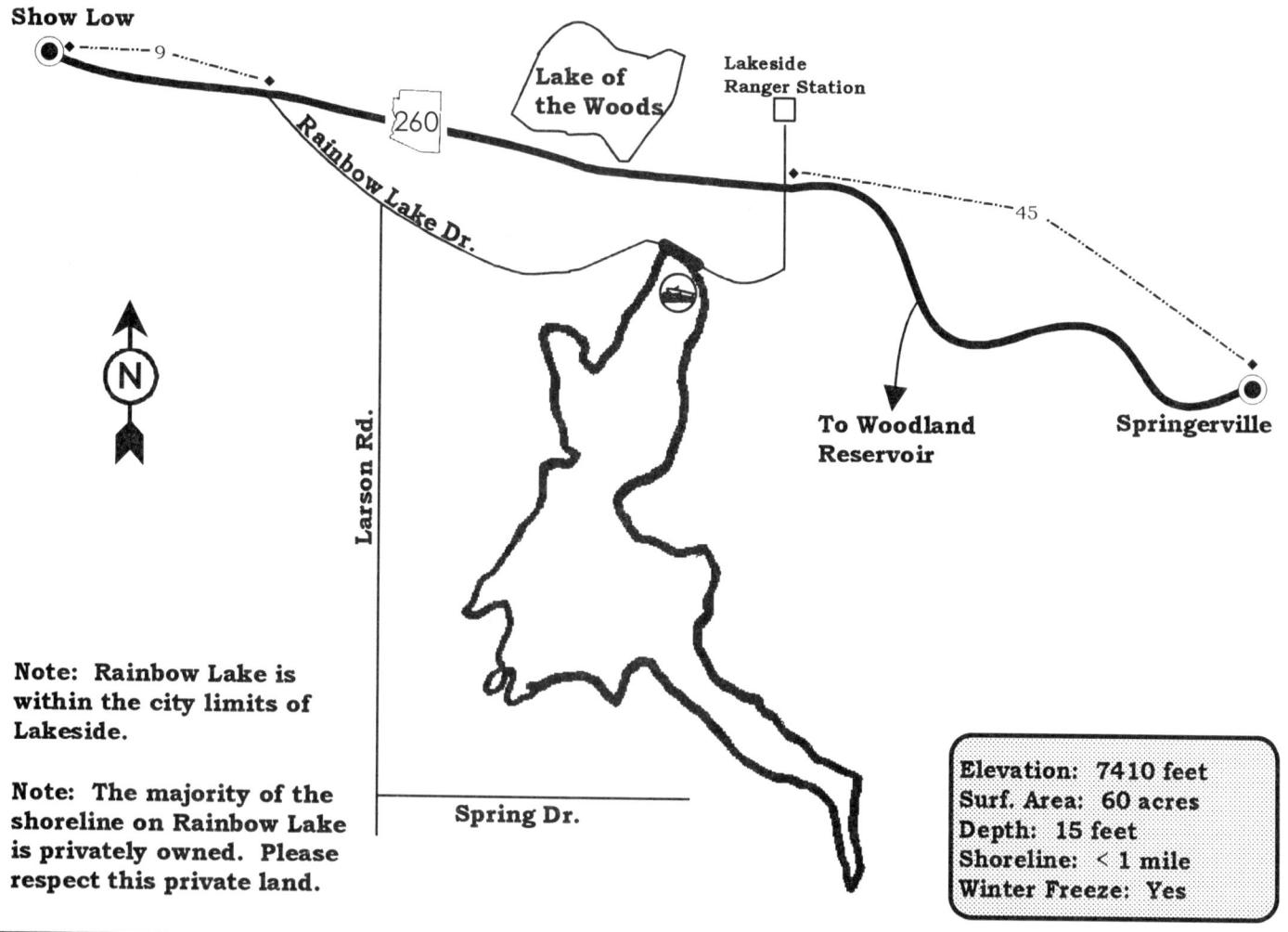

Show Low

Lake of the Woods

Lakeside Ranger Station

Rainbow Lake Dr.

Larson Rd.

Spring Dr.

To Woodland Reservoir

Springerville

Note: Rainbow Lake is within the city limits of Lakeside.

Note: The majority of the shoreline on Rainbow Lake is privately owned. Please respect this private land.

Elevation: 7410 feet
Surf. Area: 60 acres
Depth: 15 feet
Shoreline: < 1 mile
Winter Freeze: Yes

CAMPING/RVING	RECREATION	BOATING	MISCELLANEOUS
Tents/Trailers/RVs Lakeside National Forest Campground -83 sites -$7/night -water -vault toilets -tables, grills -season is May to September -numerous motels and private RV parks in Lakeside	-picnicking -canoeing -fishing: rainbow trout, brown trout, largemouth bass, sunfish, catfish NOTE: this is a "put and take" lake, don't expect much more than a pan sized catch	-8 horse power motor maximum -improved launch -lake is shallow at six feet -boat rentals are available at a private residence south and adjacent to the lake - 1140 Spring Drive (telephone number 368-8688)	-all conveniences within Lakeside -campground host on site (602) 368-6841 -Ranger station on opposite side of Arizona Highway 260 -the perimeter of the lake is privately owned - please respect property owner's rights

Information:	Apache-Sitgreaves National Forest (602) 368-5111

Woodland Reservoir is essentially within the town of Lakeside on Arizona Highway 260 in the White Mountains. At 6900 feet, the lake, managed by the Arizona Fish & Game Department, produces a variety of fish types. Not a lake for serious anglers, this is a family fun spot at which children can learn to fish and enjoy it. Woodland Lake

Park manages the 500-acre day-use facility at the lake and has some fine facilities. There's generally plenty of "action" to keep the children's attention, be it from the shore, small boat, or playground. Access is within the Lakeside/Pinetop community just southwest of Arizona Highway 260.

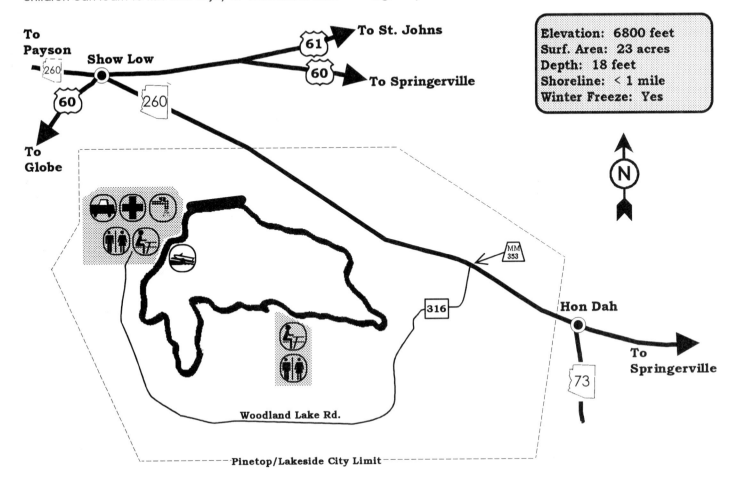

Elevation: 6800 feet
Surf. Area: 23 acres
Depth: 18 feet
Shoreline: < 1 mile
Winter Freeze: Yes

CAMPING/RVING	RECREATION	BOATING	MISCELLANEOUS
-no overnight camping, day-use-only Tent/Trailers/RVs -two national forest campgrounds located in Lakeside with very nice camping facilities - names are: Lakeside and Scott's Reservoir -various private campgrounds in Lakeside and adjacent Pinetop	-Woodland Lake Park (500 acres) (day-use facility located at lake) -picnicking: tables, grills, ramadas, drinking water, rest rooms -hiking (1.2 mile asphalt trail around lake) -tennis courts, volley ball -playgrounds -horseback riding -mountain biking -fishing: rainbow trout, brown trout, cutthroat trout, catfish, bluegills -shore fishing -no swimming	-improved launch -electric motor only -boat dock	-lake is located within Lakeside, all conveniences and facilities are there -open year round -lake (park) hours are: sunrise to 10 p.m. daily -park telephone number is 1-602-368-6700
Information:	Pinetop/Lakeside Park & Recreation Department (602) 368-6700		

COOLEY LAKE

Cooley Lake, an-11-acre pond at a 7100-foot elevation, is managed by the White Mountain Apache Indian Reservation. Camping is limited to a few designated spots with facilities minimal. Special permits and fees are required for all recreational activities on the reservation. Not far off the main drag, it is two-and-a-half miles south of the Pinetop/Lakeside or just south of Hon Dah, a quarter mile east of Arizona Highway 73. This is a bass (Florida strain) and catfish lake. Summer days are cool and relaxing. If there ever was a "brain drain" lake this is it. It is calm and peaceful with not much to do.

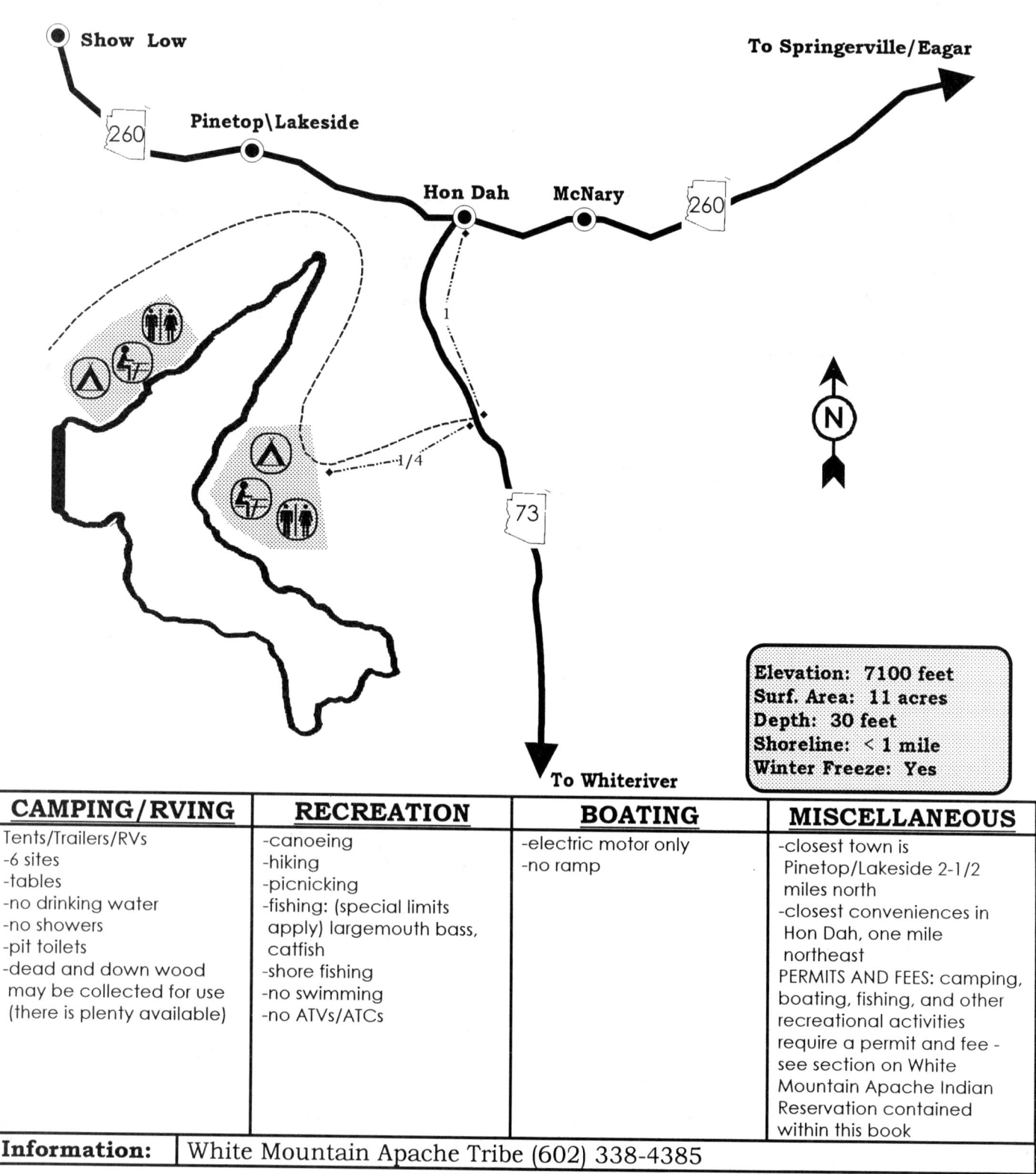

Elevation: 7100 feet
Surf. Area: 11 acres
Depth: 30 feet
Shoreline: < 1 mile
Winter Freeze: Yes

CAMPING/RVING	RECREATION	BOATING	MISCELLANEOUS
Tents/Trailers/RVs -6 sites -tables -no drinking water -no showers -pit toilets -dead and down wood may be collected for use (there is plenty available)	-canoeing -hiking -picnicking -fishing: (special limits apply) largemouth bass, catfish -shore fishing -no swimming -no ATVs/ATCs	-electric motor only -no ramp	-closest town is Pinetop/Lakeside 2-1/2 miles north -closest conveniences in Hon Dah, one mile northeast PERMITS AND FEES: camping, boating, fishing, and other recreational activities require a permit and fee - see section on White Mountain Apache Indian Reservation contained within this book
Information:	White Mountain Apache Tribe (602) 338-4385		

Shush Be Tou, "Big Bear" Lake is just up stream (less than one mile) on Bog Creek from its neighbor Shush Be Zahze "Little Bear" on the White Mountain Apache Indian Reservation. At a 7800-foot elevation, it offers a cool summer retreat which is very easy to reach. A small campground serves this small 15-acre lake. And sometimes the shore fisherman crowd the perimeter of the lake. This can be classified as a "put and take" lake for rainbows. The lake certainly freezes over at its altitude so those who can reach the lake (it's not far from the highway) may find some good ice fishing in winter. Conveniences abound along Highway 260 east or west of the lake. The lake is located 9 miles east of McNary just north (less than 1 mile) off Arizona Highway 260 at mile marker 368. This is a nice, quiet "close in," easy to reach lake.

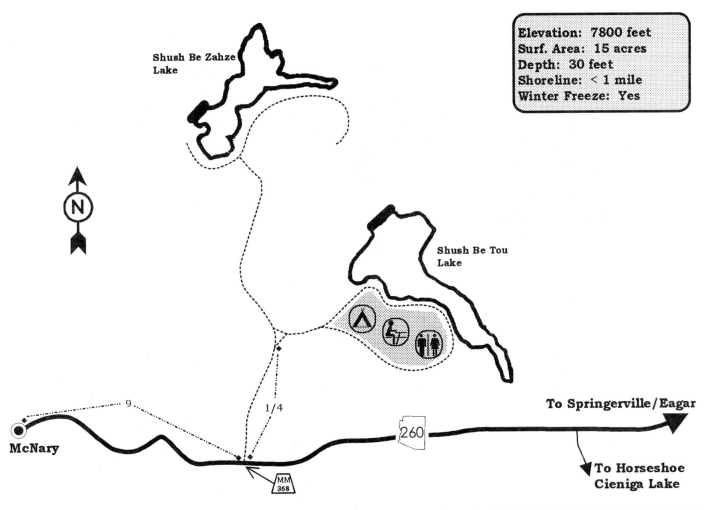

Elevation: 7800 feet
Surf. Area: 15 acres
Depth: 30 feet
Shoreline: < 1 mile
Winter Freeze: Yes

CAMPING/RVING	RECREATION	BOATING	MISCELLANEOUS
Tents/Trailers/RVs -10 sites -pit toilets -tables -no drinking water -no showers -dead and down wood may be collected for use (there's plenty of it in the area) -dogs on leash only	-canoeing -hiking -picnicking -fishing: (special limits apply) (permit/fee required) rainbow trout -shore fishing -no swimming -no ATVs/ATCs	-electric motor only -no ramp -permit and fee required	-closest town is McNary, 9 miles west on 260 -varied and plentiful facilities and conveniences along Arizona 260 east or west from lake PERMITS AND FEES: camping, boating, fishing, and other recreational activities require a permit and fee - see section on White Mountain Apache Indian Reservation contained within this book
Information:	White Mountain Apache Indian Reservation (602) 338-4385		

SHUSH BE ZAHZE LAKE

Shush Be Zahze is Apache for "Little Bear" and is adjacent to its neighbor "Big Bear," Shush Be Tou. At a 7900-foot elevation, it offers cool summer days and reasonable rainbow trout action from the shore. A very small campground is located at lakeside with minimal facilities. The lake freezes over in winter and may yield some good ice fishing. Conveniences abound along Highway 260 east or west of the lake. Shush Be Zahze is located 9 miles east of McNary just north (less than 1 mile) off Arizona Highway 260 at mile marker 368. As its neighbor, it is a quiet, "close-in," easy-to-reach lake.

Elevation: 7900 feet
Surf. Area: 18 acres
Depth: 18 feet
Shoreline: < 1 mile
Winter Freeze: Yes

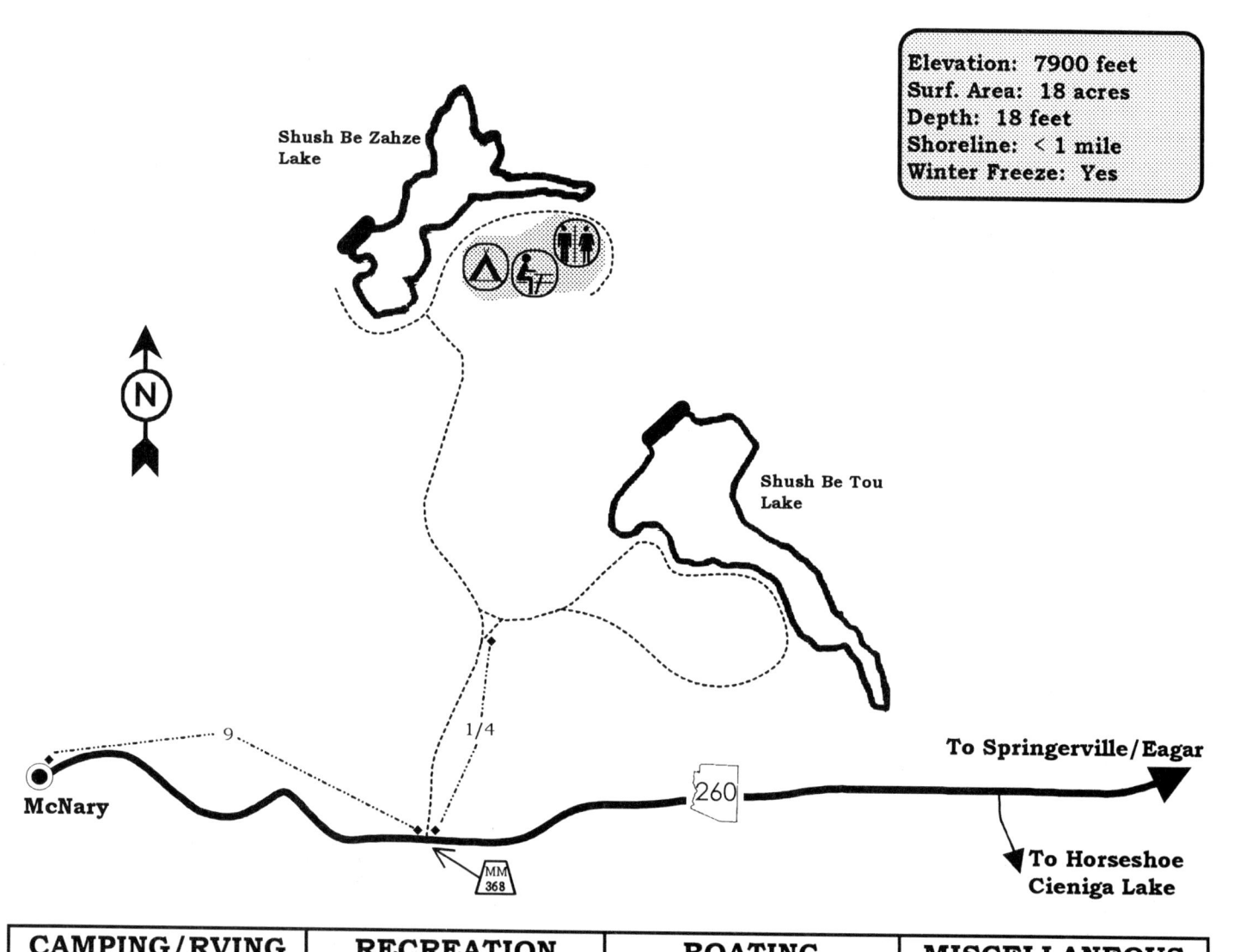

CAMPING/RVING	RECREATION	BOATING	MISCELLANEOUS
Tents/Trailers/RVs -10 sites -pit toilets -tables -no drinking water -no showers -dead and down wood may be collected for use (there's plenty in the area) -dogs on leash only	-canoeing -hiking -picnicking -fishing: (special limits apply) (permit/fee required) rainbow trout -shore fishing -no ATCs -no swimming	-electric motor only -no ramp -permit and fee required	-closest town is McNary, 9 miles west on 260 -varied and plentiful facilities and conveniences along Arizona 260 east or west from lake PERMITS AND FEES: camping, boating, fishing, and other recreational activities require a permit and fee - see section on White Mountain Apache Indian Reservation contained within this book
Information:	White Mountain Apache Indian Reservation (602) 338-4385		

Cyclone Lake is at 8100 feet elevation and is managed by the White Mountain Apache Tribe. This 37-acre lake is closed to the general public but is available "For Rent" through the White Mountain Game and Fish Department. The renter will have exclusive rights during the rental period. Camping, picnicking and fishing are available. The Game and Fish Department will make sure the lake has sufficient numbers of catchable size trout (stock if necessary), provide wood for campfires, and the requisite number of fishing permits for the group. For a group function such as a family reunion or company picnic, this is a fine "remote" choice. Access is just off Arizona 473, south of Arizona 260, between Show Low and Spingerville.

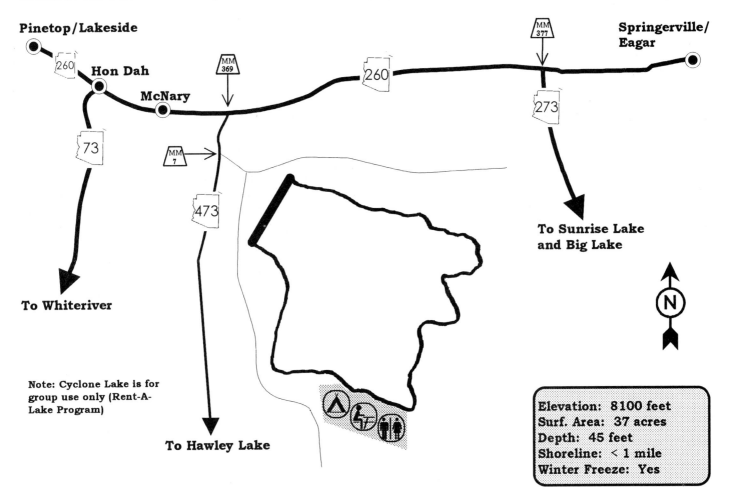

Note: Cyclone Lake is for group use only (Rent-A-Lake Program)

Elevation: 8100 feet
Surf. Area: 37 acres
Depth: 45 feet
Shoreline: < 1 mile
Winter Freeze: Yes

CAMPING/RVING	RECREATION	BOATING	MISCELLANEOUS
-Rent-a-Lake program only -permit and fee: $3/day, plus $3/person/ day -ramadas -tables -grills -primitive toilets	-hiking, picnicking -fishing (Rent-a-Lake program): cutthroat trout, brown trout and rainbow trout -special fishing limits applicable -no swimming -no ATVs/ATCs	-electric motor only -no ramp	-open May 23 to Sept. 7 (weather permitting) -Rent-a-Lake program only (choice of 1 p.m. to 11 a.m. or sunup to sundown) -firewood supplied upon request PERMITS AND FEES: camping, boating, fishing, and other recreational activities require a permit and fee - see section on White Mountain Apache Indian Reservation contained within this book
Information:	White Mountain Apache Tribe (602) 338-4385		

A-1 LAKE

At an 8900-foot elevation, A-1 Lake sits high in the White Mountains and is managed by the White Mountain Apache Indians. At 24 acres, it is relatively small yet a good grower of the trout which are stocked. A small boat is useful for fishing but certainly shore fishing yields the most at this guy. Essentially, the entire perimeter is fishable. Camping is limited to a few spots so it's not crowded in spite of the fact it is very accessible. Facilities and conveniences at lakeside are minimal. The short road to the lake or around it can be slippery when it rains, so be careful. Afternoon thunder showers are common in mid to late summer which is actually a joy to most who visit these elevations. Animal life and mountain flora abound for the day hiker or horseback rider. Remember, permits and fees are required for any recreational activities on this reservation. The lake sits just on Highway 260, at mile marker 375. You can just about touch the water as you drive by. For easy access and likely some fish and for sure some beauty, try A-1 Lake.

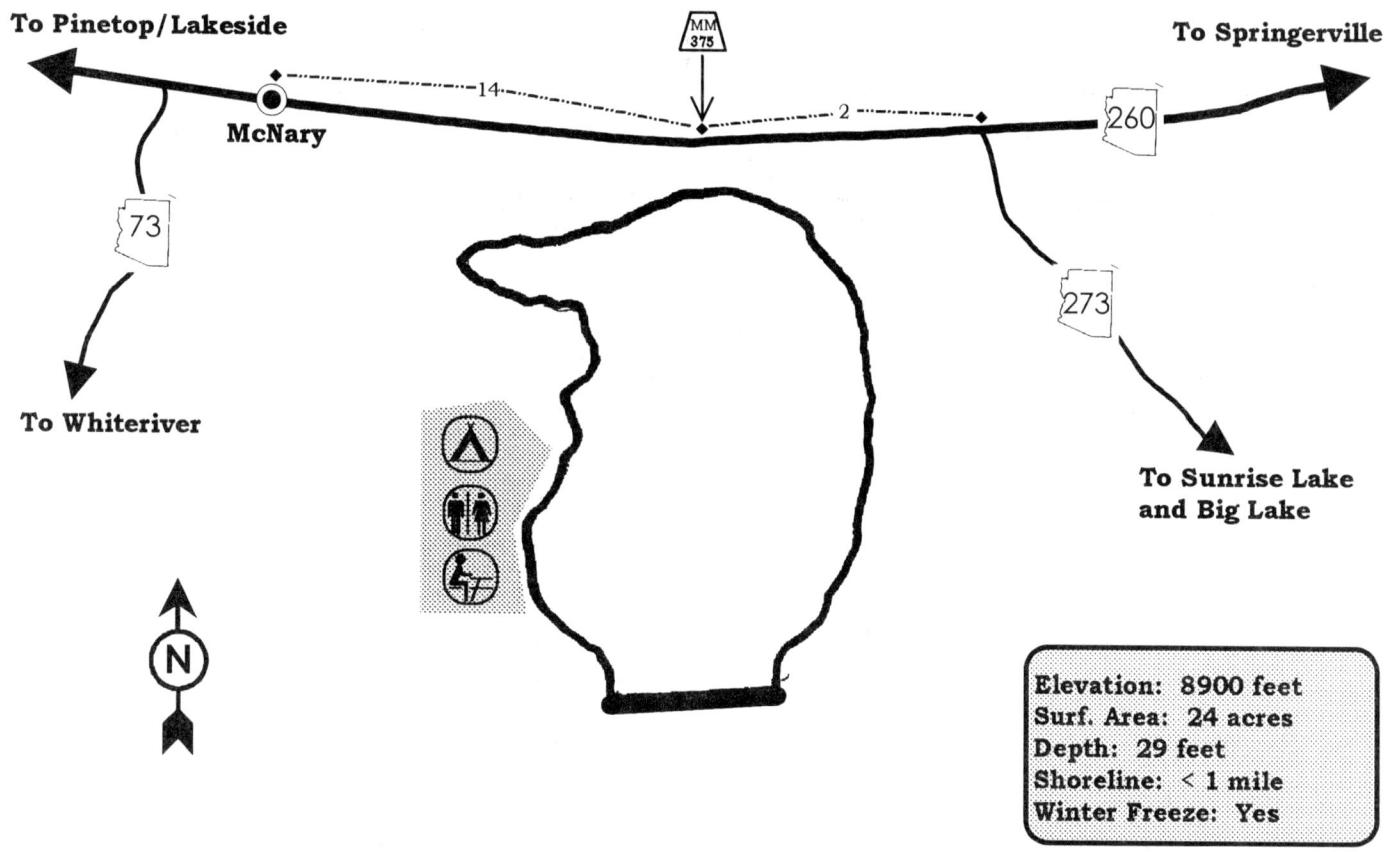

To Pinetop/Lakeside

McNary

To Whiteriver

N

To Springerville

MM 375

14

2

260

73

273

To Sunrise Lake and Big Lake

Elevation: 8900 feet
Surf. Area: 24 acres
Depth: 29 feet
Shoreline: < 1 mile
Winter Freeze: Yes

CAMPING/RVING	RECREATION	BOATING	MISCELLANEOUS
Tents/Trailers/RVs -15 sites -$6/night -tables -pit toilets -no drinking water -dogs on a leash only -camping in developed sites only -dead and down wood may be collected for use (there's plenty of it in the area)	-hiking -picnicking -canoeing -horseback riding -fishing: rainbow trout, brown trout -this lake is stocked frequently and is a good grower of fish -shore fishing -no swimming -no ATVs/ATCs	-no launch area -small inflatable or canoes, which can be carried, work best -electric motor only	-nearest town is McNary, 10 miles to the west on 260 -numerous facilities and conveniences along Arizona 260 east or west of lake -no telephone -open mid-May to mid-September PERMITS AND FEES: camping, boating, fishing, and other recreational activities require a permit and fee - see section on White Mountain Apache Indian Reservation contained within this book
Information:	White Mountain Apache Indian Reservation (602) 338-4385		

Horseshoe Cienega Lake sits on the White Mountain Apache Indian Reservation and should not be confused with Horseshoe Lake on the Verde River just north of Phoenix. This 120-acre pond sits at 8100 foot elevation and has the claim to fame of producing the state record brown trout of 16 pounds, 7 ounces and a bit less than 30 inches long. Horseshoe Cienega Lake was drained for a short period but was reopened in the spring of 1991 which preceded heavy trout stocking. Horseshoe Cienega Lake can be fished from a small boat or from the shore. the shoreline is entirely open and you can walk the lake's perimeter. Conveniences at Horseshoe

Cienega Lake are minimal with the store open only from Memorial Day to Labor Day. Of course the lake is frozen over in winter, but even during the summer months, the evening temperatures can be very cool at this elevation. Afternoon thunderstorms are common mid to late summer. Permits and fees are required for all activities at Horseshoe Cienega Lake, as for any lake on the White Mountain Apache Indian Reservation. Access to Horseshoe Cienega Lake is very simple, as it sits just a stones throw south of State Highway 260, just 19 miles east of Pinetop. The Hawley Lake turn off is just west of Horseshoe Cienega Lake, follow the signs on and from Highway 260.

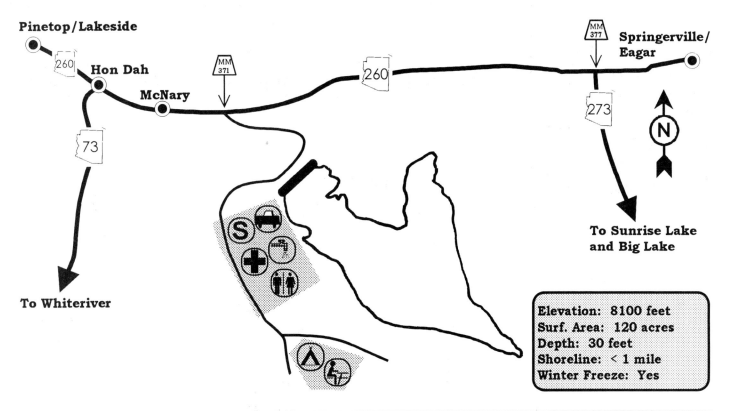

Elevation: 8100 feet
Surf. Area: 120 acres
Depth: 30 feet
Shoreline: < 1 mile
Winter Freeze: Yes

CAMPING/RVING	RECREATION	BOATING	MISCELLANEOUS
-68 primitive tent sites (fee required) -tables -drinking water -pit toilets -dogs on leash only -dead and down wood may be collected for use (there's plenty in the area)	-horseback riding -hiking -canoeing -hunting -fishing: (special limits apply) rainbow trout, brook trout, Apache trout, brown trout -shore fishing -ice fishing in winter (the entire shoreline is open, this is great for kids' fishing) -no ATVs/ATCs -no swimming	-1 unimproved launch -electric trolling motors only -boat rentals at store	-lakeside convenience store open from Memorial Day to Labor Day: bait, tackle, small groceries, boat rental, permits -many and varied conveniences along Highway 260 either east or west PERMITS AND FEES: camping, boating, fishing, and other recreational activities require a permit and fee - see section on White Mountain Apache Indian Reservation contained within this book
Information:	White Mountain Apache Indian Reservation (602) 338-4385		

HAWLEY LAKE/EARL PARK LAKE

Hawley Lake and Earl Park Lake are located on the White Mountain Apache Indian Reservation in East Central Arizona and are just a bit more than 1/2 mile apart. Hawley Lake (260 acres), like Big Lake to the east, has many conveniences, thus it draws significant crowds. At lakeside are a store, lodge, cabins, RV sites, campgrounds, laundromat, cafe, and a small marina with launch. Complete facilities and services are available just east on AZ 260. Given the electric motor only restrictions, this is predominantly a trout fisherman's lake, be it from a boat or the shore. At 8200 foot elevation, temperatures, even in the summer, can be very cool at night. But the days are magnificent. The hiker, equestrian, and relaxing campers can certainly enjoy the surrounding flora and fauna in these pine-forested hills. Both large and small game are seen frequently; the random bear will also appear. A shore hike to Earl Park Lake (47 acres), just 1/2 mile southeast of

Hawley Lake can be relaxing. There are only primitive facilities at Earl Park, camping, launch, and pit toilets. The facilities at Hawley are only open in the summer months and reservations are most certainly encouraged, almost mandatory for the lodge and cabins, which both include kitchenettes. Access to Hawley Lake is very easy. Located south of Highway 260 between Pinetop/Lakeside and Springerville. Any and all conveniences are available on the 58-mile stretch. To reach Hawley Lake, take Highway 260 east from Hon Dah for 15 miles and turn south on 473 for 9 miles. The road is paved all the way except the last 2 and 1/2 miles of well maintained gravel road. Remember, reservations are a must for the lodge and cabins with early arrival recommended for the campers. This is one busy lake. Also remember that these lakes are on the White Mountain Apache Indian Reservation and a permit/fee is required for any activity. They are available at the Hawley Lake store.

See map, next page

CAMPING/RVING	RECREATION	BOATING	MISCELLANEOUS
-24 RV sites ($5 per night or $75 per week -full hookups -showers -100 primitive campsites (permit and fee required) -drinking water -showers -tables -primitive toilets -laundromat Lodge: -1 and 2 bedroom units, $55 to $75 per night -8 cabins, various sizes; kitchenettes, gas heat, $65 to $85 per night depending on size -summer homes, 2 on each lake, daily and weekly rates -dogs on leash only -reservations recommended for RV's, lodge, cabins and homes	-sailing, canoeing -horseback riding -hiking -picnicking -fishing (special limits apply) rainbow trout, brown trout, brook trout, Apache trout cutthroat trout HINT: when trolling, use a cowbell trailed by a nightcrawler -shore fishing; the entire perimeter is accessible Note: try fishing the creek between the two lakes -ice fishing in winter -no ATVs/ATCs -no swimming allowed	-electric motor only -1 unimproved ramp at Hawley, 1 at Earl Park Lake -boat/motor rental - $10 to $34 a day depending on type of boat and the day of the week -boat dock at Hawley Lake	-no handicapped facilities -public telephones -laundromat -cafe at store (breakfast and lunch only) -store: bait, tackle, permits, small groceries, fuel, bottled propane For information, reservations, or permit/fee information, call the Hawley Lake Resort at: (602) 335-7511 PERMITS AND FEES: camping, boating, fishing, and other recreational activities require a permit and fee - see section on White Mountain Apache Indian Reservation contained within this book
Information:	White Mountain Apache Indian Reservation (602) 338-4385		

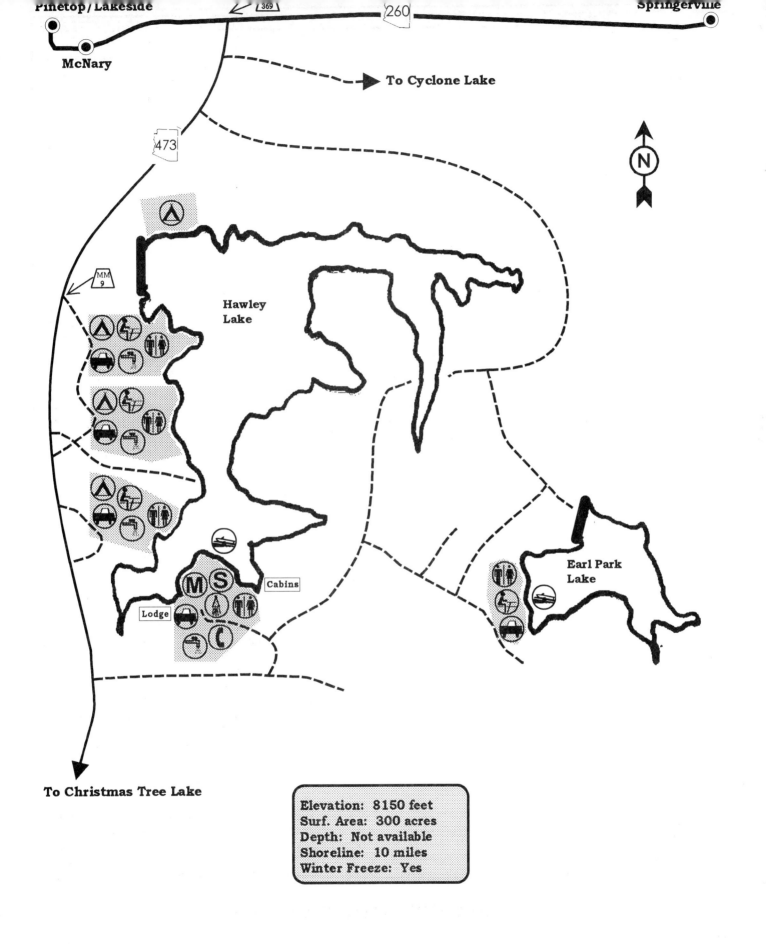

Pinetop/Lakeside

260

Springerville

McNary

369

To Cyclone Lake

N

473

MM
9

Hawley
Lake

Earl Park
Lake

Cabins

M S

Lodge

To Christmas Tree Lake

Elevation: 8150 feet
Surf. Area: 300 acres
Depth: Not available
Shoreline: 10 miles
Winter Freeze: Yes

50A

CHRISTMAS TREE LAKE

Located on the 1.6 million-acre White Mountain Apache Indian Reservation, this beauty is primarily a fisherman's lake. This 40-acre lake is closely watched by the Fish and Game Department as it holds the Apache Trout (Salmo Apache) native only to these White Mountains. This is a day-use-only lake, no overnight camping is allowed. The weather is consistent with the 8200 foot elevation. Access is off of Indian Services Route R-26, east of Arizona Highway 73, and is unpaved for the last 20 miles or so.

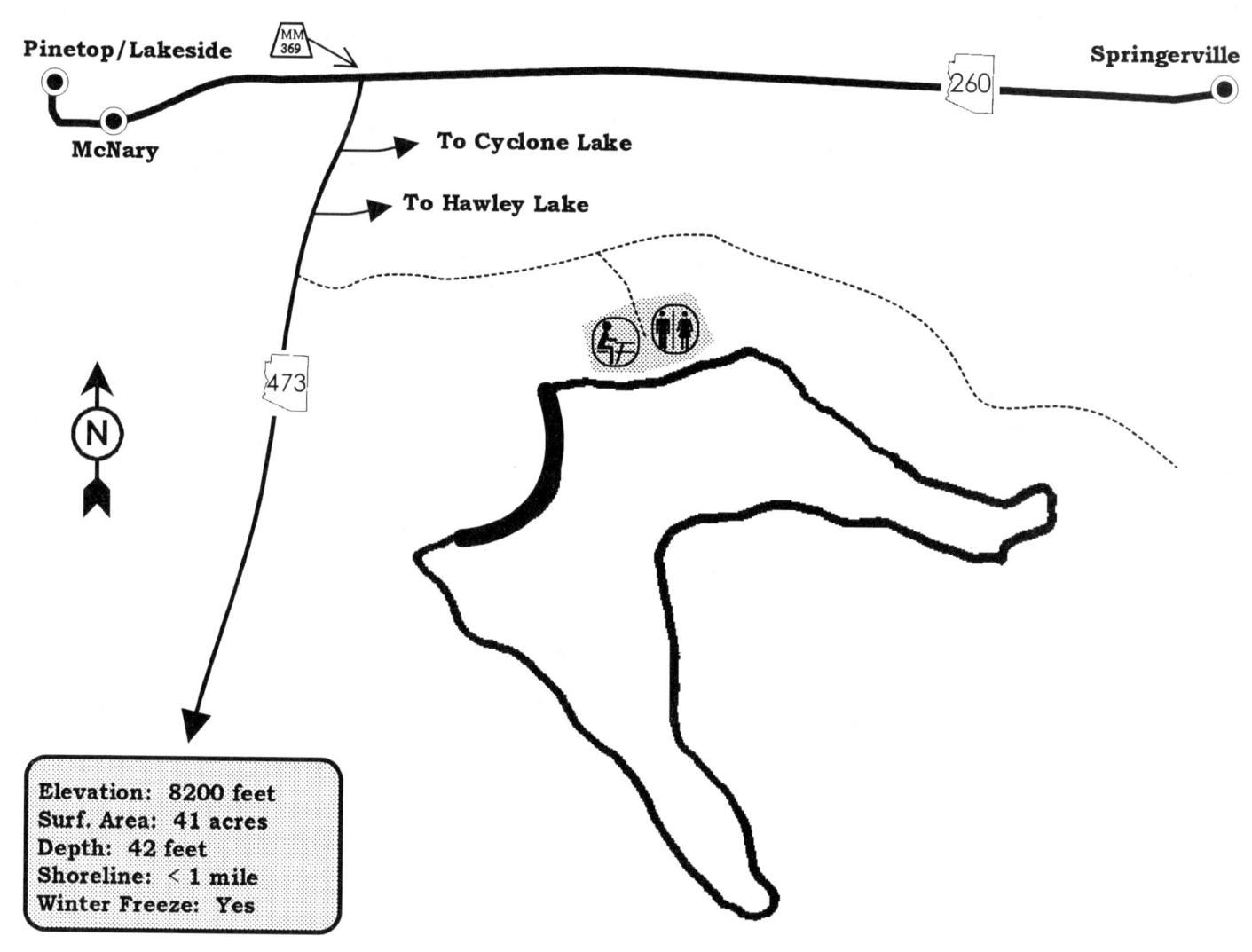

Elevation: 8200 feet
Surf. Area: 41 acres
Depth: 42 feet
Shoreline: < 1 mile
Winter Freeze: Yes

CAMPING/RVING	RECREATION	BOATING	MISCELLANEOUS
-no overnight camping allowed -primitive toilets	-picnicking, canoeing -hiking -fishing (special lake permit req.) $15/day, 1st come-1st served, sold in White River only (special limits apply) -artificial lures/flies only on barbless hook (no live bait allowed) -no swimming -no ATVs/ATCs	-electric motor only -boat permit/fee required -no ramp	-no conveniences or services -closest towns are Hon Dah and White River -open only May 23 to Sept. 7 (weather permitting) PERMITS AND FEES: camping, boating, fishing, and other recreational activities require a permit and fee - see section on White Mountain Apache Indian Reservation contained within this book
Information:	White Mountain Apache Indian Reservation (602) 338-4385		

Reservation Lake is located at the foot of Mount Baldy on the Fort Apache Reservation, 220 miles northeast of Phoenix. At 9000 foot elevation it supplies some of the states finest fishing, summer weather, and scenery. The lake is open year round but is frozen over in winter. The lake convenience store is open only Memorial Day through Labor Day. Camping and picnicking at Reservation Lake is a serene experience given the wildlife, flora, solitude and mild summer days. Fishing, much from shore, is the day's primary activity on this 280- acre lake. There are some beautiful hikes to be taken on the pine-covered hillsides. Day trips to the many other high mountain lakes, nearby streams or even the small local towns can be quite enjoyable. Insects are moderate with an occasional bear searching for supper after dark. Access to the lake is a bit difficult, with the last 25 miles unpaved, curvy, and narrow. Permits and fees are necessary for all activities on the reservation. In spite of the drive and permit requirements, this "off the beaten path" haven is perfect for the "outdoorsy" and quiet.

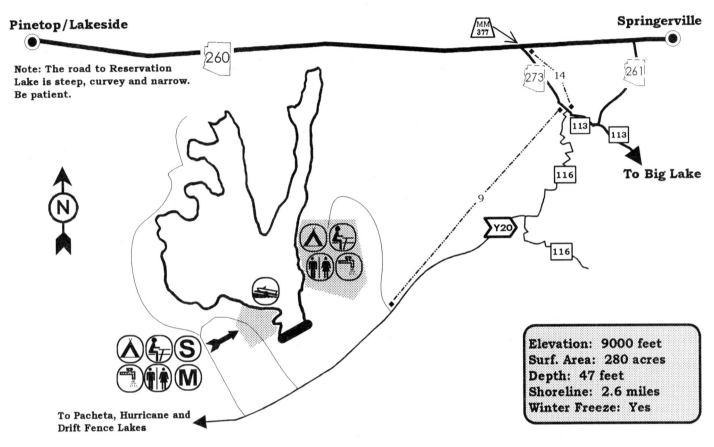

Note: The road to Reservation Lake is steep, curvey and narrow. Be patient.

Elevation: 9000 feet
Surf. Area: 280 acres
Depth: 47 feet
Shoreline: 2.6 miles
Winter Freeze: Yes

To Pacheta, Hurricane and Drift Fence Lakes

CAMPING/RVING	RECREATION	BOATING	MISCELLANEOUS
Tents/Trailers/RVs -developed campsites -primitive cabins available -permit/fee required -primitive rest rooms -drinking water -dead and down wood may be collected for use (there is plenty of it) -no showers -dogs on leash only	-hiking -picnicking -horseback riding -fishing: rainbow trout, brook trout, brown trout (special limits apply) HINT: when trolling use a cowbell trailed by a crawler -shore fishing -hunting -no ATVs/ATCs -no swimming	-electric motor only -1 improved ramp -1 primitive launch -boating permit/fee is $2/day or $10/year	-convenience store: bait, tackle, permits, gas, boat rentals, battery charging. -closest town is Greer -no telephone PERMITS AND FEES: camping, boating, fishing, and other recreational activities require a permit and fee - see section on White Mountain Apache Indian Reservation contained within this book
Information:	White Mountain Apache Tribe (602) 338-4385		

PACHETA LAKE

Another of the remote, quiet, and beautiful Fort Apache Indian Reservation Lakes, Pacheta Lake sits at an 8200-foot elevation. It is essentially a replication of the other White Mountain lakes, quiet, wooded, frozen over in winter, and cool and pleasant in the summer. With 68 acres it's as remote as you can get. If you're looking for solitude, this is it. Even more isolated would be a summer's hike up or down Pacheta Creek. One heck of a beautiful venture for the stream angler. Minimal facilities are available at this lake located five miles south of Reservation Lake. Remember to bring in everything you need (except wood, there's plenty lying around).

Conveniences are rare. The surrounding forests contain exquisite flora and much wildlife with, of course, its compliment of insects. There is a road around the lake which may be useful for shore fishing access. Access is south of Arizona Highway 260, at mile marker 377, to Arizona 273. Follow the signs to Reservation Lake, then continue five miles south up the signage. You can come in from the east through White River/Fort Apache but the going's much tougher. As it is, there's 30 miles of narrow, dusty, curvy, steep gravel/dirt road to navigate. If you're looking for summer trout, quiet and cool, the White Mountain Apache lakes are the spot.

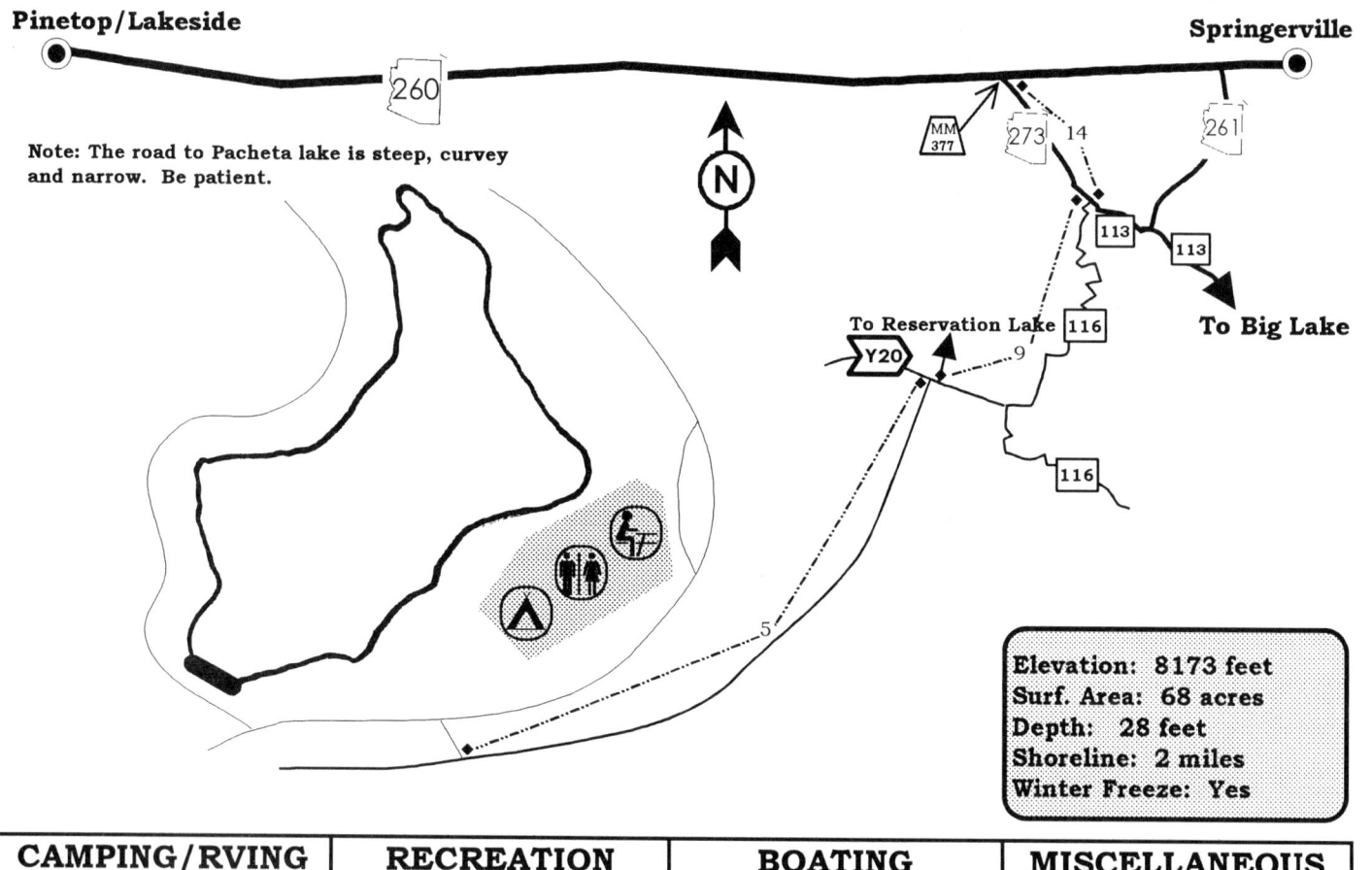

Note: The road to Pacheta lake is steep, curvey and narrow. Be patient.

Elevation: 8173 feet
Surf. Area: 68 acres
Depth: 28 feet
Shoreline: 2 miles
Winter Freeze: Yes

CAMPING/RVING	RECREATION	BOATING	MISCELLANEOUS
Tents/Trailers/RVs -15 sites -no hookups -pit toilets -no showers -no drinking water -dogs on leash only -dead and down wood may be collected for use (there's plenty of it)	-hiking -picnicking -horseback riding -hunting (permit required) -fishing: (special limits apply) rainbow trout, brown trout -shore fishing -no swimming -no ATVs/ATCs	-electric motor only -no launch ramp -permit and fee required	-nearest town is Greer -open mid-May to Sept 15 -nearest convenience is Reservation Lake store: bait, tackle, gas, battery charge, food -no telephone PERMITS AND FEES: camping, boating, fishing, and other recreational activities require a permit and fee - see section on White Mountain Apache Indian Reservation contained within this book
Information:	White Mountain Apache Tribe (602) 338-4385		

At 16 acres, Drift Fence Lake sits in a meadow of aspen and spruce on the White Mountain Apache Indian Reservation. At 9000 feet, the lake feels and sees four seasons and has some of the states finest summer weather and scenery. Camping is allowed at the lake and solitude will be the name of the game. The picnicker, hiker, horseback rider, or angler will all enjoy the quiet, peaceful, and beautiful surroundings. A permit and fee are required for any or all activities on the reservation. Insects are moderate but the flora and wildlife are plentiful. Fishing is the primary activity at Drift Fence Lake. Fishing in the fall is better than springtime.

The lake freezes in winter and given the shallowness generally loses its fish. The lake needs to be restocked yearly. Fly fisherman will do well. Day trips to the many other high mountain lakes and nearby streams or the small local towns can be quite enjoyable. Access to the lake is a bit difficult with the last 28 miles unpaved, curvy, hilly, and narrow. Access is south of Arizona Highway 260 at mile marker 377 on 273, then Forest Road 116 to Indian Road Y-20. The simpler instructions are to follow the signs to Reservation Lake and from there follow the signs to Drift Fence Lake 2-1/2 miles southwest. In spite of the drive, permits and fees, you will love this high-mountain retreat.

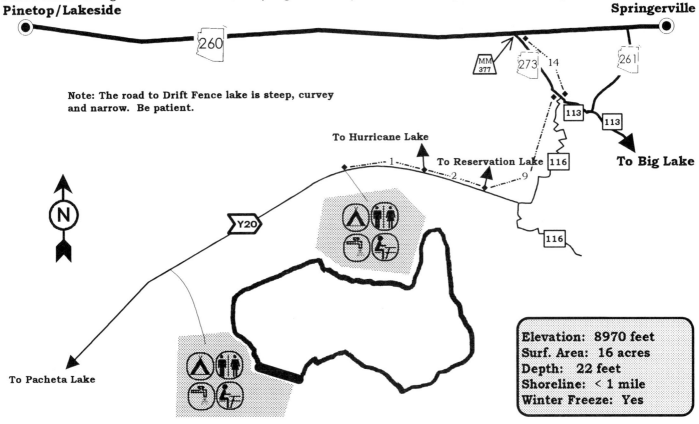

Note: The road to Drift Fence lake is steep, curvey and narrow. Be patient.

Elevation: 8970 feet
Surf. Area: 16 acres
Depth: 22 feet
Shoreline: < 1 mile
Winter Freeze: Yes

CAMPING/RVING	RECREATION	BOATING	MISCELLANEOUS
Tents/Trailers/RVs -12 sites -tables -pit toilets -no showers -drinking water -dead and down wood may be collected for use (there's plenty of it in the area) -dogs on leash only	-hiking -picnicking -canoeing -horseback riding -hunting (permit required) -fishing: rainbow trout, brook trout -shore fishing -no swimming -no ATVs/ATCs	-electric motor only -no launch ramp -permit and fee required	-open mid May to Sept 15 -nearest town is Greer -nearest convenience is Reservation Lake store, 2.5 miles away: bait, tackle, gas, battery charge, food -no telephone PERMITS AND FEES: camping, boating, fishing, and other recreational activities require a permit and fee - see section on White Mountain Apache Indian Reservation contained within this book
Information:	White Mountain Apache Tribe (602) 338-4385		

HURRICANE LAKE

Hurricane Lake is located 3 miles west of Reservation Lake on the White Mountain Apache Indian Reservation. At 900-feet elevation, the surrounding spruce and fir forest is fabulous. There is no camping allowed at Hurricane Lake. This 19-acre angler's lake offers the Salmo-Apache trout. A special Hurricane Lake permit is required and is available only in White River. Twenty permits are issued each day on a first-come, first-served basis. There are also special limits which apply to this lake. Please be sure you are cognizant of the rules and regulations on the reservation and in particular those applicable to Hurricane Lake. This lake would be a good choice for a day trip if you're camping at Reservation Lake, just near by. Weather is fabulous in midsummer months. Beware though of those late afternoon thundershowers. This lake offers a special challenge to those diehard trout fishermen looking for "bragging rites." Access to Hurricane lake is not the easiest. Just follow the signs from Reservation Lake.

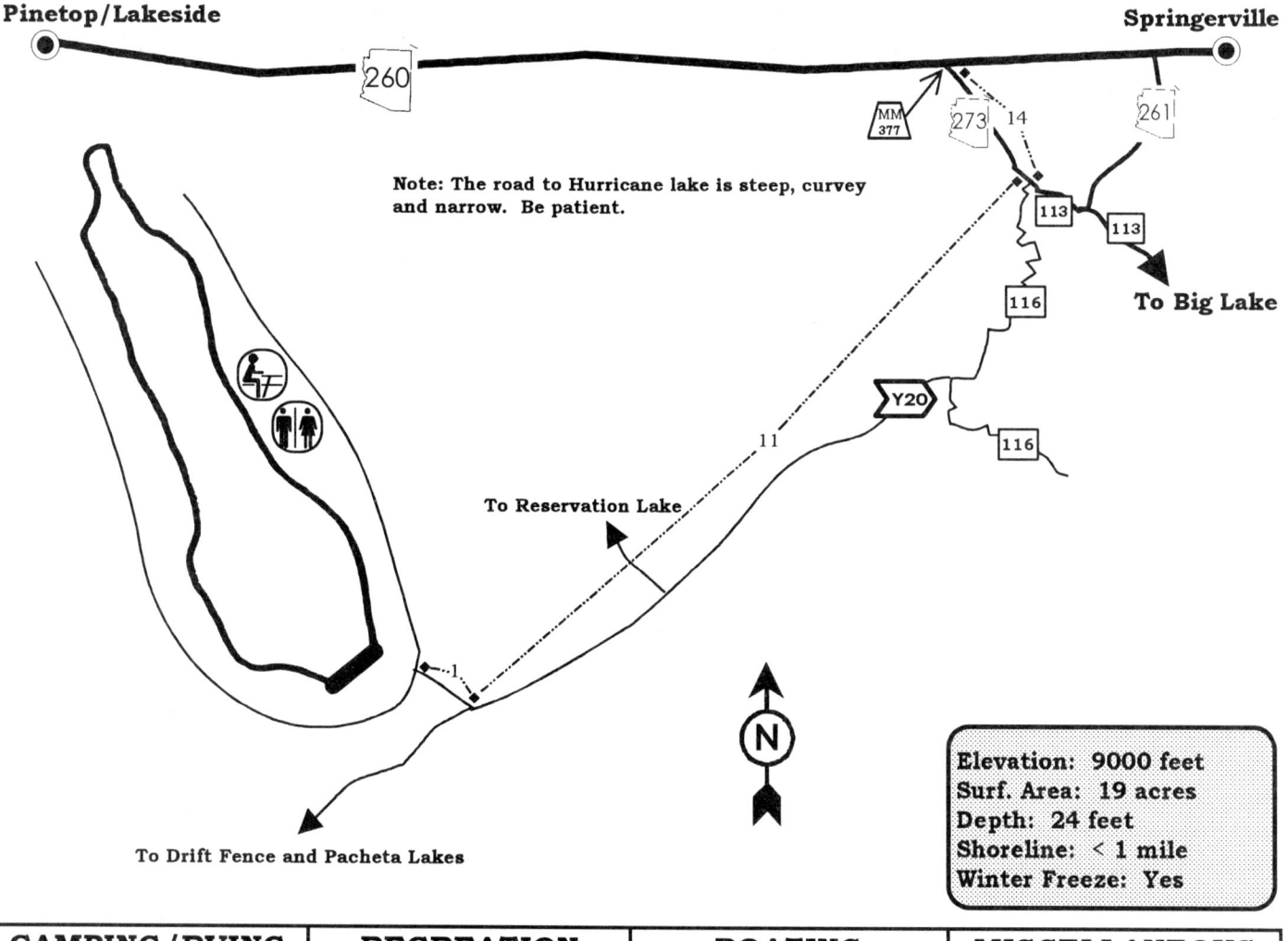

Note: The road to Hurricane lake is steep, curvey and narrow. Be patient.

Elevation: 9000 feet
Surf. Area: 19 acres
Depth: 24 feet
Shoreline: < 1 mile
Winter Freeze: Yes

CAMPING/RVING	RECREATION	BOATING	MISCELLANEOUS
-no overnight camping allowed at lake -Recommendation: camp at Reservation Lake just 3 miles away - developed campgrounds surround the lake with all necessary conveniences at the lake store	-picnicking, canoeing -fishing: (20 special permits per day only) 1st come - 1st served $15 each - these special permits are only sold in White River -artificial flies/lures only on a single barbless hook (no live bait allowed) -local limit is 1 Apache trout 16' or longer	-electric motor only -no launch ramp -recommend a canoe or small inflatable	-open May 27 through Sept 6 (weather permitting) -closest town is Greer PERMITS AND FEES: camping, boating, fishing, and other recreational activities require a permit and fee - see section on White Mountain Apache Indian Reservation contained within this book
Information:	White Mountain Apache Tribe (602) 338-4385		

Tonto Lake sits at a 7800-foot elevation in a very remote area of the White Mountain Apache Indian Reservation. Open to the public on weekends only (Friday, Saturday, and Sunday). Special lake permits are required. There are three picnic areas around the lake. The summer weather is typical of the area, pleasant daytime temperatures, with an occasional thunderstorm in the afternoon. One small campsite sits near the dam at the south end of the lake. At 80 acres, there is plenty of room for the few anglers that will venture over the difficult terrain required to reach Tonto Lake. Access is difficult no matter which direction you come in, be it from the north past Reservation lake or from the west through White River. Please remember to acquire the special lake permits required for Tonto Lake. Remember also to bring in all you need. You're pretty isolated.

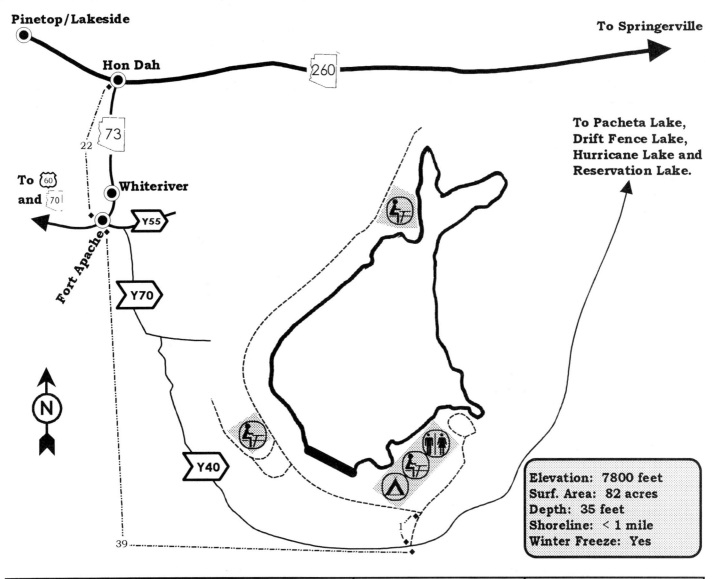

Elevation: 7800 feet
Surf. Area: 82 acres
Depth: 35 feet
Shoreline: < 1 mile
Winter Freeze: Yes

CAMPING/RVING	RECREATION	BOATING	MISCELLANEOUS
Tents/Trailers/RVs -camping on Friday and Saturday nights only -pit toilets -no drinking water -no showers -dead and down wood may be collected for use (there is plenty available) -dogs on leash only	-hiking -picnicking -canoeing -horseback riding -fishing: (special lake permit required) (special limit applies) -shore fishing -no swimming -no ATVs/ATCs	-electric motor only -boat launch area -permit/fee required	-closest town is Maverick, 5 miles to the northeast PERMITS AND FEES: camping, boating, fishing, and other recreational activities require a permit and fee - see section on White Mountain Apache Indian Reservation contained within this book
Information:	White Mountain Apache Indian Reservation (602) 338-4385		

BECKER LAKE

Becker Lake, located in northeastern Arizona is managed by the Arizona Game and Fish Department. Becker Lake has a long history of ups and downs as a fishery, suffice it to say, it's back on line with much good news expected in the future. Becker, with 85 acres is exclusively a fisherman's lake with trout, trout, and more trout. Action from a boat is likely the best, but shore fishing or wading work well also. Fly fisherman are in abundance at Becker exercising the more traditional trout catching methods. At 6900 feet, this lake freezes over in winter and is a summer fisherman's getaway. With no overnight camping at the lake, you'll need to stay at one of the area's private campgrounds or in town two miles south. Access is paved on US Highway 60, 2 miles north of Springerville.

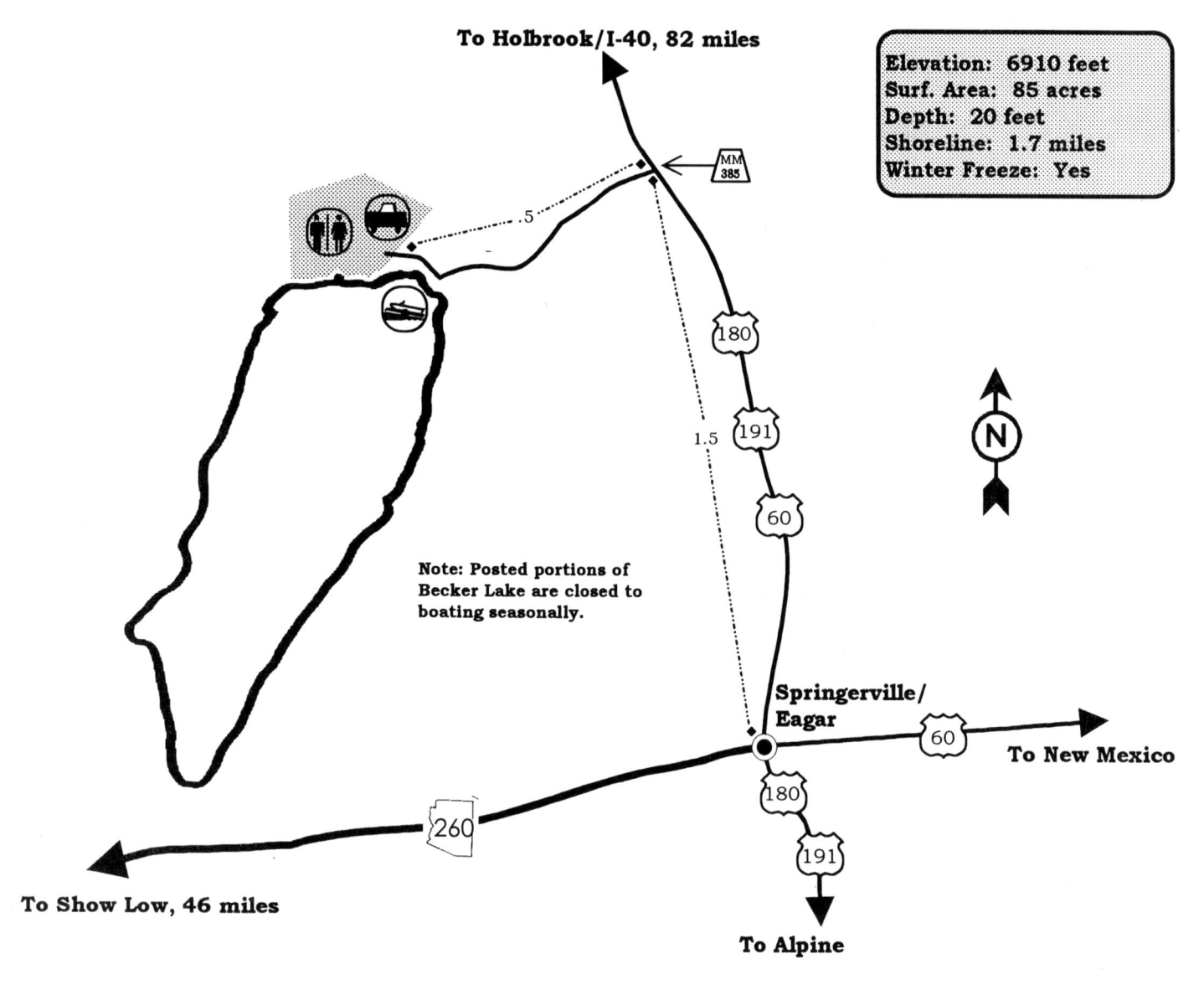

To Holbrook/I-40, 82 miles

MM 385

Elevation: 6910 feet
Surf. Area: 85 acres
Depth: 20 feet
Shoreline: 1.7 miles
Winter Freeze: Yes

Note: Posted portions of Becker Lake are closed to boating seasonally.

Springerville/ Eagar

To New Mexico

To Show Low, 46 miles

To Alpine

CAMPING/RVING	RECREATION	BOATING	MISCELLANEOUS
-no camping allowed at lake -private campground 1/2 mile from lake -complete lodging facilities in Springerville two miles south of the lake	-canoeing -sailing, sailboarding -fishing: (special limits apply) rainbow trout, brown trout -shore fishing	-electric motor only -watercraft are prohibited from entering posted portions of Becker Lake from April 1 through July 31 -improved ramp	-closest town is Springerville, 2 miles to the south -primitive rest rooms
Information:	Arizona Game and Fish Department (602) 367-4281		

If there is beauty found in the White Mountains, it is at Lee Valley Lake which sits at the foot of Mount Baldy. At 9400-foot elevation, this lake is managed by the Apache-Sitgreaves National Forest. Fishing is the order of the day at Lee Valley with the rare Apache Trout, Browns, but mostly the Arctic Grayling. Special rules and limits apply. A small lake of 45 acres, it certainly freezes in winter given the elevation. There is no camping at the lake but numerous campgrounds exist within a six-mile radius be they on the White Mountain Apache Indian Reservation or in the surrounding national forest. Summer afternoons are pleasant with cool, cool evenings. Don't be surprised at the late afternoon thunder showers during midsummer. Insects are moderate and wildlife abounds be it big or small. A pleasant day can be spent just hiking and observing the flora and fauna. The horseback rider will enjoy the same pleasures as the hiker but can cover more ground. A "horse camping-only" campground, named Gabaldon, lies only nine miles north. Access is moderate going south from Arizona Highway 260 on Arizona 273 and heading west on Forest Road 113E. A dusty gravel/dirt road comprises more than 1/2 the challenge once you're off of 260. If all else fails, just follow the signs off 273.

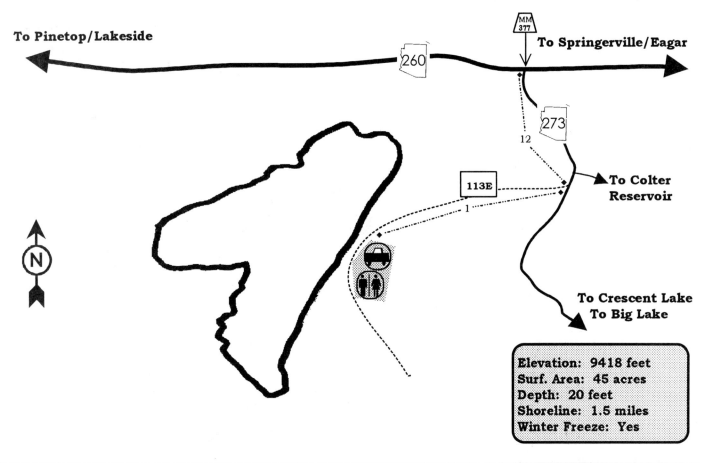

Elevation: 9418 feet
Surf. Area: 45 acres
Depth: 20 feet
Shoreline: 1.5 miles
Winter Freeze: Yes

CAMPING/RVING	RECREATION	BOATING	MISCELLANEOUS
Tents/Trailers/RVs -no overnight camping at lake -campgrounds at other nearby lakes both on the White Mountain Apache Indian Reservation or on the Apache- Sitgreaves National Forest -camping in developed campsites only -pit toilets	-hiking, horseback riding -picnicking -canoeing -fishing: brook trout, arctic grayling NOTE: (special limits apply) (no live bait allowed, artificial lures only) -catch and release all day	-electric motor only -launch ramp	-nearest convenience or town is Greer, 11 miles away -Recommendation: pay particular attention to fishing rules and limits -season - May 15 to Nov. 1 -access roads not cleared in winter -plenty of firewood lying around for campfires
Information:	Apache-Sitgreaves Indian Reservation (602) 333-4372		

SUNRISE LAKE

Sunrise Lake sits at a 9100-foot elevation on the northeastern edge of the White Mountain Apache Indian Reservation. Popular, Sunrise Lake is a favorite, thus usually busy. Nearly 900 acres when full, Sunrise is a prolific trout grower. Special limits and rules apply to the boating and fishing of Sunrise but that does not hinder the great catches. The troller, fly fisherman, or cast and retrieve kind-of-person will all do well. If one method doesn't work, change to another. The sailor or sail boarder will relish the frequently windy lake. You'll see from the barren surroundings that there's plenty of room for the wind to pickup. The horseback rider has many open miles to roam. A large campground with primitive facilities sites 1/2 mile from the lake. A motel, restaurant, store, gas station are right there at the lake. If you're up skiing at Sunrise during winter months, you can try your luck at some ice fishing. The weather is what you might expect at this location and altitude; summer days are warm with cool evenings. Afternoon thundershowers (welcomed by most visitors) are common in mid to late summer month. Access to Sunrise is too simple. Heading east from Pinetop/Lakeside on Arizona Highway 260 turn south (right) on Arizona 273 which is mile marker 377. Look for the snow fences on your right. Follow the road three miles to the store and you are on top of the facility.

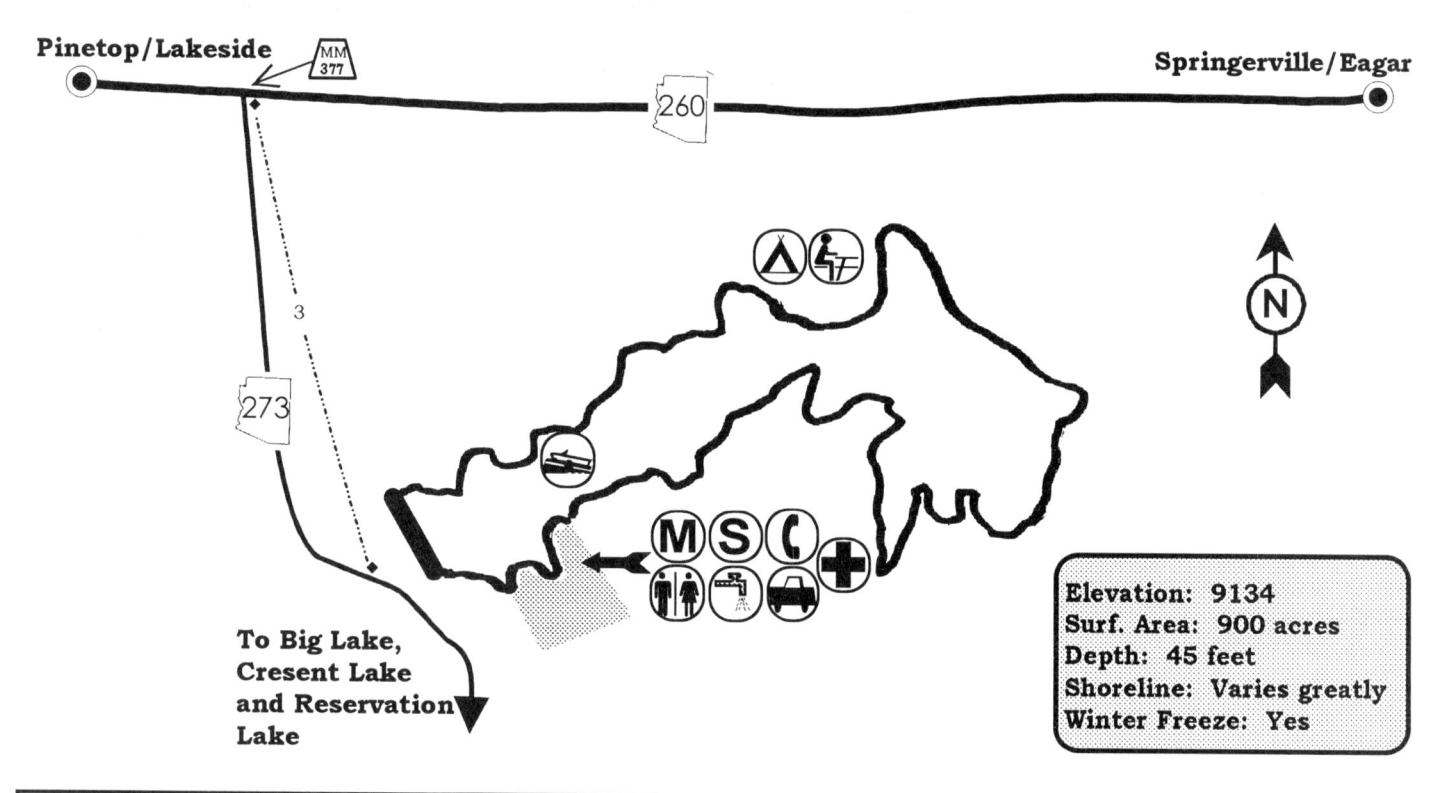

Pinetop/Lakeside — MM 377 — 260 — Springerville/Eagar

273

3

To Big Lake, Cresent Lake and Reservation Lake

Elevation: 9134
Surf. Area: 900 acres
Depth: 45 feet
Shoreline: Varies greatly
Winter Freeze: Yes

CAMPING/RVING	RECREATION	BOATING	MISCELLANEOUS
Tents/Trailers/RVs -200 sites -permit/fee required -pit toilets -drinking water, tables, grills -no hookups, no showers -dead and down wood may be collected for use - no wood in immediate area but plenty on side roads on reservation -campground 1/2-mile from lake -season of use is mid-May to mid-September -dogs on leash only	-hiking, horseback riding -picnicking -sailing, sail boarding, canoeing -permits & fees required -fishing: rainbow trout, brook trout -shore fishing -ice fishing NOTE: special rules and limits apply - artificial lures and flies only -no swimming -no ATVs/ATCs	-10 horse power motor or less -1 improved ramp -boat rentals at store -upper end of the lake is shallow and weedy -permit & fee required	-closest town is 5 and 1/2 miles to Greer -restaurant/motel at lake-store open in summer: telephone, boat rentals, gasoline, groceries, bait, tackle, permits -store open mid-May to mid-September PERMITS AND FEES: camping, boating, fishing, and other recreational activities require a permit and fee - see section on White Mountain Apache Indian Reservation contained within this book

Information:	White Mountain Apache Tribe (602) 338-4385

Colter Reservoir, formed by the east fork of the Little Colorado River, sits at the base of Mount Baldy at a 9300-foot elevation within the Apache-Sitgreaves National Forest. There are no conveniences or facilities whatsoever at this lake. This lake is not stocked with fish and serves only as an irrigation reservoir. But for the equestrian, hiker, or day-use picnicker, this remote, seldom visited reservoir has all the scenic beauty of Arizona's White Mountains. The canoer will also relish the 100 acres of solitude. Weather in summer is sunny warm days, cool evenings and frequent afternoon thunderstorms in mid to late summer. The wildlife and flora are fabulous throughout the area. There is a "horse camping only" campground a few miles north. Access is moderate, going south from Arizona 260 (mile marker 377) on to 273 and then heading east on Forest Road 113E. Simply follow the signs to Lee Valley Reservoir and it's just on the east side of 273, less than 1 mile. But remember, you have to walk to the lake. There is no drive-in access to the shoreline.

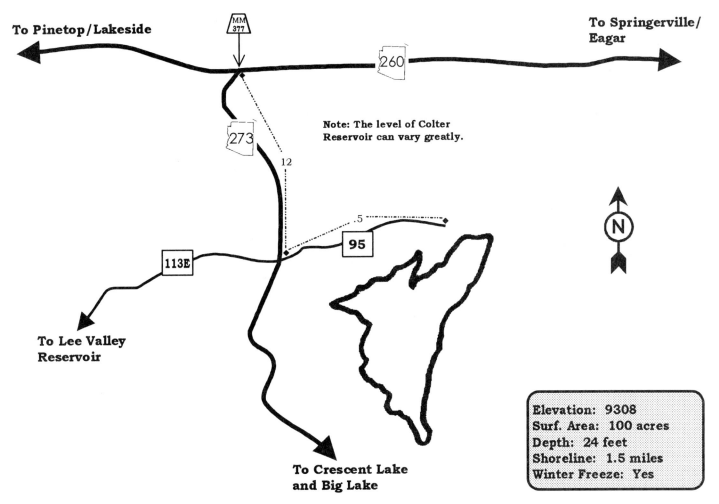

To Pinetop/Lakeside

MM 377

260

To Springerville/ Eagar

Note: The level of Colter Reservoir can vary greatly.

273

12

N

.5

95

113E

To Lee Valley Reservoir

To Crescent Lake and Big Lake

Elevation: 9308
Surf. Area: 100 acres
Depth: 24 feet
Shoreline: 1.5 miles
Winter Freeze: Yes

CAMPING/RVING	RECREATION	BOATING	MISCELLANEOUS
Tents/Trailers/RVs -no developed sites -no road access directly to the lake -primitive camping allowed throughout forest -developed campgrounds are located nearby on the Apache-Sitgreaves National Forest or on the White Mountain Reservation	-hiking -picnicking -sailing -horseback riding -fishing: lake not stocked, not likely that you will catch anything -snoozing	-no ramp -electric motors only	-nearest town is Greer, 11 miles away -plenty of firewood - dead and down wood may be collected for used (there's plenty in the area) -be aware of fire restrictions and rules -access road not cleared in winter
Information:	Apache-Sitgreaves National Forest (602) 333-4372		

BUNCH / RIVER / TUNNEL RESERVOIRS

The trio, Bunch, River and Tunnel Reservoirs are locally known as the "Greer" lakes. These lakes are managed by the Apache-Sitgreaves National Forest and sit at 8200 foot elevation. Predominantly for fisherman, trout is the name of the game here. Totaling approximately 500 acres, River Reservoir is by far the largest, about 3 times larger than either of the other two. There is a boat ramp on each lake but shore fishing is common. Camping is located in either of 2 national forest campgrounds and flank Arizona Highway 373 just 2 miles form the lake. The summer days are pleasant at this altitude; an excellent respite during Arizona's summer. Access is easy on Forest Road 87B, 1/2 mile north of Greer, off Arizona Highway 373.

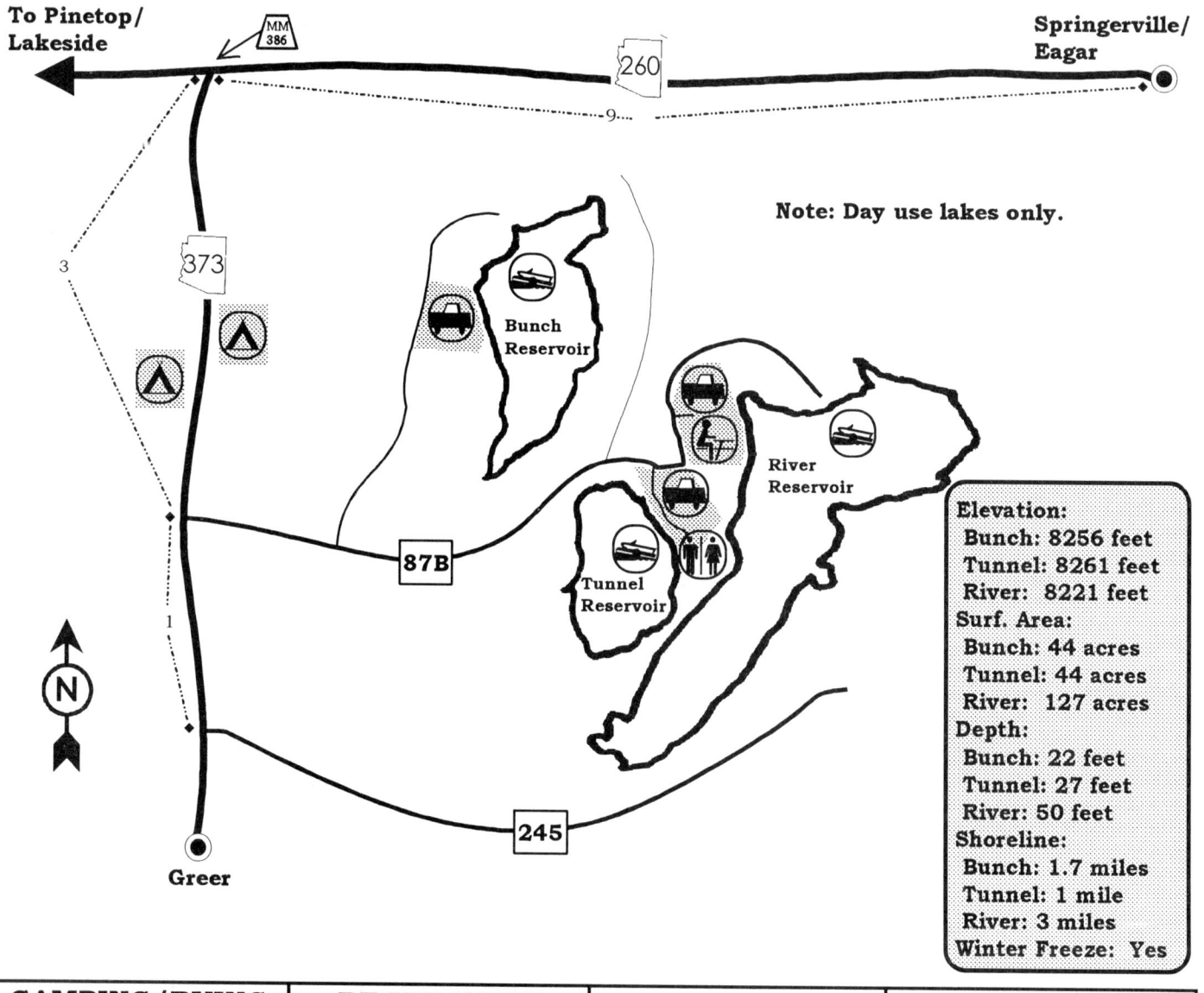

Note: Day use lakes only.

Elevation:
Bunch: 8256 feet
Tunnel: 8261 feet
River: 8221 feet
Surf. Area:
Bunch: 44 acres
Tunnel: 44 acres
River: 127 acres
Depth:
Bunch: 22 feet
Tunnel: 27 feet
River: 50 feet
Shoreline:
Bunch: 1.7 miles
Tunnel: 1 mile
River: 3 miles
Winter Freeze: Yes

CAMPING/RVING	RECREATION	BOATING	MISCELLANEOUS
-day-use-only lake Tent/Trailer/RV -2 campgrounds (Rolfe C. Hoyer and Bonny Creek) one mile from lake -drinking water -toilets, dump stations -recommend reservations during summer weekends call: 1-800-283-2267	-hiking -picnicking -horseback riding -canoeing -fishing: rainbow trout, brown trout -shore fishing	-1 improved ramp on each lake -electric motor only	-closest town is Greer, one mile south -the level of these lakes can vary significantly -this lake freezes over in winter, try ice fishing -managed season is May to November
Information:	Apache-Sitgreaves National Forest (602) 333-4372		

A "day-use-only" lake on the Apache-Sitgreaves National Forest, Crescent Lake is essentially a fisherman's lake at an 8950-foot elevation. Similar to Big Lake, just next door, it can produce some rather large fish with some excellent catches in late fall (Oct/Nov). At 130 acres and 4.5 miles of shoreline, much of it accessible by a road, it serves both those with boats and without. Boat rentals are available at the modest lakeside store. Fly fishermen can be particularly successful in this shallow, weedy lake. Numerous campgrounds are nearby, just north or south of the lake. The weather, insects, and crowds are similar to the other White Mountain lakes which are easily accessible. Access is south of Arizona 260 on Arizona 273 then a couple of miles on a well maintained dirt road. Crescent Lake is easy to get to.

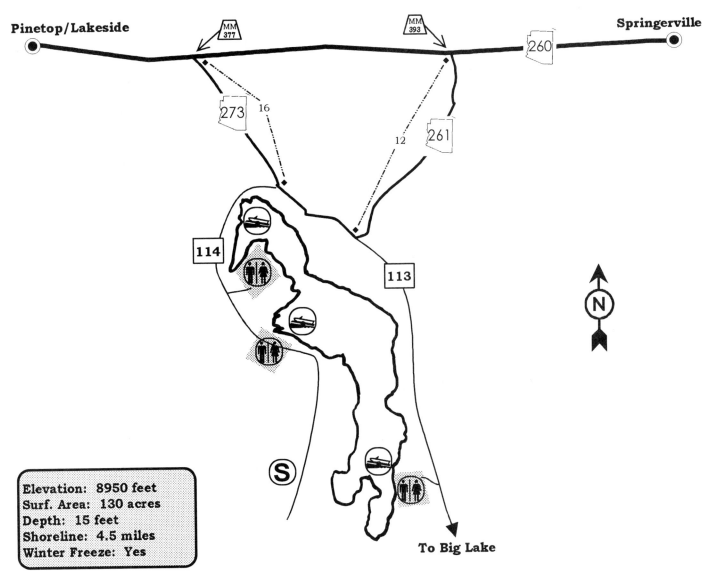

Elevation: 8950 feet
Surf. Area: 130 acres
Depth: 15 feet
Shoreline: 4.5 miles
Winter Freeze: Yes

CAMPING/RVING	RECREATION	BOATING	MISCELLANEOUS
-no camping at lake, day-use facilities only NOTE: numerous national forest campgrounds are nearby offering excellent camping facilities for tents, trailers or RVs. -pit toilets	-swimming -hiking -picnicking -canoeing, sailing -fishing: rainbow trout, brook trout -shore fishing -toilets for day use	-8 horse power motor maximum -1 improved ramp -3 primitive launch areas -lake is shallow and weedy	-small store at lake: boat rentals groceries, bait, tackle -other conveniences at Big Lake store, 2 miles south -nearest town is Eagar, 24 miles north
Information:	Apache-Sitgreaves National Forest (602) 333-4372		

BIG LAKE

Contained within the nearly 2-million acre Apache-Sitgreaves National Forest, Big Lake at 9200-foot elevation is one of the more popular high-mountain lakes in the state. Big Lake sits just east of 11,500 foot Mount Baldy in a forest of ponderosa pine, spruce, and aspen. Big Lake hosts 4 camp grounds with over 200 total developed camp sites. None of the four camp grounds are directly on the lake, but the two closest are Brookchar and Cutthroat (both approximately 100 yards from the water's edge).. These two camp grounds handle tents only - no trailers or RVs. Reservations are recommended during the "open" summer months, which run from Memorial Day (or a bit earlier) to Labor Day (or a bit later). Campers may camp at Big Lake year round with no fee when it is officially closed. The fisher people, particularly those with children will be grateful for the routine success. Big Lake is stocked frequently with rainbow and brook trout, sometimes up to 400,000 a year. With 8 miles of shoreline, the 450 acres of Big Lake serves those with a boat or without. Motors are limited to 8 horsepower. The canoers and sailors are pleased about that. Hikers and mountain bikers can enjoy the newly cut 10 miles of nature trails, both large and small game roam the forests and any afternoon may be "frittered" away just watching them. Deer, elk, antelope, bear, turkey, javelina, countless small ground animals, and fowl make this a photographer's haven. For those a bit more adventuresome, a horseback ride through these forests from meadow to meadow will offer both sensuous and academic pleasure. A stable with horse rentals resides at the south end of Big Lake. The lake-side convenience store is well stocked with necessary camping/fishing equipment and food stuffs. Boat/motor rentals and private docks are available. Weather at Big Lake is consistent with the elevation. Winter at 9200 foot elevation is cold with plenty of white stuff. Summer months contain pleasant/warmish days with cool evenings. Just perfect. Late afternoon thunderstorms are common in the latter half of summer. They can be fun also. Given the beautiful surroundings, comfortable atmosphere, and successful fishing, summer months can be very busy. Weekends are nearly a stampede. Camping reservations are certainly recommended. If you want a boat/motor reserved recommendations are helpful there also. You can access Big Lake a few ways. Proceed south for Arizona Highway 260 at mile marker 377 on to Arizona Highway 273 or south from 260 at mile marker 393 on Arizona Highway 261. Arizona Highway 261 is paved nearly all the way to the lake, but both roads offer easy access with the worst a well maintained gravel road. You can also get to Big Lake from the east. Get on Forest Service Road 249 from US Highway 191 just north of Alpine, Arizona and 19 miles later you'll be there. This way is kind of a fun trip.

See map, next page

CAMPING/RVING	RECREATION	BOATING	MISCELLANEOUS
Tents/Trailers/RVs -no RV hookups -210 developed sites -Labor Day to Memorial Day no camping fee -tables -grills -drinking water -flush toilets -dump station -14 day limit -Reservation - call: 1-800-283-CAMP -$6/night	-hiking, picnicking -canoeing, sailing -swimming -napping -horseback riding at Clear Creek Stables horse rentals, 1, 2, 4 hours, all day or overnight questions/reservations: (602) 333-4174 -fishing: rainbow trout, brook trout, cutthroat trout -shore fishing -hunting -no day-use fee	-1 improved launch -8 horsepower maximum motor -boat rentals at store -daily and afternoon rates -boat docking for private boats -boat rental/boat dock reservations: (602) 367-5126 extension 0145	-convenience store at lake: bait, tackle, sporting goods, drinks, limited groceries, ice, gasoline, oil, camping supplies, tire repair, hunting and fishing license -nearest town is Springerville, 28 miles -closest conveniences in Greer, 17 miles north -a day trip to Crescent Lake or Mexican Hay Lake may well include some quieter fishing -dead and down firewood may be collected for use
Information:	Apache-Sitgreaves National Forest (602) 333-4372		

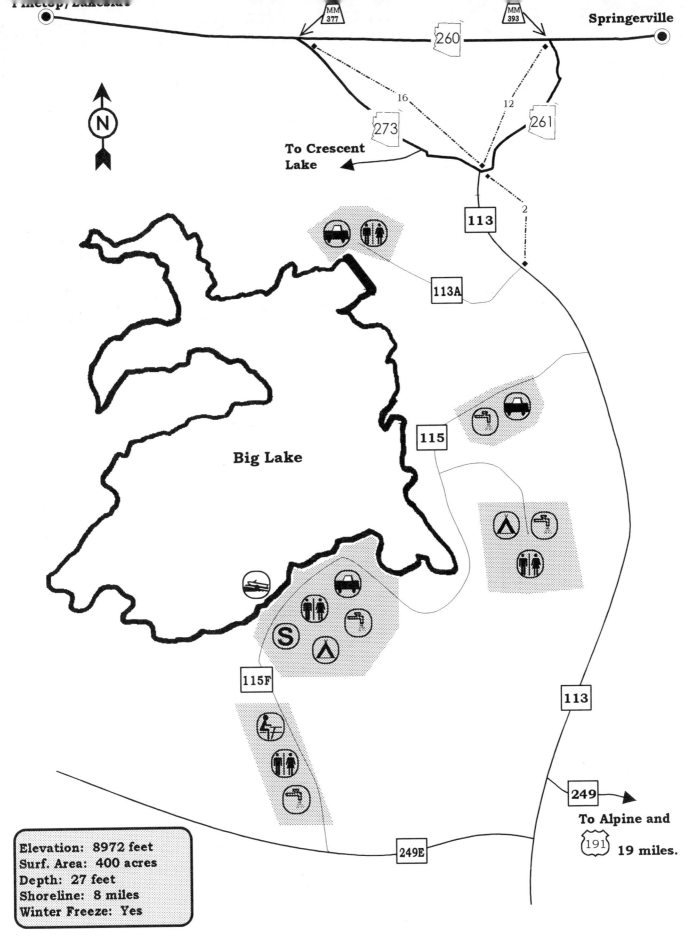

Pinetop/Lakeside

MM 377

MM 393

Springerville

260

16

12

273

261

To Crescent Lake

113

2

113A

115

115

S

115F

249

To Alpine and 191 19 miles.

249E

Elevation: 8972 feet
Surf. Area: 400 acres
Depth: 27 feet
Shoreline: 8 miles
Winter Freeze: Yes

Big Lake

BOOT LEG LAKE

Boot Leg Lake is located in the White Mountain Apache Indian Reservation just 2 miles west of Arizona Highway 73, on a reasonably rough road. The elevation is 6800 feet at this 10-acre pond which houses some very large bass (catch and release only). Just a few miles from the town of Hon Dah, on Arizona 260 it is convenient for those "close in" campers who prefer services nearby.

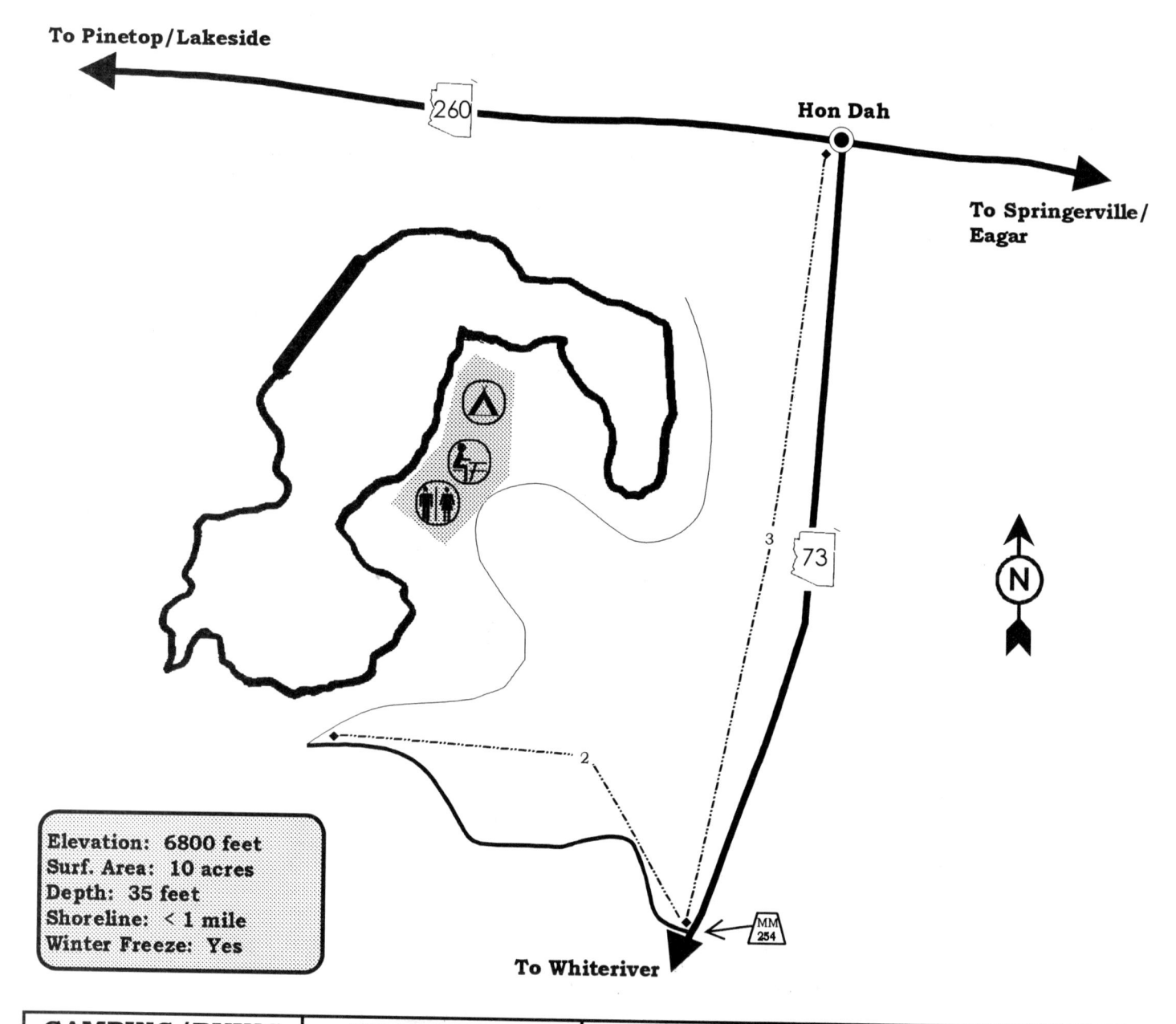

To Pinetop/Lakeside

260

Hon Dah

To Springerville/Eagar

73

N

3

2

MM 254

To Whiteriver

Elevation: 6800 feet
Surf. Area: 10 acres
Depth: 35 feet
Shoreline: < 1 mile
Winter Freeze: Yes

CAMPING/RVING	RECREATION	BOATING	MISCELLANEOUS
-tent camping (permit/fee required) -open year round -primitive toilets -tables -dead and down wood may be collected for use	-picnicking, canoeing -hiking -fishing: (special lake permit req.) catfish, trout, sunfish, largemouth bass (all bass must be released immediately) -no swimming -no ATVs/ATCs	-electric motor only -no ramp -boat permit and fee req.	-Closest town is McNary PERMITS AND FEES: camping, boating, fishing, and other recreational activities require a permit and fee - see section on White Mountain Apache Indian Reservation contained within this book
Information:	White Mountain Apache Tribe (602) 338-4385		

At an 8400-foot elevation, Lake Sierra Blanca is contained within the Apache-Sitgreaves National Forest. This is another "day-use-only," "fisherman's lake," that's too small (5 acres) and too shallow and weedy to build up the facilities. There is no camping at the lake or even nearby. There are no facilities or conveniences at the lake. Lake Sierra Blanca is located seven miles west of Alpine on Forest Road 249. Alpine is 28 miles south of Springerville on the Coronado Trail (US Highway 191). Like Mexican Hay Lake it is a fisherman's get-a-way during the busy summer weekends on the other area lakes.

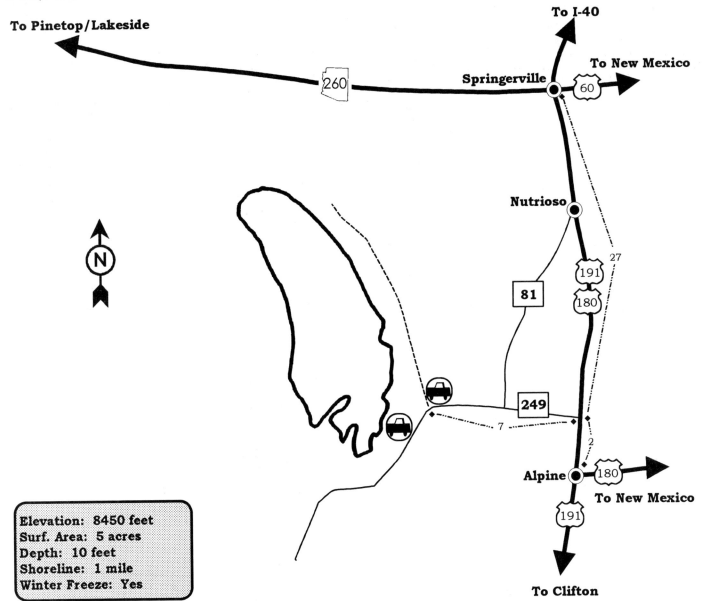

To Pinetop/Lakeside

To I-40

To New Mexico

260

Springerville

60

N

Nutrioso

27

191

81

180

249

7

2

Alpine

180

To New Mexico

191

To Clifton

Elevation: 8450 feet
Surf. Area: 5 acres
Depth: 10 feet
Shoreline: 1 mile
Winter Freeze: Yes

CAMPING/RVING	RECREATION	BOATING	MISCELLANEOUS
-day-use only -no camping at or near lake -numerous campgrounds in the 10- to 20-mile radius in the Apache-Sitgreaves National Forest	-fishing: rainbow trout -shore fishing NOTE: fly fishing seems the most productive in this weedy, slightly difficult-to-fish lake	-electric motor only -no ramp -recommend small inflatable or canoe	-nearest town is Alpine, 7 miles to the east

Information:	Apache-Sitgreaves National Forest (602) 339-4384

LUNA LAKE

Luna Lake is just a couple of miles from the New Mexico border and resides within the Apache-Sitgreaves National Forest. With 120 acres at a 7900-foot elevation, it is an excellent choice for any recreational activity. A well maintained forest service campground is adjacent to the lake plus three group camping sites. The tall pines, shimmering aspens, blue spruce, and ponderosa pine fill this high mountain country with some of the southwest's best visual pleasure. Wildlife is abundant, be it big game or ground animals. The hiker, equestrian or casual user will certainly enjoy the ambiance. The lake serves the angler well, be it from a boat or from the 3.3 miles of shoreline. Trollers or fly fisherman will be successful. Side trips to the Gila National Forest, just southwest of the lake across the border in New Mexico, would be a pleasure as would an afternoon in Alpine just four miles east. A beautiful, friendly town which has all the comforts necessary for visitors. Access is south of Springerville on US Highway 180/191. The lake is 4 miles east of Alpine on 180, take Forest Road 570 just 1/8 mile to the campground.

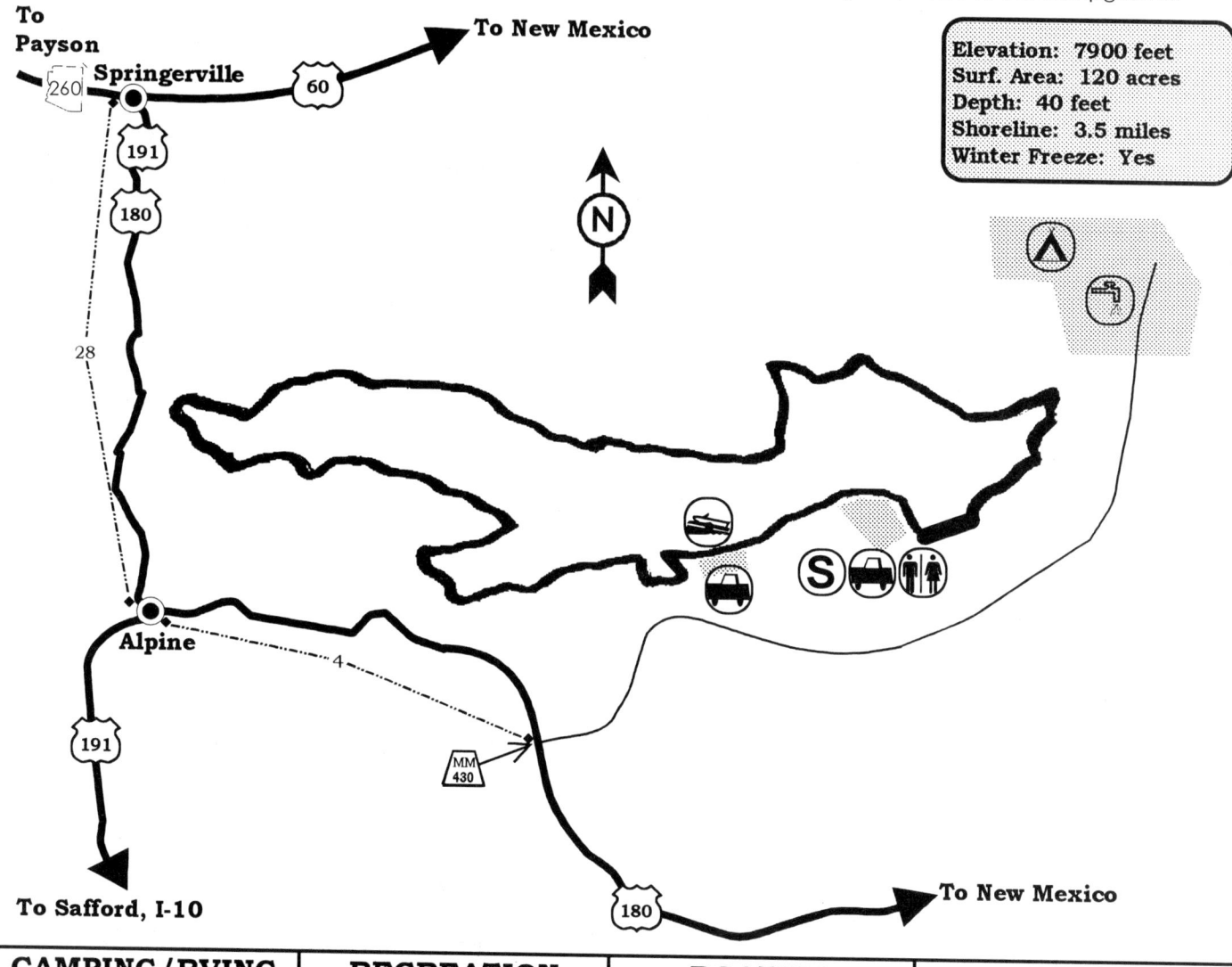

Elevation: 7900 feet
Surf. Area: 120 acres
Depth: 40 feet
Shoreline: 3.5 miles
Winter Freeze: Yes

CAMPING/RVING	RECREATION	BOATING	MISCELLANEOUS
Tents/Trailers/RVs -50 sites -$6/night -tables -pit toilets -drinking water -3 group campgrounds	-picnicking -sailing, canoeing -hiking -horseback riding -fishing: rainbow trout, brook trout -shore fishing -ice fishing HINT: fly fishing or trolling work very well	-8 horse power motor maximum -1 boat launch -watercraft are prohibited in posted areas of lake from April 1 through July 31	-complete facilities and conveniences in town of Alpine, just 4 miles west on Highway 180 -no phone at the lake -small store at the lake: boat/motor rental, bait, tackle, ice, snacks

Information:	Apache-Sitgreaves National Forest (602) 339-4384

Hulsey Lake is a 4-acre pond which sits at 8600 foot elevation near the New Mexico boarder. There is no camping at the lake proper but a modest national forest campground is located 3 miles south of the lake. The angler, picnicker, and hiker are the predominant beneficiaries of this "day-use-only" lake. The angler does best in early spring. The picnicker and hiker do well as long as there is no snow on the ground. The beauty of the surrounding forest is awesome, don't forget your camera. The flora and wildlife are abundant. If you're in the area, don't forget to visit the small town of Alpine, just 7 miles south of the lake. Access to Hulsey Lake is east of Arizona Highway 191 on Forest Road 56 (at marker 421) just 4 miles north of Alpine. Follow Forest Road 56 for 2 miles to 56A which takes you to the parking area. There is no vehicle access to the shoreline. The roads can be tough in wet weather.

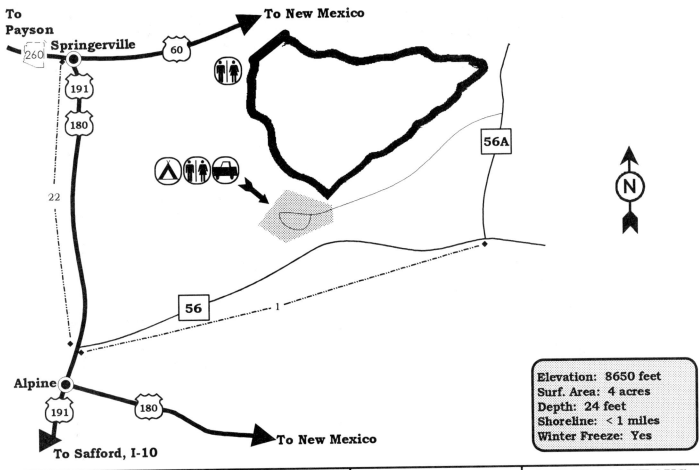

Elevation: 8650 feet
Surf. Area: 4 acres
Depth: 24 feet
Shoreline: < 1 miles
Winter Freeze: Yes

CAMPING/RVING	RECREATION	BOATING	MISCELLANEOUS
-no camping at lake shore, day-use only -nearest developed campgrounds 3 miles south of lake at Apache-Sitgreaves National Forest Campgrounds Alpine Divide Tents/Trailers/RVs -$5/night -12 sites -tables, grills -pit toilets, drinking water -campground host on site	-picnicking -hiking -canoeing -horseback riding -fishing: rainbow trout -shore fishing NOTE: fishing is best in early spring	-electric motor only -no improved launch -recommend a small canoe or inflatable on this modest 4-acre lake	-lake freezes in winter - try ice fishing -nearest town is Alpine, 7 miles south - full services and conveniences are available -dirt road access may get difficult in rainy weather -Escudilla Mountain wilderness located just a few miles east of lake, give it a visit
Information:	Apache-Sitgreaves National Forest (602) 339-4384		

NELSON RESERVOIR

Nelson Reservoir is another Apache-Sitgreaves National Forest "day-use-only" lake. Just 10 miles south of Springerville on US Highway 191, it serves the local shore fishermen well. There are two paved launch ramps by which one may access this 84-acre lake. The physically disabled can make good use of the "handicapped fishing station." There are five picnic spots just perfect to lounge away an afternoon. Camping facilities are at least 10 miles north or 14 miles south. At 7400 feet the summer days are cool and the lake freezes over in winter. Access is just off the highway so ice fishing is doable in winter. Access is 10 miles south of Springerville on US 191. The lake is right on the roadway, to the west. You can't miss it.

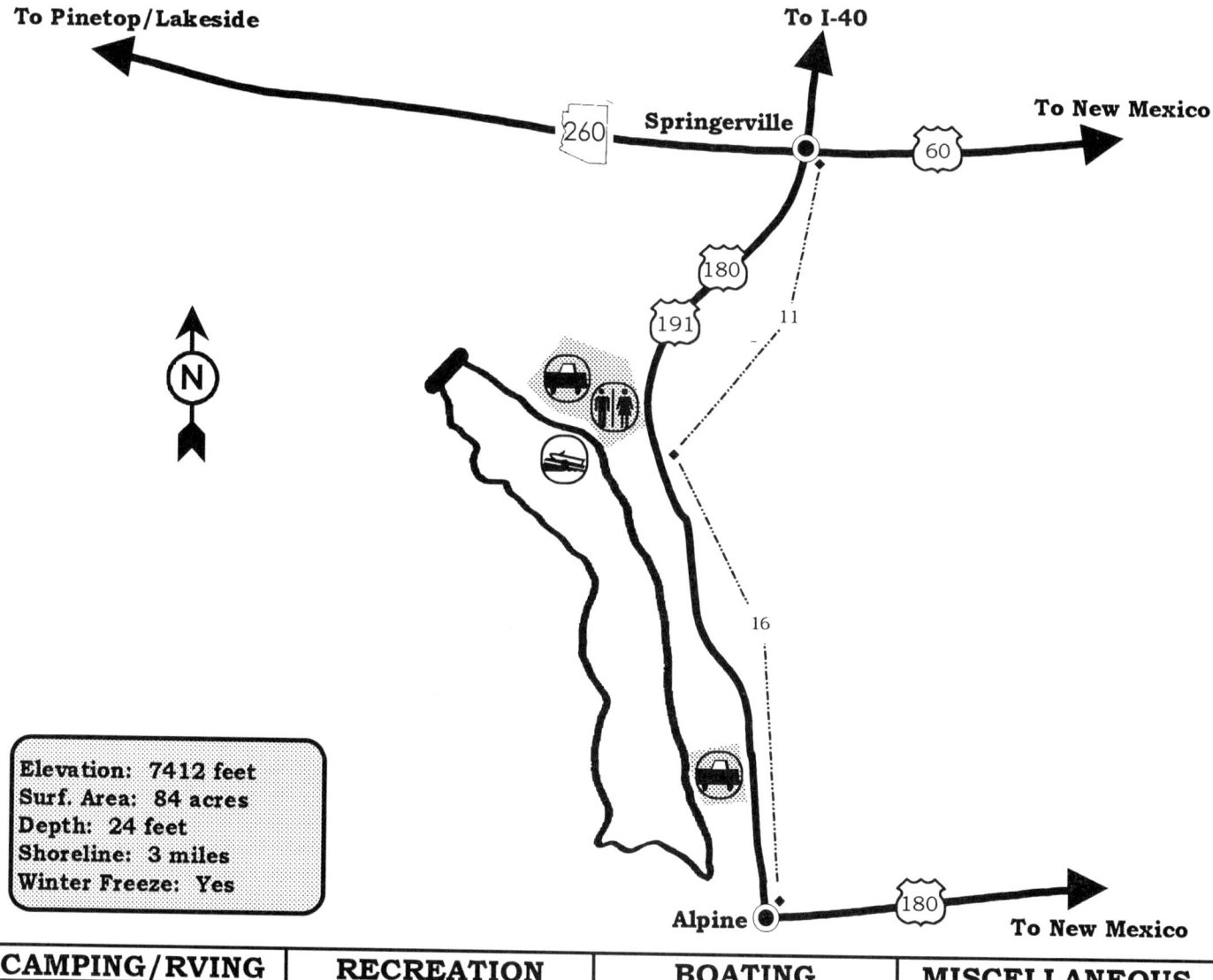

Elevation: 7412 feet
Surf. Area: 84 acres
Depth: 24 feet
Shoreline: 3 miles
Winter Freeze: Yes

CAMPING/RVING	RECREATION	BOATING	MISCELLANEOUS
-no overnight camping, day-use only -nearest camping is 10 miles north in Springerville at private campgrounds or 14 miles south at Apache-Sitgreaves National Forest Campground named Alpine Divide	-canoeing -hiking -picnicking (five picnic areas at lake) -horseback riding -fishing: rainbow trout, brown trout, brook trout, cutthroat trout -fishing stations for the handicapped -shore fishing -day-use rest rooms	-2 paved launch ramps -electric motor only	-closest town is Springerville, 10 miles to the north -lake freezes in winter - try ice fishing

Information:	Apache-Sitgreaves National Forest (602) 333-4372

Properly named for the flora that surrounds the lake, Mexican Hay Lake is in the White Mountains on the Apache-Sitgreaves National Forest. A "day-use-only," "fisherman's lake," it is frequently the hottest spot in the state for trout. At 164 acres, a boat is still a good bet given the weedy shoreline. Fly fishermen do well here. There are no facilities or conveniences at the 8910-foot elevation lake. Camping at the lake is prohibited, with the closest campground a dozen or more miles away. This lake is one you might try when the other area lakes are buzzing with summer weekend crowds. Access to Mexican Hay Lake is paved all the way when you take Arizona 261 south 7 miles from Arizona 260, just west of Eagar.

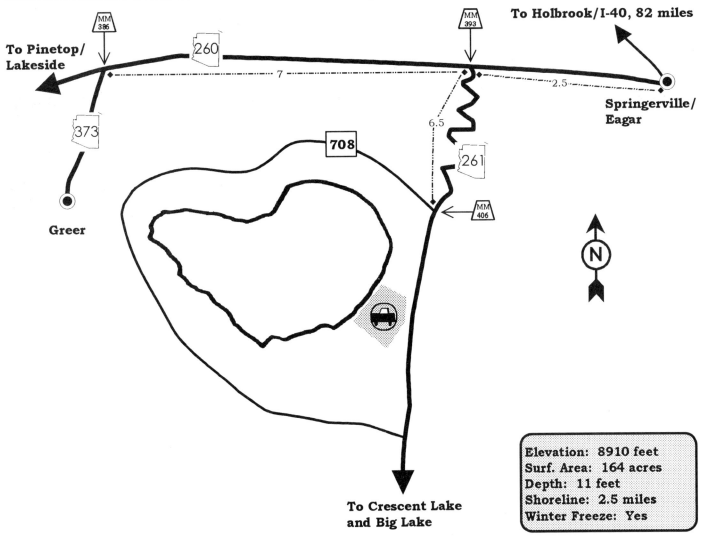

Elevation:	8910 feet
Surf. Area:	164 acres
Depth:	11 feet
Shoreline:	2.5 miles
Winter Freeze:	Yes

CAMPING/RVING	RECREATION	BOATING	MISCELLANEOUS
-day-use only -no camping facilities at or near the lake -closest developed camping is greater than 12 miles away	-fishing: rainbow trout -shore fishing is difficult due to weedy shoreline NOTE: fly fishermen do well in this shallow and weedy lake	-lake is shallow and weedy	-nearest town is Eagar, 7 miles northeast of lake -Mexican Hay Lake is on the route to other lakes in the Apache- Sitgreaves National Forest or on the way to the Fort Apache Indian Reservation - you'll know when to fish this lake when you see the crowds as you drive by - it's right on the highway
Information:	Apache-Sitgreaves National Forest (602) 333-4372		

GEORGE'S LAKE

At a 5500-foot elevation, George's Lake sits at the remote southern edge of the White Mountain Apache Indian Reservation. There are a few (six or so) campsites on this relatively barren lake. A boat will work but the shoreline will work for this non-trout lake. It is recommended that you bring in everything you need as conveniences are not close by. Access is south from White River on Apache Road Y-70 for 9 miles. Turn right or southwest on Apache Road Y-10 for another 11 miles. You'll pass Nash Tank on your left, keep going. The lake is visible from the road. Remember to obtain all your permits before going to the lake. Access is also doable from the south via the San Carlos Indian Reservation.

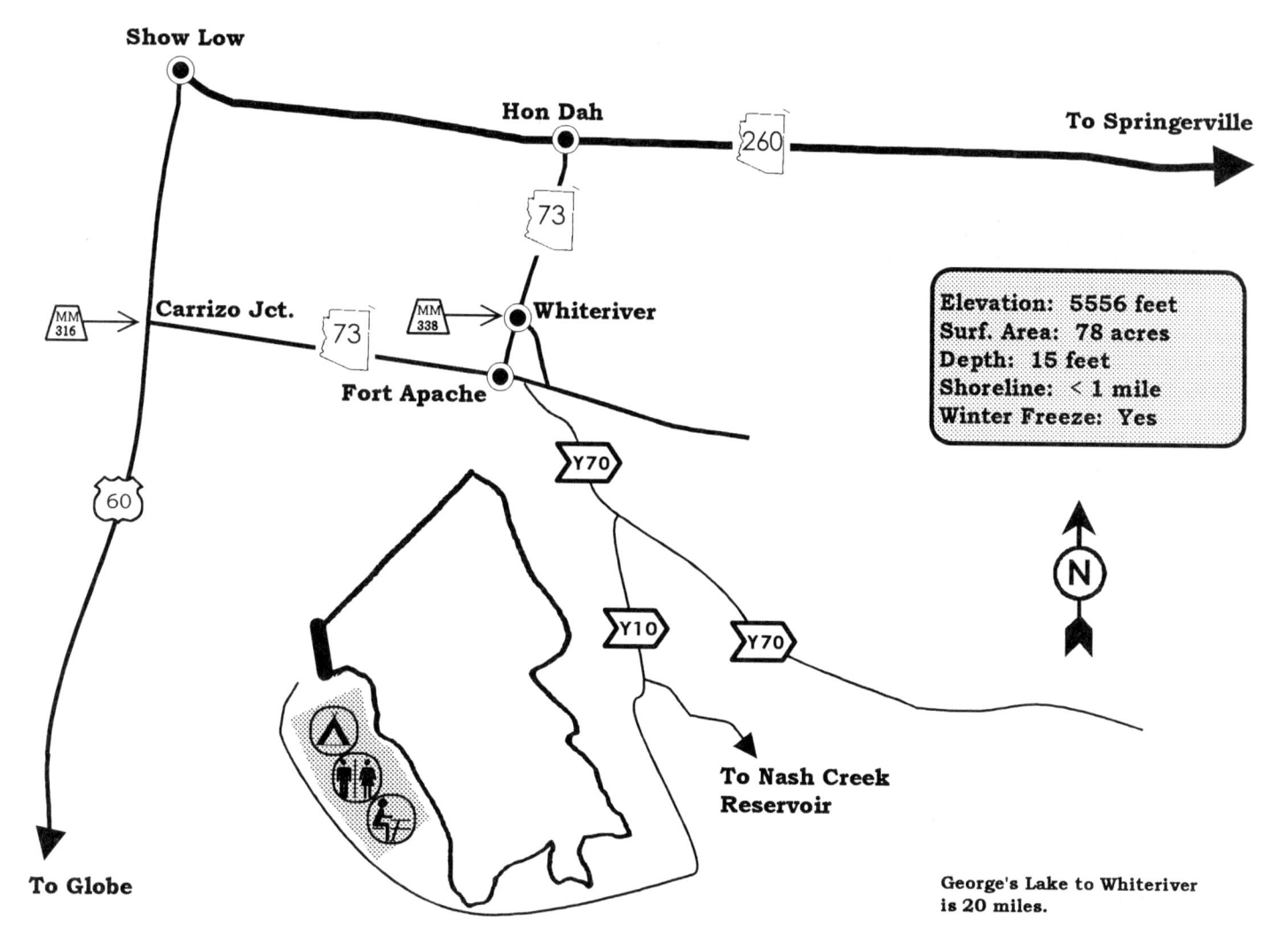

Elevation: 5556 feet
Surf. Area: 78 acres
Depth: 15 feet
Shoreline: < 1 mile
Winter Freeze: Yes

George's Lake to Whiteriver is 20 miles.

CAMPING/RVING	RECREATION	BOATING	MISCELLANEOUS
Tents/Trailers/RVs -6 developed sites -permit & fee required -pit toilets -no drinking water -tables -dead and down wood maybe collected for use -dogs on leash only -no showers	-hiking -canoeing -sailing -horseback riding -shore fishing: catfish, largemouth bass -no ATVs/ATCs -no swimming	-electric motor only -no launch ramp -permits and fee required	-nearest town or conveniences are located 20 miles northwest in White River PERMITS AND FEES: camping, boating, fishing, and other recreational activities require a permit and fee - see section on White Mountain Apache Indian Reservation contained within this book
Information:	White Mountain Apache Tribe (602) 338-4385		

Lyman Lake is contained within the Lyman Lake State Park in west central Arizona. At 1500 acres, Lyman is the largest lake in the White Mountain vicinity, and with no motor restrictions, it is the "water skiers delight." This is now particularly true with the new water ski course. This lake and its facilities are open year round and at 5980-foot elevation the weather ranges from warm/hot in the summer to cool/pleasant in the winter. Anglers will enjoy the variety of fish, particularly midweek when the skiing traffic is reduced. Fishing is available from a boat, from shore, or from the piers at waters edge. Camping is convenient and pleasant with all the necessary facilities at hand. Campers and day users can swim, bike, canoe, sail, ride their horses, or lounge as they please. Handicapped facilities are more than adequate, Lyman ranks among the best lakes in the state for those with impairments. Keep a close eye on the buffalo as you enter and exit the park. These big guys are a site to behold. The park staff are courteous and helpful, some of the best in the state. Paved access to Lyman Lake is just off of Highway 191, 18 miles north of Highway 60 at Springerville. From the north, Lyman is 69 miles south of Interstate 40 at Holbrook.

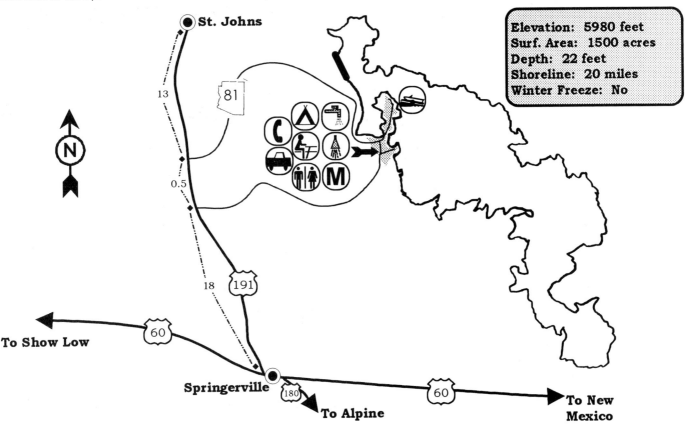

Elevation: 5980 feet
Surf. Area: 1500 acres
Depth: 22 feet
Shoreline: 20 miles
Winter Freeze: No

CAMPING/RVING	RECREATION	BOATING	MISCELLANEOUS
RV/Trailer -25 sites with hookups -drinking water, electricity -$12/night -37 developed sites Tents/Trailers/RVs -$7/night -grills, tables, ramadas -drinking water, hot showers -flush toilets, dump station -no reservations -campsites removed from waters edge -group campsites available	-picnicking, hiking -swimming beach -water skiing -sailing, canoeing, jet skiing -horseback riding -fishing: catfish, largemouth bass, walleye, perch, northern pike, trout -shore fishing -fishing from pier at locations around lake -day-use fee $3/vehicle	-2 improved ramps -no motor restrictions (all boat/motor types allowed) -boat rental at store -fuel and oil at store -courtesy dock -day-use fee covers boating costs NOTE: exclusive waterski course on the dam end of the lake, special rules apply, special permit and fee - see attendants at park office	-small convenience store at lake: bait, tackle, permits, gas, boat rentals -battery charging -public telephone -information booth -visitor's center, first aid -nearest towns: St. John's, 13 miles north Springerville, 18 miles south PERMITS AND FEES: SEE SECTION ON ARIZONA STATE PARKS CONTAINED WITHIN THIS BOOK
Information:	Lyman Lake State Park (602) 337-4441		

ACKRE LAKE

Remote in the southeastern section of the Apache-Sitgreaves National Forest sits Ackre Lake. At an 8608 foot elevation, this is a "day-use" fishing lake with no camping allowed. A small lake with 2 acres and .4 miles shoreline, it has no facilities or conveniences. Ackre Lake sits in a high, pine forest and frequently freezes solid making the available catch just the current year's stocking. Camping is available at various national forest campgrounds very nearby. One of them has equestrian facilities. Ackre Lake is quiet and secluded, perfect for those who search for cool temperatures and solitude. Access is south from Arizona 260 at Springerville on US Highway 191 for 57 miles, then 1 mile up a bumpy, windy, poorly maintained road. From the south, go north on US Highway 191, 102 miles from US Highway 70. The southern route is curvy and hilly.

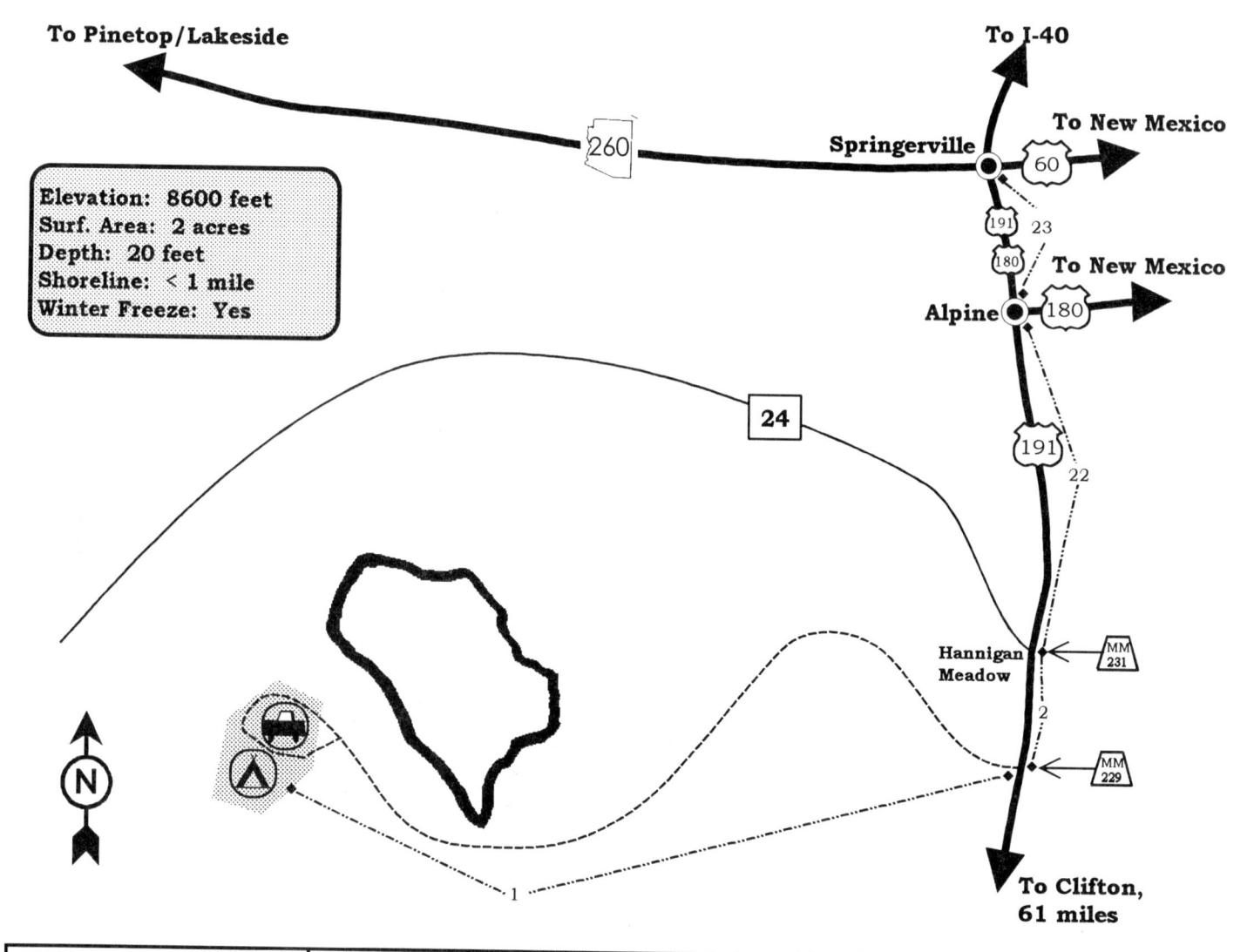

Elevation: 8600 feet
Surf. Area: 2 acres
Depth: 20 feet
Shoreline: < 1 mile
Winter Freeze: Yes

CAMPING/RVING	RECREATION	BOATING	MISCELLANEOUS
-no camping at lake, day-use only NOTE: there are three national forest campgrounds just a few miles north or south on US Highway 666, the facilities vary at each locations -campground names are: K.P. Cienega Hannagan Stray Horse	-hiking -horseback riding -fishing: brook trout NOTE: no live bait allowed, lures and flies only -shore fishing	-electric motor only -no ramp NOTE: lake is two acres and only 10 feet deep	-no vehicle access to within 100 feet of lake -nearest conveniences at Hannagan Meadows, 4 miles north -nearest town is Alpine, 26 miles north on US Highway 191 -horse corrals located a K.P. Cienega Campground
Information:	Apache Sitgreaves National Forest (602) 339-4384		

Point of Pines Lake is a small (28 acres) spectacular high-mountain lake (6205 feet elevation) on the San Carlos Indian Reservation. Campers, picnickers, hikers, fishermen, and horseback riders will find privacy, nay solitude. Given its remoteness, remember to bring in every thing you need. Facilities at the lake are minimal. The surroundings are typical of this elevation with large and small wildlife abundant. Certainly a side trip to Dry Lake, just a few miles to the east is well worth the trip. Weather is perfect in summer months, warm days, cool evenings, with some thunder showers likely in late summer afternoons. Winter months are markedly cooler here, actually cold. Access to Point of Pines Lake is easier than it looks. You'll have pavement just about all the way to the lake. From the west, US Highway 70 west of Globe, Arizona turn north on to Indian Service Route 8 (a.k.a. Road 1000), proceed approximately 55 miles to Road 1571. Turn left for another three miles an you'll be there. All but the last three miles is paved. Access can also be from the east on Indian Route 14 (a.k.a. Road 1800) from US Highway 666, 12 miles north of Clifton. As a destination, Point of Pines Lake will meet all your needs if you're looking to get away from the crowds. The trip to Point of Pines will also give you some great appreciation of the wilderness of the San Carlos Reservation, Permits and fees are required for any recreational activity on the San Carlos Reservation. Permits are available at a variety of stores in the towns surrounding the Reservation. Remember also to pick up a copy of the rules and regulations. Recently some excellent maps have been made available and they may be purchased anywhere the permits are sold. For further information, call the number listed below.

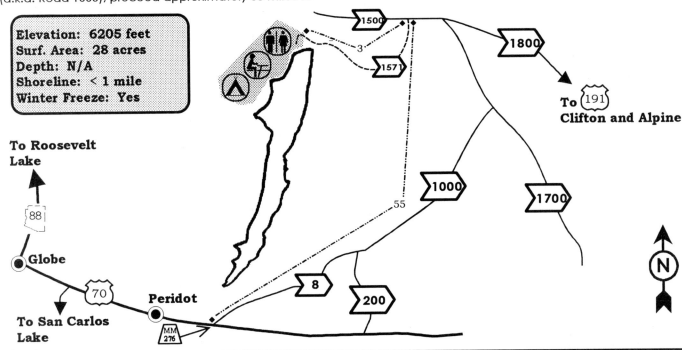

Elevation: 6205 feet
Surf. Area: 28 acres
Depth: N/A
Shoreline: < 1 mile
Winter Freeze: Yes

CAMPING/RVING	RECREATION	BOATING	MISCELLANEOUS
Tents/Trailers/RVs -primitive camping around the lake -dogs on leash only -potable water is available at the Ranger Station 3 1/2 miles from the lake -dead and down wood may be collected for use	-swimming -hiking -picnicking -horseback riding -canoeing -fishing: rainbow trout -fishing permit and fee required -special fishing limits and rules apply -shore fishing -hunting -permit and fee required for any day-use activity on the reservation	-electric motor only -unimproved launch area -boating permit and fee required	-open year round -nearest town is San Carlos -complete facilities and conveniences are located in Globe/Miami to the east PERMITS AND FEES: camping, boating, fishing, and other recreational activities require a permit and fee - see section on San Carlos Apache Indian Reservation contained within this book
Information:	San Carlos Apache Indian Reservation (602) 475-2343		

TALKALAI LAKE

Talkalai Lake resides on the 1.8-million acre San Carlos Indian Reservation, in east central Arizona, and is formed by the Elgo Dam on the San Carlos River. At 2600 foot elevation, Talkalai Lake is an oasis of solitude just 4 miles northeast of San Carlos, Arizona. If you're looking for warm water fish, privacy, or a picturesque oasis, Talkalai Lake is the spot. This 640-acre beauty of blue and green sits in a valley of bleached white hillsides. Facilities at Talkalai Lake are minimal with a few scattered picnic tables, ramadas, and pit toilets. Fishing and napping are the predominant activities here. The shoreline is lush and green with plenty of shade which are rare commodities in this otherwise barren area. Fishing from shore is rather difficult given the perimeter of the lake is rung by reeds. There is a primitive boat launch for small boats or inflatables. Boating is limited to an 8-horsepower motor. Given the difficulty of access, not the distance, it is recommended you bring everything in you need, including firewood. Those who visit Talkalai Lake are torn between sharing the knowledge of this beauty with friends or keeping quiet so it remains unused. Remember that permits and fees are required for any recreational activity on the San Carlos Reservation. Permits are available in the town of San Carlos and in many retail outlets in the towns around the Reservation. Remember also to obtain a copy of the regulations when you purchase your permit. Access to Talkalai Lake is through San Carlos, Arizona off Arizona State Route 170, north from US Highway 60. The specific directions are as follows. Proceed east form Globe on US Highway 70, turn north on Arizona 170 to San Carlos (3 miles). At mile marker 275 you'll find White Mountain Avenue, turn right. Proceed 1.9 miles to an unmarked dirt road leading east (right). You have to cross a small stream but that should be no problem. Follow this road for 1.1 miles. At the top of the hill, you'll see the lake below. Turn right at Road 1110 (marked by a very small sign on a stick) to the lake 1.9 miles. You will come to two forks in the road - stay left at both of them. The road can be washed out in places so be careful. Patience is thekey, the drive is not long - just four miles from town but hill, curvy, and sometimes bumpy. It is recommended that a 4-wheel drive be used but a high clearance vehicle will work also. For those who brave this short but toughish road will be rewarded with all the beauty central Arizona has to offer.

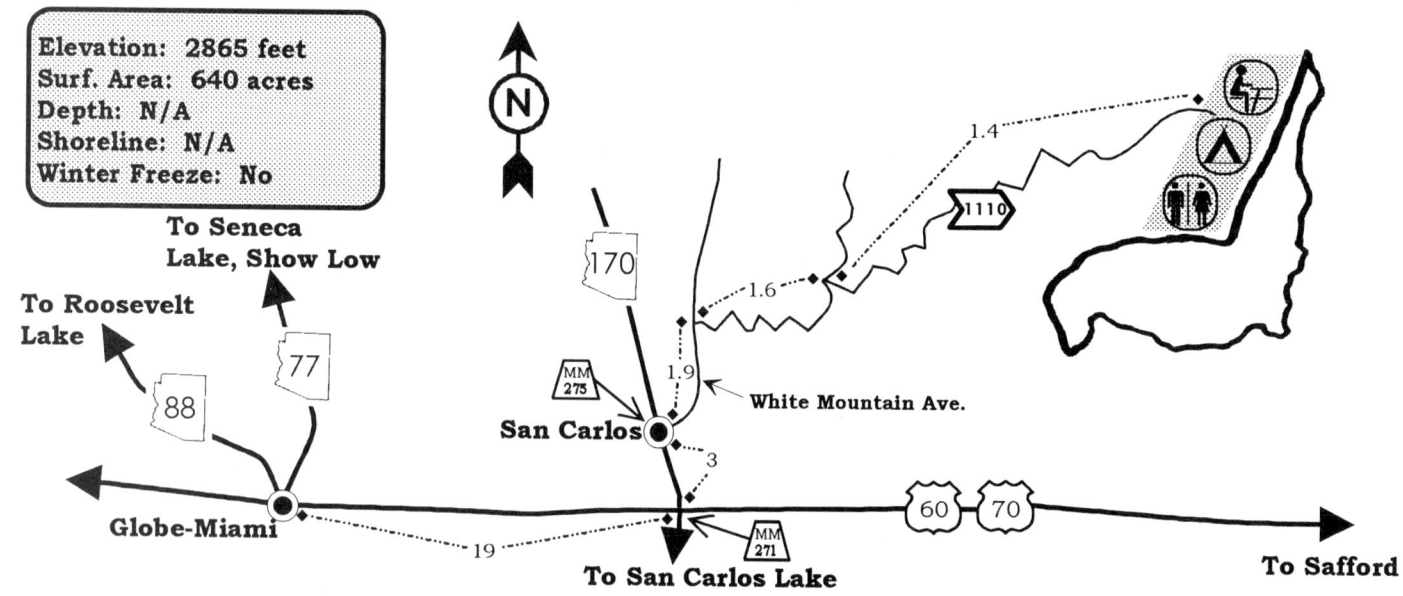

	Elevation:	2865 feet
Surf. Area:	640 acres
Depth:	N/A
Shoreline:	N/A
Winter Freeze:	No

CAMPING/RVING	RECREATION	BOATING	MISCELLANEOUS
Primitive camping only (permit and fee required) -tables -ramadas -pit toilets -dogs on leash only -no drinking water Remember: bring in your fire wood	-canoeing -hiking -picnicking -horseback riding -napping -fishing: bass, catfish, crappie -trotlining for catfish -hunting -permit and fee required -no swimming	-8 horse power maximum rated outboard motor -primitive launch -permit and fee required	-nearest town is San Carlos, (4 miles) -complete facilities and conveniences located in Globe, 22 miles to the east PERMITS AND FEES: camping, boating, fishing, and other recreational activities require a permit and fee - see section on San Carlos Apache Indian Reservation contained within this book
Information:	San Carlos Apache Indian Reservation (602) 475-2343		

San Carlos Lake resides on the 1.8-million acre San Carlos Indian Reservation in east central Arizona. At 17,410 acres when full, San Carlos Lake has 160 miles of shoreline which is nearly all accessible over newly constructed and well maintained roads. When full, this "Jewel" of the Reservation is the largest lake within Arizona. Created by Coolidge Dam on the Gila River, San Carlos Lake sits at 2500-foot elevation and is used by the wide variety of water recreators: water skiers, fishermen, jet skiers, pleasure/power boaters, sailors, wind surfers, and canoers. It must be noted here that water skiers and jet skiers are limited to the eastern 1/4 of the lake. (See boating below). Some camping facilities are newly constructed with primitive camping allowed on nearly the entire perimeter of the lake. There is a single improved launch ramp, but access is not limited as there are many primitive launch areas around the lake. The water level of San Carlos Lake varies significantly over the course of a year, but this does not inhibit its recreational uses. Hikers and sightseers will relish this land with fully four seasons of recreation. San Carlos Reservation is geographically and ecologically diverse, ranging from mid-altitude deserts to high-country forests. The plant and animal life are as diverse as the ranging

elevations. Fishing is certainly the predominant activity at San Carlos Lake. Currently San Carlos is the home of state records for both flathead catfish and black crappie. But foremost, San Carlos Lake is renown for its catches of largemouth bass. The shoreline of San Carlos Lake is barren and shade is scarce. Weather is consistent with the elevation. Summers are hot, hot, hot. Winter months are as perfect as Arizona has to offer. Recreational use of waters and lands of the San Carlos Reservation require permits and fees. They are obtainable on the Reservation or at many retail outlets in the towns surrounding the lake. Recently some excellent detailed maps of San Carlos Lake and the Reservation have become available for purchase at these same outlets. Be sure to pick one up. They will guide you to some wondrous outdoor adventures and scenery. Access to San Carlos Lake is very easy. Roads to and around the lake are well maintained and marked. The lake itself sits 20 miles east of Globe, Arizona, just south of Highway 70, turn south at mile marker 271 and follow the superb paved road 8 miles to the various spurs to the lake shore. They are well marked. Remember, this is private land. Please honor the residents and territories of this fantastically, beautiful and functional wilderness.

See map, next page

CAMPING/RVING	RECREATION	BOATING	MISCELLANEOUS
Trailers/RVs Soda Canyon -7 sites, full hookups -$15/night Tents/Trailers/RVs (permits and fees required) -Camping allowed on the perimeter of the lake -Some developed campsites -tables -grills -ramadas -pit toilets -water only at Soda Canyon -pets on leash only -boat camping -dump station	-hiking -picnicking -canoeing -swimming -sailing -sail boarding -jet skiing -water skiing -fishing: channel catfish, flathead catfish, bluegill, largemouth bass, crappie -hunting, trapping -horseback riding -permit and fee required	-no motor restrictions -1 improved launch located at Soda Canyon but its use varies with the rise and fall of the water level -unlimited launching around the lake at many and varied locations -gasoline available at San Carlos Lake Store -no water skiing or jet skiing within 400 yards of any shore, except as published regulations allow NOTE: water skiing and jet skiing are limited to the eastern 1/4 of the lake. Check with local authorities for specific boundaries	-convenience store at east end of lake: permits, gasoline, propane, marine supplies, food, ice, snacks, fishing gear -Store phone number is: 1-602-475-2756 -nearest city is Globe, 20 miles to the east -Remember to bring in your fire wood PERMITS AND FEES: camping, boating, fishing, and other recreational activities require a permit and fee - see section on San Carlos Apache Indian Reservation contained within this book
Information:	San Carlos Apache Indian Reservation and Wildlife Department (602) 475-2343		

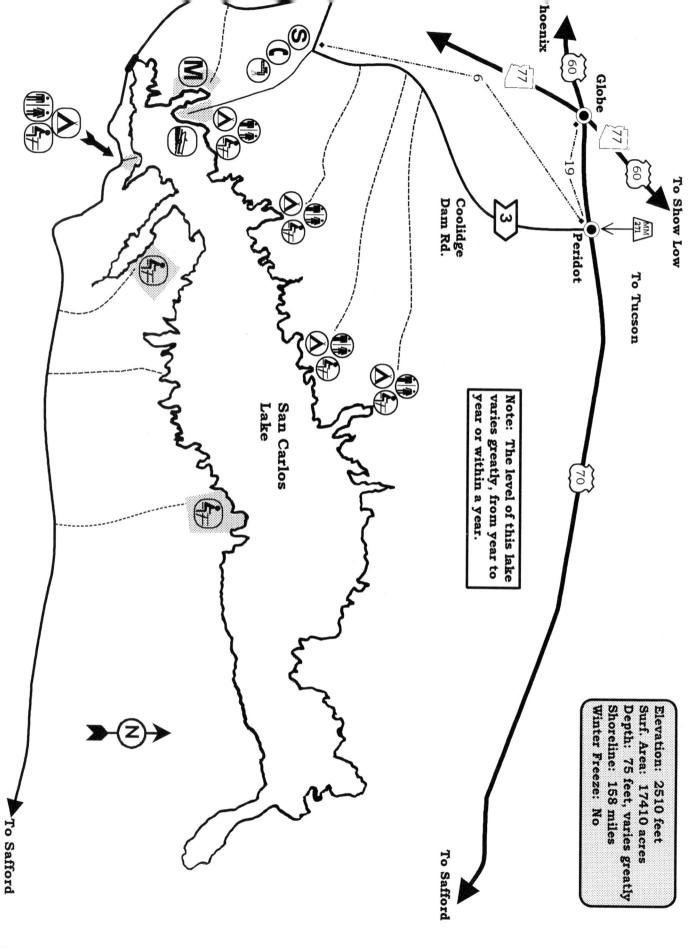

San Carlos Lake

Coolidge Dam Rd.

To Phoenix

Globe

To Show Low

To Tucson

Peridot

To Safford

To Safford

Note: The level of this lake varies greatly, from year to year or within a year.

Elevation: 2510 feet
Surf. Area: 17410 acres
Depth: 75 feet, varies greatly
Shoreline: 158 miles
Winter Freeze: No

Seneca Lake rests on the northwest corner of the 1.8-million-acre San Carlos Indian Reservation. For the last few years the facilities at Seneca Lake have sat idle and unmaintained. The near future may hold some upgrades and reopening of the existing RV facilities. But for now, this location remains a "wanna-be" lake. The 25 acres of Seneca Lake sit at 4840 foot elevation as a warm water fishery, offering bass, catfish and bluegill. A small boat is useful for fishing as the perimeter is rung by reeds. Likely the best this area has to offer is Seneca Falls, a 100-foot plus waterfall, less than a half mile from the lake. Those adventurous will be found repelling the walls of the canyon from which the falls cascade. Hikers will find the terrain rocky and hilly. Weather is hot hot in the summer with pleasant temperatures in winter time. Access to Seneca Lake could not be simpler. It sits on the west side of Arizona Highway 60, just 36 miles north of Globe/Miami. The scenic ride through the Salt River Canyon, whether from the north or south will be visually fantastic.

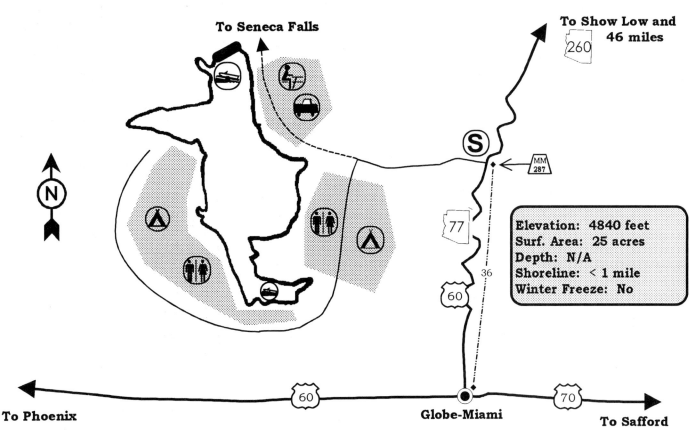

Elevation: 4840 feet
Surf. Area: 25 acres
Depth: N/A
Shoreline: < 1 mile
Winter Freeze: No

CAMPING/RVING	RECREATION	BOATING	MISCELLANEOUS
Primitive camping only (permit and fee required) -tables -grills -pit toilets The campgrounds has the appearance of RV facilities with full hookups, but as of this printing, they are not operational -dogs on leash only	-hiking -repelling -canoeing -picnicking -fishing: bass, catfish, bluegill -hunting -permit and fee required	-electric motor only -2 improved launches -permit and fee required	Store -minimal conveniences -nearest town is Globe, 36 miles south -nearest gas and conveniences at store located 6 miles north at the Salt River Bridge PERMITS AND FEES: camping, boating, fishing, and other recreational activities require a permit and fee - see section on San Carlos Apache Indian Reservation contained within this book
Information:	San Carlos Apache Indian Reservation (602) 475-2343		

76

ROOSEVELT LAKE

Given its size, location, facilities, and natural attributes, Roosevelt Lake is likely the most popular lake in Arizona. Any and all recreational water users find exactly what they need at this 17,000-acre reservoir. Located just east of Phoenix, it draws significant crowds, but not so that you can't find solitude. All water sports can be enjoyed here, but the fisherman and water skiers are most predominant. Various warm water species fill the lake with largemouth bass, smallmouth bass, crappie, and catfish claiming the most, best, and likely true "Fish Stories." When someone tells you they filled a cooler full of two-pound crappies in a half a day during the spring - believe them. If you hear of 30 bass a day - also believe them. About the monster catfish - again - believe them. Roosevelt Lake currently holds the state record for carp at 33 and 1/2 pounds and smallmouth bass at 7 plus pounds. It is a rare weekend that you'll not find a bass tournament headquartered at "Windy Hill." Generally, the water skiers and jet skiers do not conflict with the fisherman or those with sailboats. Camping is allowed on the entire perimeter of the lake with the north side more difficult to access. A four-wheel drive is recommended. RVs and trailers should stay on the south side. Boat camping on the 88 miles of shoreline is an excellent choice for those that want solitude. Drinking water is at a premium, so bring in all you'll need. Developed camping is available at the newly constructed Cholla Recreation Site, east of the dam. There is a large concrete launch ramp at this site. There is also a fish cleaning station. The campgrounds are located up the hill from waters edge. The campgrounds include hot showers, flush and vault toilets, and two playgrounds. There is generally a host on site during the winter months. The weather at Roosevelt is similar to Phoenix, given the elevation and proximity. Summer days are very hot with an occasional thunderstorm in late afternoons. Keep your eyes open for the local wildlife, many of the famed red cardinals and coyotes are about. You'll hear them howling at dusk. The cattle feeding around the lake will not bother you if you don't bother them. There are some newly constructed group camping sites at "Grape Vine," east of the dam. Groups of 100 can be accommodated and the facilities are excellent. Access to "Grape Vine" group camp area is on a dirt road east of the dam. Follow the signs. Everyone can find enjoyment at Roosevelt Lake be it the hiker, equestrian, boater, swimmer, hunter, or sailor. There are a few snakes around, beware. A day trip to the Tonto National Monument can be pleasurable. Much to see and learn about the native inhabitants of the area. The visitor's center is located south of Route 88 near Windy Hill and the 2 miles are paved. Just watch the roadside signs. Roosevelt Lake can be accessed easily. From Globe/Miami, take Route 88 for 32 miles to the dam. From the west, take Route 188 from State Highway 87 or for those with adventure, take Apache Trail closest to Roosevelt, it's gravel but very well maintained. There are some steep climbs and hairpin turns, so be careful. The vista along this road offers Arizona's finest view of its mountains, canyons, and lakes. Roosevelt Lake and the surrounding terrain has much to offer. It is recommended that you acquire a detailed map of the area so you'll not waste time searching and can maximize your pleasure.

See map, next page

CAMPING/RVING	RECREATION	BOATING	MISCELLANEOUS
Tents/Trailers/RVs -unlimited primitive camping around the entire lake - no fee -camping is allowed at marina Developed camping Tents/Trailers/RVs Cholla Recreation Site -206 sites -no hookups -fees $10 to $16 -flush and vault toilets -drinking water, hot showers -playgrounds, hiking trails -no reservations Group camping -reservations: (602) 467-3200 Boat camping	-hiking, rock hounding -house boating, canoeing -swimming -water skiing, jet skiing -hunting/trapping -sailing: the winds can be perfect for large or small sailing vessels -fishing: largemouth bass, smallmouth bass, crappie, bluegill, carp, channel catfish, flathead catfish (slot limit in effect for largemouth bass) -shore fishing -golf in Globe/Miami HINT: quail and dove hunting can be excellent on the north side of the lake	-no motor restrictions -4 paved ramps -various unimproved ramps -boat rental at marina: pontoon, ski boats, fishing boats, ski rental, -boat storage and repair at marina -marina: fuel, oil, bait, tackle, slips, ice, beer/soda -marina phone number (602) 467-2245 NOTE: posted portions of Tonto Arm are closed from November 15 to February 15 - see local regulations HINT: M & S Marine does a fine job on boat repair	-general store at marina: gasoline (auto/boat), LP gas (bulk), deli, groceries, tackle, boating supplies, telephone on dock -varied but limited services are available on 15-mile stretch just east of marina: boat storage, boat repair, liquor, telephones -nearest town is Globe/Miami, 32 miles east of dam on State Route 88 (all services) -Roosevelt Lake Resort (602) 467-2276 -26 motel rooms -bar/lounge, gift shop -reservation recommended -6 RV spaces with full hookup $12/night, located at east end of lake, 1/2 mile off Highway 88
Information:	Tonto Basin Ranger District (602) 225-5296		

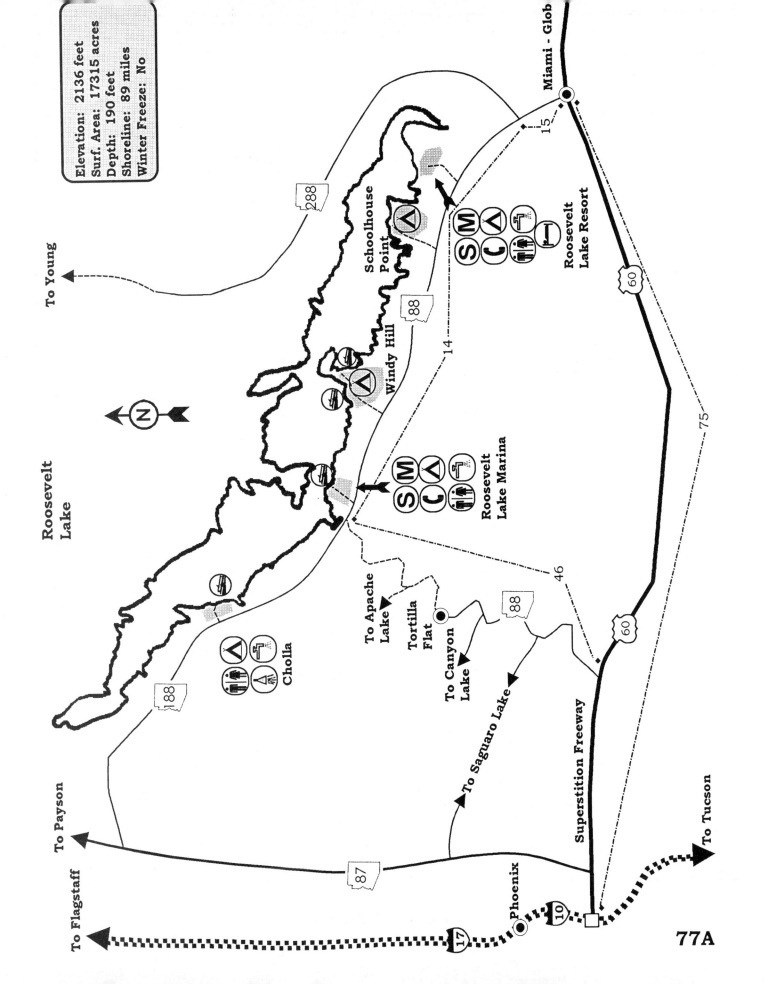

Elevation: 2136 feet
Surf. Area: 17315 acres
Depth: 190 feet
Shoreline: 89 miles
Winter Freeze: No

Roosevelt
Lake

To Young

To Payson

To Flagstaff

To Tucson

Phoenix

Superstition Freeway

To Saguaro Lake

To Canyon Lake

Tortilla Flat

To Apache Lake

Cholla

Windy Hill

Schoolhouse Point

Roosevelt Lake Marina

Roosevelt Lake Resort

Miami - Glob

77A

APACHE LAKE

Apache Lake is the second lake in the Salt River Project chain and is managed by the Tonto National Forest. At 1900 foot elevation it is generally hot during the summer months but is busy given it 65 mile proximity to Phoenix. Camping/RVing is at either the Apache Lake Resort facilities or at Burnt Corral public campground to the east. Boat campers enjoy the numerous "sandy beaches" along the 42 miles of shoreline on this 17-mile long lake, located in very rugged terrain. Water skiers are common but more so the fishermen given the variety of fish and generally good catches.   Apache Lake has received recent acclaim for its walleye pike, a rare find in Arizona, and its smallmouth bass. At 2700 acres there is plenty of room on this "canyon lake" which has depths ranging from "flats" to 260 feet. This changing underwater contour facilitates the variety of aquatic life. Access is just north of Arizona 88 (Apache Trail), you can see the lake from the road and it is a spectacular drive. Whether from the east (Phoenix) or from the west (Roosevelt) you will need some patience and care as either direction is 10 to 12 miles of an unpaved (generally well maintained) gravel road. The ride itself is worth the effort in spite of the difficulties of the 2.2 miles of Fish Creek Hill.

Elevation: 1914 feet
Surf. Area: 2650 acres
Depth: 264 feet
Shoreline: 42 miles
Winter Freeze: No

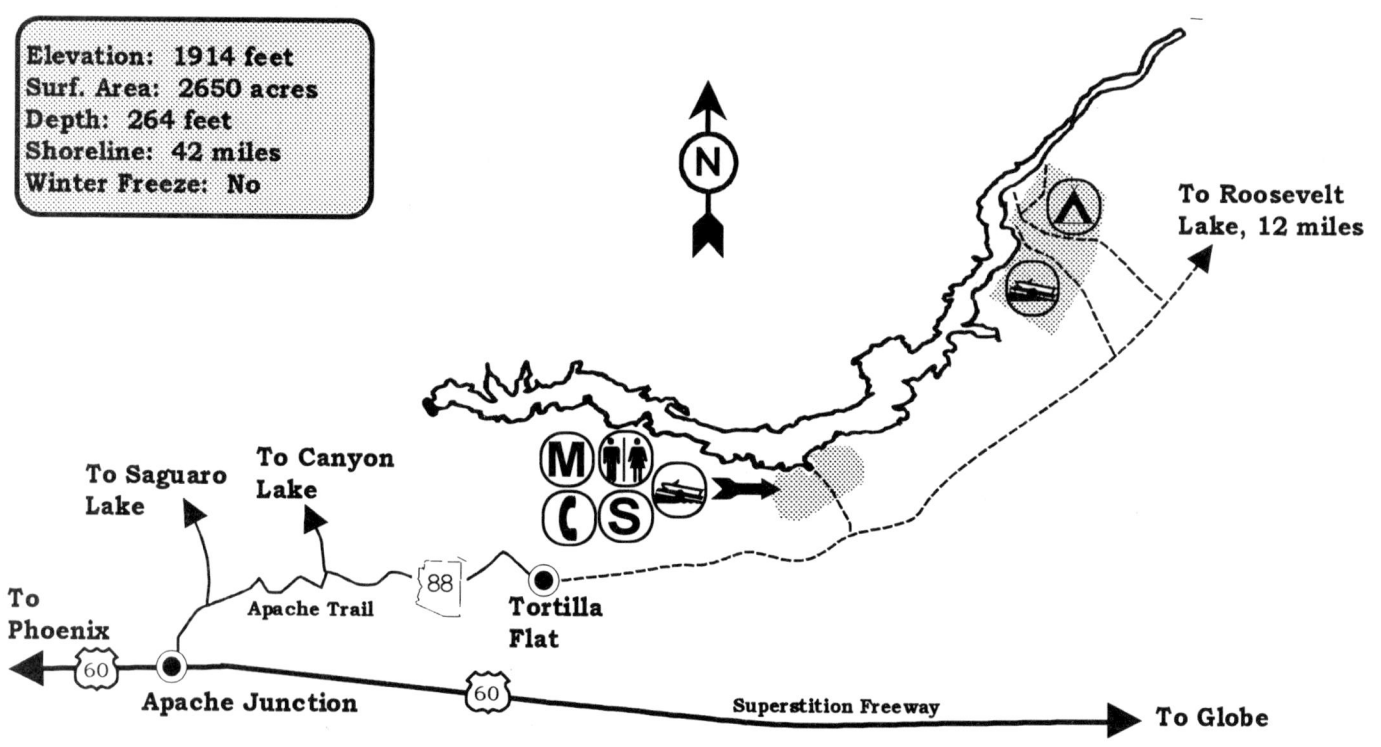

CAMPING/RVING	RECREATION	BOATING	MISCELLANEOUS
Tents/Trailers/RVs -Burnt Corral (public and currently under renovation) fee TBD, 78 developed campsites, tables, grills, water, no hookups, no showers -Apache Lake Resort is privately owned; 12 RV spots, full hookups, $15 fee, open tent camping around resort $2 general-use fee - recommend reservations -boat camping on lake's numerous sandy beach areas	-hiking, picnicking -water skiing -jet skiing -sail boarding -canoeing -fishing; walleye, crappie, bluegill, smallmouth bass, largemouth bass, rainbow trout, channel catfish -shore fishing	-2 improved ramps, 1public, 1 private - $2 fee -no motor restrictions -upper lake closed to skiers -marina: boat storage and repair, fuel/oil, boat and pontoon rentals, bait, tackle	-motel at lake -lake level varies overnight -open all year -restaurant -store -laundry -Apache Lake Resort (602) 467-2511
Information:	Tonto National Forest (602) 467-2236		

Canyon Lake is a "full service" recreational body of water located 50 miles east northeast of Phoenix. Canyon Lake, at a 1600-foot elevation, resides between Apache Lake and Saguaro Lake within the Tonto National Forest. The lake is part of the Salt River Project and has 950 plus acres and depths of 140 feet. The climatic condition are generally the same as Phoenix on any given day. The lake is aptly named as it is housed in nearly a 10-mile canyon with steep rugged walls. Most of its 28 miles of shoreline are rocky but some sections have sandy beaches which can be camped by boat. Shore fishing can be difficult but fishing is the main attraction with a "variety bag" likely. Water skiers or just pleasure boaters typically fill the lake on most weekends. Sometimes access to the lake is just closed due to overcrowding so, get there early. Camping at the lake is limited, but a casual, well maintained national forest campground named Tortilla lies just a mile or two east of the main lake access. Picnicking, hikers, sailors, horseback riders, or any day-user will find adequate facilities/conveniences. The resort has a restaurant, marina (most services), and steamboat cruises. Access is paved all the way on the beautiful winding State Route 88, just 15 miles east of Apache Junction. The ride up or down Route 88 (Apache Trail) is worth the effort by itself. Access can also be from the east through Roosevelt down Route 88.

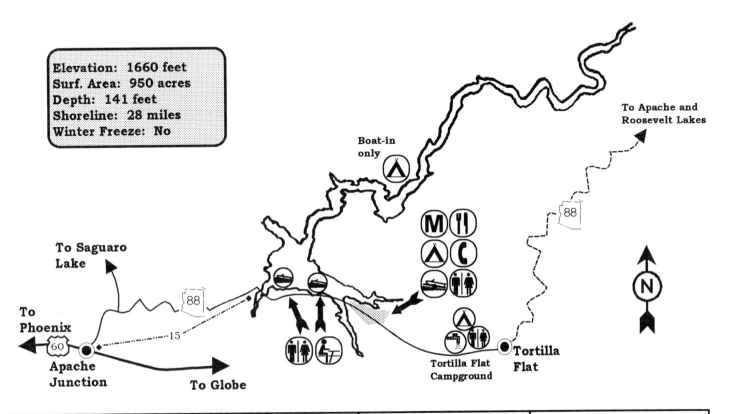

CAMPING/RVING	RECREATION	BOATING	MISCELLANEOUS
Tents/Trailers/RVs -boat camping Laguna Beach (private) -$8/night -tables, grills -no hookups -rest rooms Tortilla Campground one mile east of the lake on Arizona 88 -76 developed sites -$6/night -handicapped rest rooms -drinking water -some campsites are creekside	-swimming, picnicking -sailing, canoeing -water skiing, sail boarding -handicapped facilities at picnic area -no pets or glass containers in picnic area -fishing: walleye, largemouth bass, rainbow trout, crappie, catfish, yellow bass -shore fishing	-no motor restrictions -3 launch ramps -upper end of lake closed to power boats -marina: full service, wet/dry storage, bait, tackle, sundries, marine equipment, repair, fuel -boat rental: ski boats, fishing boats, row boats, and canoes	-nearest town is Apache Junction, 15 miles west on Arizona 88 -some conveniences located at Tortilla Flat just east of lake access -telephone at resort -steamboat cruises from resort area -lakeside restaurant (full service and food to go)
Information:	Canyon Lake Marina (602) 986-5546		

SAGUARO LAKE

Saguaro Lake is managed by the Tonto National Forest and is the last lake in the Salt River Project chain. Fishing and water skiing are the primary activities at this location. At 1530 feet elevation and the proximity of Phoenix, the summer months are hot and very, very crowded. Occasional "closings" result from insufficient parking space. Early arrival is recommended. Anglers should avoid the midday pleasure boaters by choosing the early or late hours of day. Overnight stays are limited to tent camping on the lake via boat. Canyon Lake is the primary input to Saguaro and the level of this 10-mile long lake can vary significantly, even overnight. The shoreline is rugged in this mountainous cavern. There are plentiful services at the marina, restaurant and convenience store. Saguaro is an excellent choice for midweek boating (fishing, skiing or cruising) or just a casual picnic during any season. Bicycler's will revel in the beauty of the Usery Pass just a few miles southwest of the lake. Access is off Bush Highway, 40 miles northeast of Phoenix.

Elevation: 1530 feet
Surf. Area: 1200 acres
Depth: 120 feet
Shoreline: 22 miles
Winter Freeze: No

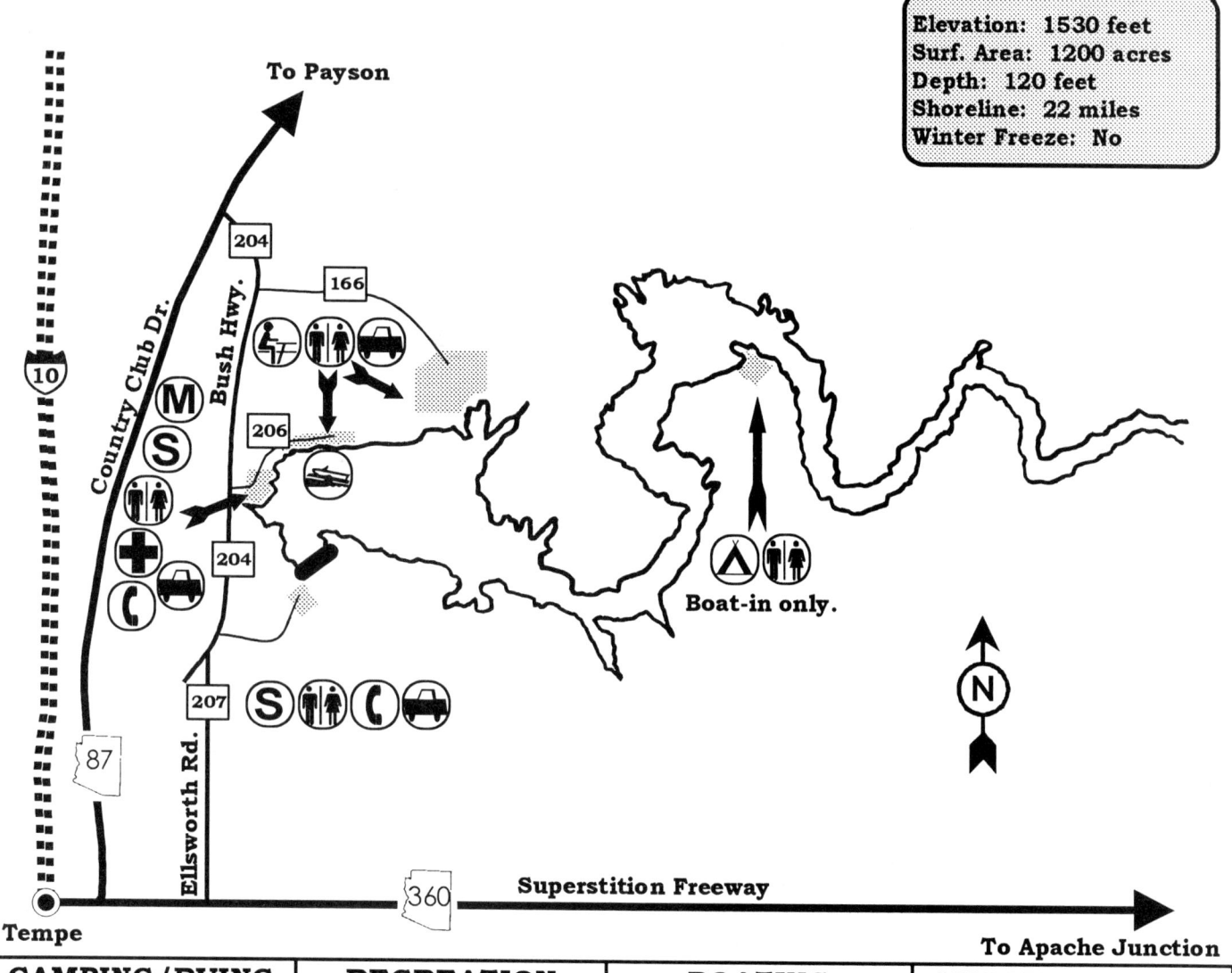

CAMPING/RVING	RECREATION	BOATING	MISCELLANEOUS
-boat camping only (tent) -rest rooms -no RV facilities -no electricity -no showers -no reservations -14 day stay limit	-swimming, sailing -water skiing -hiking, picnicking -fishing: walleye, carp, largemouth bass, brown trout, bluegill, channel cat, yellow bass, crappie -shore fishing is difficult	-3 improved ramps -full service marina: fuel, storage, bait, tackle, boat and pontoon rentals, repair -no motor restrictions -upper lake closed to skiing	-restaurant -convenience store -"Steamboat" lake cruise -first Aid at Ranger Station -closest hospital is in Mesa -Saguaro Lake Marina phone number is: (602) 986-5546
Information:	Tonto National Forest (602) 225-5200		

Managed by the Tonto National Forest, Bartlett Lake, at 1350 acres is one very busy lake. Located 48 miles northeast of Phoenix., at 1700 foot elevation, it is generally hot in summer and very convenient to a variety of lake users. Campers, anglers, skiers, jet skiers, and sailors race to this Verde River reservoir each weekend. The conditions for each of these aquatic activities is superb, but it is not uncommon to see a fisherman "shaking" their finger at a skier or jet skier who blasts by too close. Bartlett has long been known for giant catfish of 50 plus pounds. Crappie fishing can also be excellent, just look for the "armada" of boats clustered together. For day-users, it is recommended to arrive early such to obtain a parking spot and to avoid delays resulting from the lake being closed due to overcrowding. (Just too many boats. Summer months will find longish lines at the boat ramp on Saturday and Sunday mornings. The entire shoreline can be camped, with boat camping very popular up river or on the east shore. Forest Road 459 (dirt) parallels the west shore for approximately 5 miles facilitating access to the lake shore. Until just recently, facilities at Bartlett Lake have been minimal. Better days are ahead. Construction is underway on a full service marina. Over the next few years a full service (500 boat) marina with wet and dry storage, fuel, boat repair, general store, fish cleaning station, boat rental, restaurant, day-use beach, and tour boat will be constructed. The slips have started construction this fall of 1993 and will include both 30 amp power service and potable water. There will also be rest rooms and showers, security, pump out facilities and expanded parking. Prices and rates for both wet and dry storage have been set. Deposits are currently being taken by their "preoperating office," in Tempe. Advertisement for the marina services appear weekly in the Arizona Republic sport's section. Access to Bartlett is paved entirely and is 17 miles east of Cave Creek and Carefree on the Bartlett Dam Road. All conveniences are available in these towns.

See map, next page

CAMPING/RVING	RECREATION	BOATING	MISCELLANEOUS
Tents/Trailers/RVs open to all camping -no developed sites -no services -no fees -no dump station -no showers -no drinking water -primitive rest rooms -boat camping (east shore)	-hiking -swimming -water skiing, jet skiing -sail boating -horseback riding -fishing: bluegill, largemouth bass, flathead and channel catfish, crappie -shore fishing -sail boarding (not recommended on weekends - too crowded) -hunting/trapping -no picnic facilities	-1 improved ramp -upper lake closed to water skiing -varying lake levels, be careful -no motor restrictions **Under Construction:** full service marina currently under construction (fall 1993) -wet storage (power/potable water) (max boat length 30 feet) -dry storage (covered and uncovered) (max boat length 24 feet) (boat launch for dry storage) -fuel -boat repair -pumpout -boat rentals	-bring your own firewood -nearest towns are Cave Creek and Carefree, 15 miles west **Under Construction:** (fall 1993) -general store -restaurant -beach (day-use only)
Information:	Tonto National Forest (602) 488-3441		

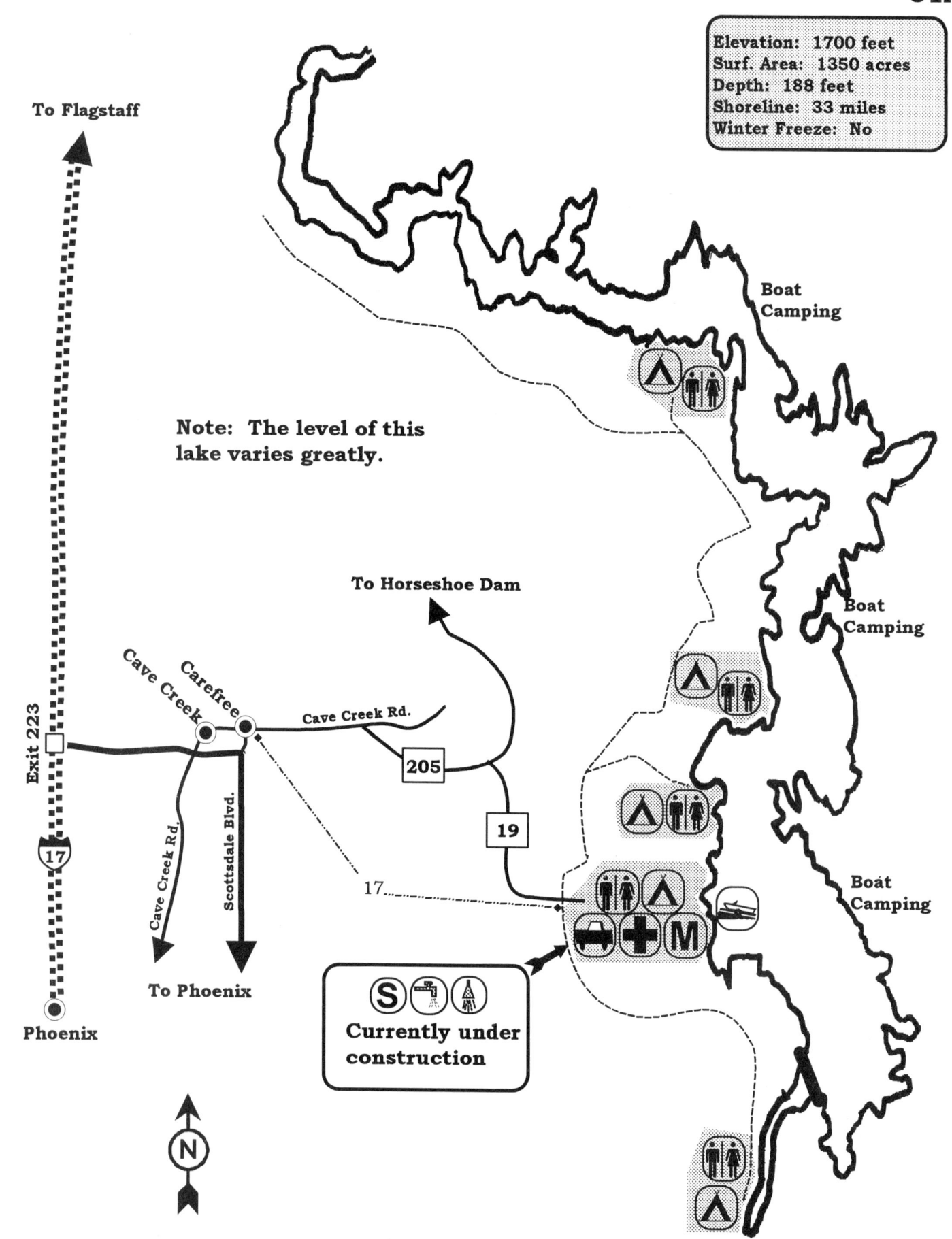

Elevation: 1700 feet
Surf. Area: 1350 acres
Depth: 188 feet
Shoreline: 33 miles
Winter Freeze: No

To Flagstaff

Boat Camping

Note: The level of this lake varies greatly.

To Horseshoe Dam

Boat Camping

Cave Creek

Carefree

Cave Creek Rd.

205

Boat Camping

Exit 223

17

19

17

Cave Creek Rd.

Scottsdale Blvd.

To Phoenix

Phoenix

S Currently under construction

N

Horseshoe Lake, like Bartlett its sister lake to the south, is a reservoir on the Verde River and has many of the same attributes. Managed by the Tonto National Forest, the conveniences and facilities are essentially non-existent. The elevation is 2200 feet and summer months are generally very warm. Fishing and sailing are the orders of the day at Horseshoe due to the "no skiing," "no jet skis" and the 20 mph limit on this somewhat remote lake.

Over recent years, Horseshoe's size has fluctuated significantly and frequently. It is currently full at 2700 acres. Camping, like Bartlett, is primitive, you need to bring everything in, and remember to bring it back out. Horseshoe Lake is located 51 miles northeast of Phoenix with the last 12 miles on reasonably well maintained dust/dirt road. Access is on Horseshoe Dam Road north from Bartlett Dam Road.

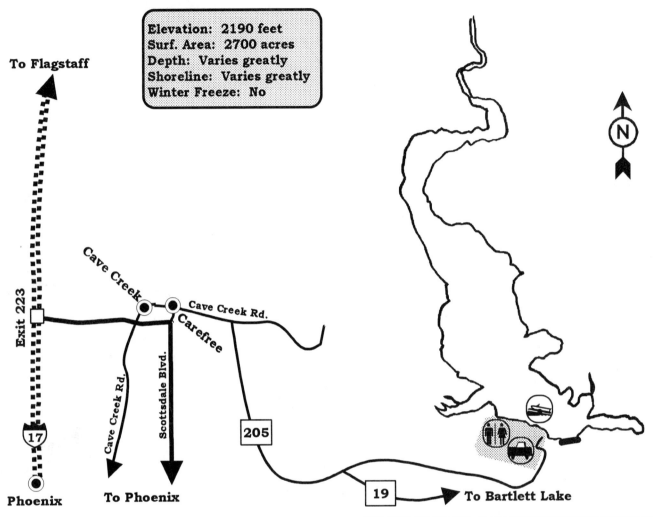

Elevation: 2190 feet
Surf. Area: 2700 acres
Depth: Varies greatly
Shoreline: Varies greatly
Winter Freeze: No

CAMPING/RVING	RECREATION	BOATING	MISCELLANEOUS
Tents/Trailers/RVs -primitive rest rooms -no developed sites: open camping -no drinking water, no showers -no services, no dump station -public campgrounds and open camping on the Verde River directly south of lake, just off the access road	-swimming, but it is generally muddy -sailing -fishing: largemouth bass, smallmouth bass, crappie, channel and flathead catfish, carp -shore fishing	-no motor restrictions -1 improved ramp -varying lake levels, be careful -20 mph limit -no water skiing allowed -no jet skis allowed	-bring in your own firewood -no facilities or conveniences at lake -nearest towns are Cave Creek and Carefree Warning: many big black ants
Information:	Tonto National Forest (602) 488-3441		

ROPER LAKE / DANKWORTH POND

Roper Lake is contained within the 319-acre Roper Lake State Park, one of Arizona's many fine state facilities. A small lake at 33 acres, it sits at the base of Mount Graham at 3100-foot elevation and is open year round. The summers are warm to hot, none the less, this lake gets plenty of use. Fishing, swimming and sailing are the primary aquatic activities. Campers are served well with the local facilities. Handicapped individuals are very well served at this state park. A winter visitors' delight is the natural mineral hot springs located both at Roper Lake and at Dankworth Pond (just down the road a few miles). The Dankworth Pond unit is for day-use only, primarily fishing, picnicking, and swimming. Day-use facilities at this state park are plentiful and of good quality. Access to Roper Lake is off US Highway 70 at Safford. Take Highway 191 south for 5 miles and you are there. A few miles farther south and you'll be at the Dankworth Pond unit.

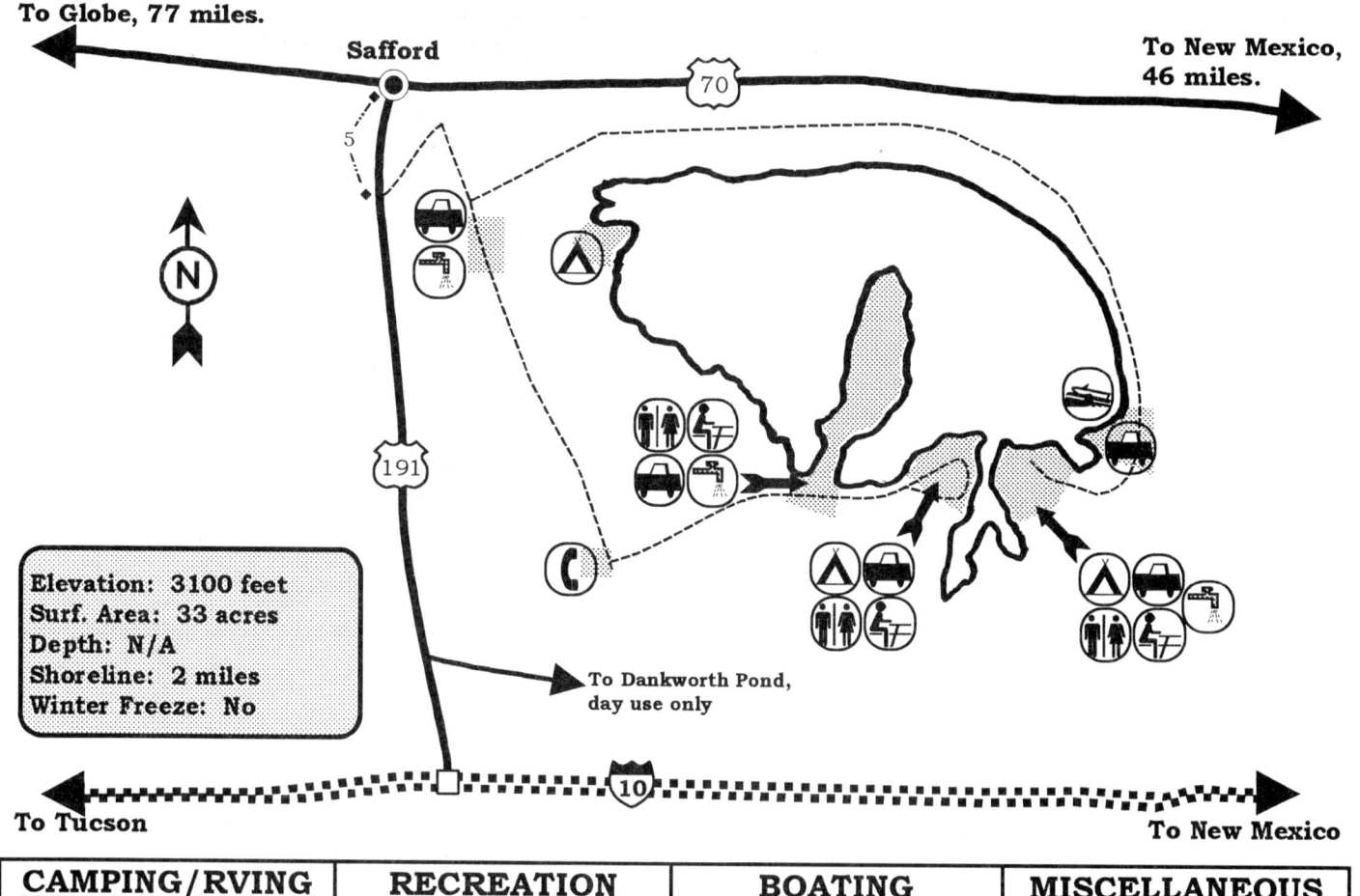

Elevation: 3100 feet
Surf. Area: 33 acres
Depth: N/A
Shoreline: 2 miles
Winter Freeze: No

CAMPING/RVING	RECREATION	BOATING	MISCELLANEOUS
Tents/Trailers/RVs -RV/trailer sites - 20 with electricity and water - $12/night -55 developed sites for tents, trailers, RVs, no hookups $7/night -group site available -rest rooms, showers -drinking water -dump station -no camping at Dankworth Pond - day-use only	-canoeing, sailing -swimming -picnicking: (3 day-use areas, some at waters edge) ramadas, grills, tables -hiking - nature trails -fishing: crappie, largemouth bass, sunfish, catfish, stocked rainbows in winter -shore fishing -fishing at Dankworth Pond can be fairly good -mineral hot springs -day-use fee $3/vehicle	-electric motor only -1 paved launch -courtesy dock -no launch ramp at Dankworth Pond -day-use fee covers boat launch	-handicapped rest rooms available -public telephone -nearest town is Safford, six miles away -Dankworth Pond located just south of Roper Lake -park fees cover both the Roper Lake facility and the Dankworth Pond unit PERMITS AND FEES: SEE SECTION ON ARIZONA STATE PARKS CONTAINED WITHIN THIS BOOK
Information:	Roper Lake State Park (602) 428-6760		

High on Mount Graham sits Riggs Flat Lake an 11-acre beauty managed by the Coronado National Forest. At an 8500-foot elevation, the lake freezes over in winter and is inaccessible due to roads not being cleared. From a small boat or from shore, there are various trout and not all small guys either. There is very comfortable camping adjacent to the lake with adequate facilities. For those adjusted to the altitude, a hike is the perfect pastime. Riggs Flat Lake is located 40 miles from Safford. The lake itself is 12 miles south of General Swift Trail (Arizona Highway 366) 35 miles west of the 191 and 366 junction. The access is paved except the last 12 miles which is dirt but still navigable by those with 2-wheel drive. The drive is both scenic and difficult, as it is one of the curviest in the state. Those prone to motion sickness should take care. With a patient driver, one can make an excellent day trip visiting Riggs Flat Lake. The drive is beautiful.

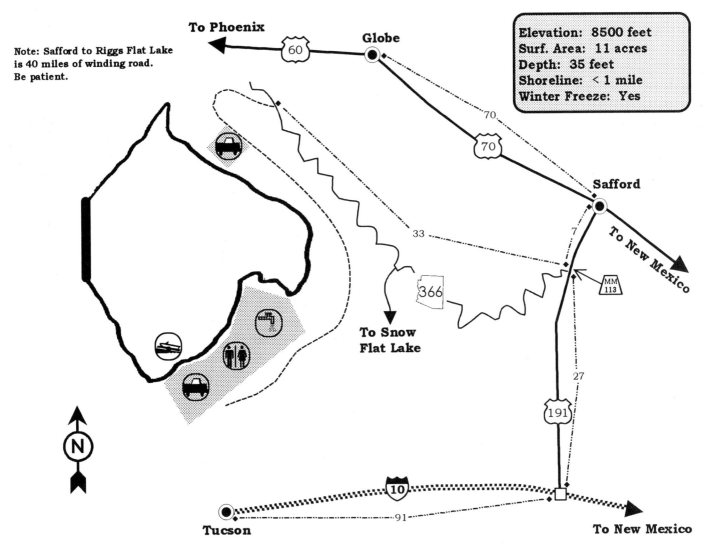

Note: Safford to Riggs Flat Lake is 40 miles of winding road. Be patient.

Elevation: 8500 feet
Surf. Area: 11 acres
Depth: 35 feet
Shoreline: < 1 mile
Winter Freeze: Yes

CAMPING/RVING	RECREATION	BOATING	MISCELLANEOUS
Tents/Trailers/RVs -26 sites -$5/night/family -drinking water -tables -fire pits -pit toilets	-canoeing -hiking -picnicking -sailing -fishing: rainbow trout, brown trout, brook trout -shore fishing	-electric motor only -boat launch area	-thunderstorms usual in mid to late summer afternoons -nearest town is Safford, 40 miles east -snow closes road in winter -nearest conveniences are located at a small store at the 366 and 191 junction
Information:	Coronado National Forest (602) 428-4150		

84

SNOW FLAT LAKE

It takes a bit of an imagination to call the one-half-acre pond at Snow Flat a lake. Located at 8700 feet in the Pina Leno Mountains in the Coronado National Forest, it really has nothing to offer other than wet. Fishing, that is to say fish, are non-existent. One might enjoy paddling around in a canoe or small inflatable but that's the only purpose this lake serves other than a watering hole for the resident wildlife. Camping at the lake is primitive but national forest campgrounds are nearby. Certainly the most popular activity is hiking with numerous trails in the area. Snow Flat is located 1 mile southwest of Arizona Highway 366 which is paved for 23 miles from the westerly turn off from US Highway 191, 6 miles south of Safford. Snow Flat is settled between the 10,000-foot peaks of Heligraph Peak and Webb Peak. The road is one of the states curviest and not for those prone to car/motion sickness. The elevation can also be difficult on the body.

Note: Safford to Snow Flat Lake is 29 miles of winding road. Be patient.

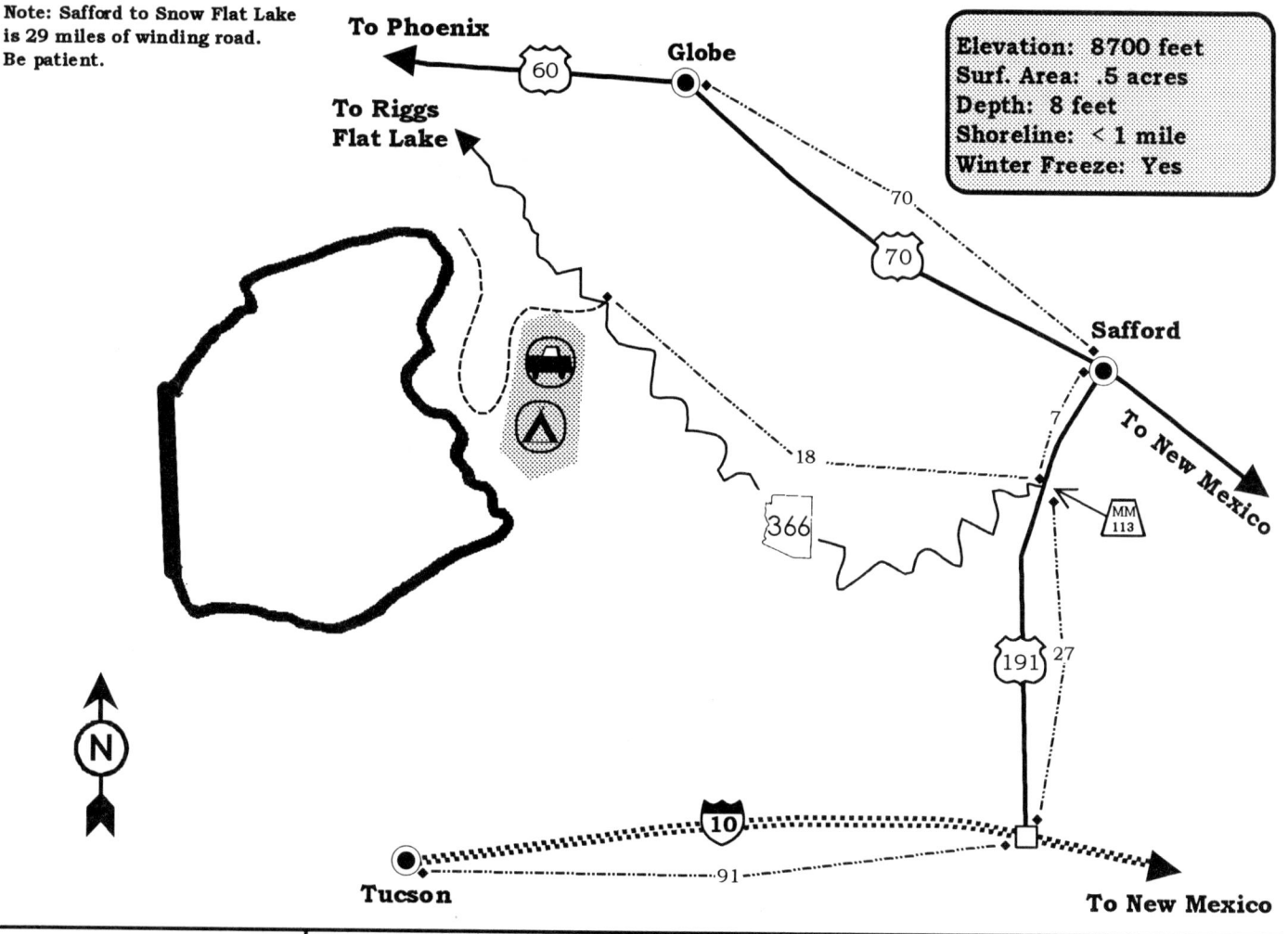

Elevation: 8700 feet
Surf. Area: .5 acres
Depth: 8 feet
Shoreline: < 1 mile
Winter Freeze: Yes

CAMPING/RVING	RECREATION	BOATING	MISCELLANEOUS
Tents/Trailers/RVs -primitive camping at the lake shore -no facilities -two national forest campgrounds (Shannon and Hospital Flats) within two miles of the lake -20 total sites -$5/night -drinking water -pit toilets	-canoeing -hiking -picnicking -napping -fishing is not recommended since there is nothing to catch -more napping	-watercraft are prohibited on Snow Flat Lake	-thunderstorms usual on mid to late summer afternoons -nearest town is Safford, 29 miles to the north east -nearest conveniences at small store at junction of 366 and 191
Information:	Coronado National Forest (602) 428-4150		

Rucker Canyon Lake sits in a superbly scenic canyon in the Chiricahua Mountains just south of the Chiricahua Wilderness and is managed by the Coronado National Forest. The lake sits at 6300 feet and is little more than a pond. Certainly, the surrounding area is some of the most magnificent in southern Arizona. The forested wilderness areas are incomparable. Fishing, mostly from shore, can be good in other than summer months. The lake is stocked routinely in cooler weather. Camping is within five smallish national forest campgrounds at or near the lake. Facilities are typical of the national forest system.

The drive or ride on Rucker Canyon Road (Forest Road 74) is superb and is worth the effort even for a day trip. Probably the most rewarded among those that utilize the Coronado National Forest are the hikers and this is particularly true near Rucker Canyon Lake. The hike can be a bit tough but given the flora, fauna, and formations, well worth it. Take Rucker Canyon Road (Forest Road 74) east from US Highway 191 at a point 29 miles north of Douglas. Follow this road for 22 miles to Forest Road 74E. Turn left and follow this road 6 miles to the lake.

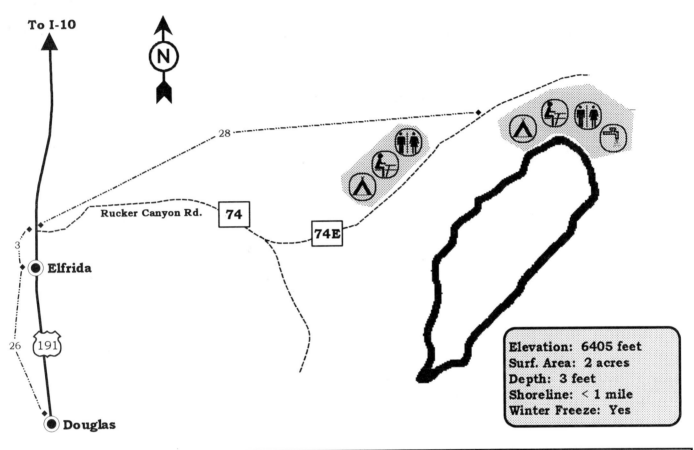

Elevation: 6405 feet
Surf. Area: 2 acres
Depth: 3 feet
Shoreline: < 1 mile
Winter Freeze: Yes

CAMPING/RVING	RECREATION	BOATING	MISCELLANEOUS
Tents/Trailers/RVs -5 national forests campgrounds at or adjacent to lake - Rucker, Rucker Lake, Cypress Park, Bathtub, and Camp Rucker -$5/day -tables -grills -pit toilets -drinking water	-canoeing -hiking -picnicking -horseback riding -fishing: rainbow trout (not stocked in warm summer months) -shore fishing -$2.50/vehicle day-use fee -no swimming	-electric motor only -this lake is only a couple of acres, anything other than a small inflatable or canoe would be ridiculous	-nearest town is Douglas, 44 miles south
Information:	Coronado National Forest (602) 364-3468		

PARKER CANYON LAKE

Parker Canyon Lake sits at 5400 foot elevation in the Coronado National Forest in south central Arizona. This site is a bit remote, which makes it perfect for those looking to get away from the crowds. The surrounding landscape is typically tall grasses with scrub oak. Small game hunters love the area. Fishing on Parker Canyon Lake can yield both cold and warm water species. Trout are stocked routinely during the winter months with bass, catfish, and bluegills predominant in summer. This lake boasts the state inland waters record for channel catfish at a bit over 32 pounds and 39 inches in length. Success can be had from a boat or the shoreline. Weather here is moderate with summer days warm and evenings cool. A 30 degree Fahrenheit temperature change during the day is not uncommon. Recent renovations facilitate the handicapped. Although not totally "handicappedized" it is one of the better locations in the state for those with physical disabilities. Hunters, bird watchers, hikers, equestrians, and campers all do very well here. Both bald and golden eagles winter in the area. There is a relatively level trail which circles the lake and is 5 and 1/2 miles in length, perfect for a casual day time stroll. There is a group camp area for up to 60 people: reservations are necessary for its use. The individual campground is called Lakeside, but is not directly on the lake, rather it is 3/4 of a mile from waters edge, but it is paved to the lake. A stay at Parker Canyon Lake can be dotted with day trips to Tombstone or Mexico, and a variety of old mining towns with "Old West" atmospheres. Access to the lake is east of Tucson on Interstate 10, turn south on State Route 83 all the way to the lake. The last 25 miles is a well maintained, gravel road, all else is paved.

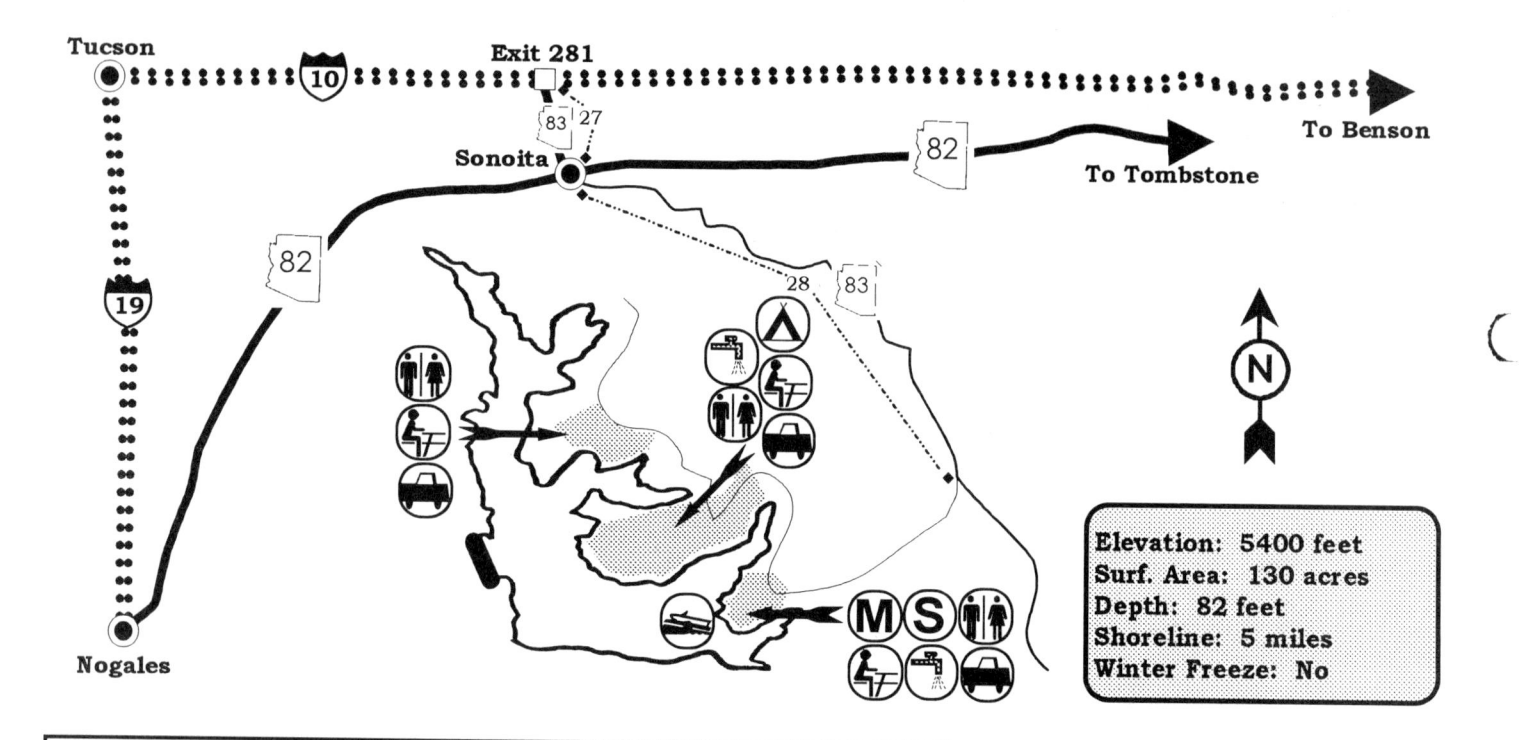

Elevation: 5400 feet
Surf. Area: 130 acres
Depth: 82 feet
Shoreline: 5 miles
Winter Freeze: No

CAMPING/RVING	RECREATION	BOATING	MISCELLANEOUS
Tents/Trailers/RVs Lakeview Campgrounds -65 sites -$8/vehicle/night -tables, grills, fire places -drinking water -pit toilets -dead and down wood may be collected for use Group camp area -60 people max -handicapped facilities -reservations: call (602) 458-0761	-sailing, canoeing -hiking -picnicking -hunting -horseback riding -bird watching -fishing: stocked trout, largemouth bass, catfish, sunfish -shore fishing -no swimming -day-use fee is $5/vehicle/day	-8 horse power motor maximum -paved launch ramp -boat rentals at marina (with or without motors) -there is no gasoline sold on site	-the campground store and marina are open year round -convenience store/marina phone #: (602) 455-5847 -bait -tackle -fishing license -snacks -beverages -handicapped facilities at store/ marina and campgrounds -closest town is Sonoita (28 miles)
Information:	Coronado National Forest (602) 378-0311		

Patagonia Lake is contained within the 640-acre Patagonia Lake State Park just a few miles north of the Mexican border. At 265 acres, it is the areas longest lake and is well suited to all water recreation. Patagonia lake is a reasonably busy lake, solitude is not its strong point. With its 100 campsites and the fine facilities, the overnighter will do well. Day-use facilities are abundant. The angler will have the best luck in the warmer months but winter trout stocking will also keep the fisherman busy. The lake is at a 3800-foot elevation which gives moderate to hot weather in the summer and cool to pleasant during winter months. This is a fine year-round usable park. Shade is scarce so bring some covering in the heat of summer. There are special boating rules for summer time water-skiers and jet skiers (see below). The east half of the lake is a no-wake area. Please observe posted boating rules. This park has moderate handicapped facilities. Access is paved all the way to the lake. Take Arizona State Highway 82 north from Nogales for 12, miles then turn north for 4 miles. Follow the posted signs.

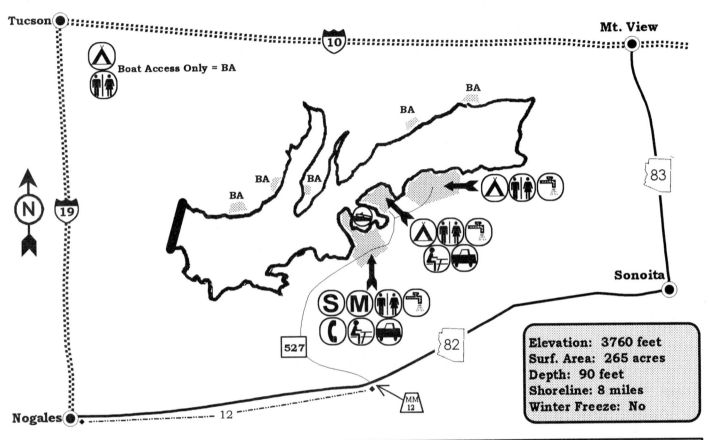

CAMPING/RVING	RECREATION	BOATING	MISCELLANEOUS
Trailer/RVs 10 sites: water, electricity -$12/night Tents/Trailers/RVs -300 developed sites: $7/night -dump station -drinking water, showers -handicapped rest rooms -dogs on leash only	-hiking - nature trails -sailing, canoeing -jet skiing -swimming (sandy beach area) -picnicking: ramadas, tables, grills -group picnic area -fishing: largemouth bass, bluegill, catfish, crappie, trout stocked in winter -shore fishing -bird watching is superb -day-use fee $3/vehicle	-no motor restrictions -2 improved ramps -boat rentals at store -courtesy dock -day-use fee covers boating costs NOTE: no water skiing, jet skiing or towing behind boats on weekends or holidays between May 1 and October 1 NOTE: the eastern half of the lake is a no-wake area, please observe posted regulations	-telephone -convenience store at lake: food, bait, boat rental, fishing, tackle, license, fuel/oil -store phone number is: (602) 287-6063 -closest town is Patagonia PERMITS AND FEES: SEE SECTION ON ARIZONA STATE PARKS CONTAINED WITHIN THIS BOOK
Information:	Patagonia Lake State Park (602) 287-6965		

PENA BLANCA LAKE

Pena Blanca Lake is contained within the Coronado National Forest and is one of the more southern lakes in the state. At 3832-foot elevation, it is plenty warm in the summer, but very pleasant during the winter months. A small lake at 45 acres and three miles of shoreline it is predominately an anglers lake with the usual summer Arizona catches augmented by stocked rainbow trout during the cooler months. The motel, restaurant and convenience store at lake side are adequate. The lake and its facilities are open yearlong. Access is 10 miles west of Interstate Highway 19 on Arizona Highway 289 which is paved all the way. This is an easy-to-find, easy-to-get-to lake.

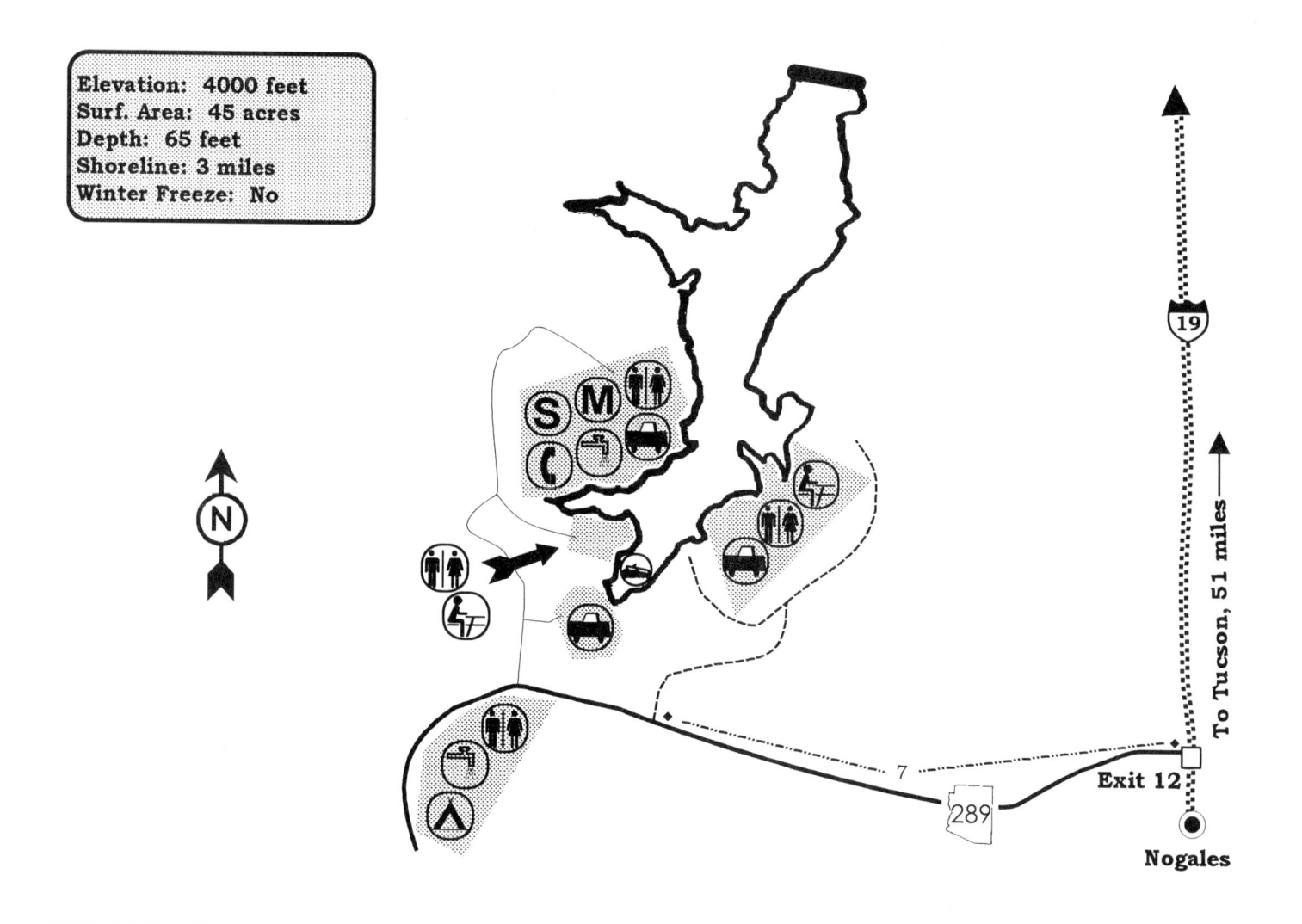

Elevation: 4000 feet
Surf. Area: 45 acres
Depth: 65 feet
Shoreline: 3 miles
Winter Freeze: No

To Tucson, 51 miles

19

Exit 12

289

7

Nogales

CAMPING/RVING	RECREATION	BOATING	MISCELLANEOUS
Tents/Trailers/RVs White Rock Campground 1/4 mile from lake -15 sites -$5/night -primitive rest rooms -grills, tables -drinking water -no showers -dispersed camping at various locations in the canyons near lake	-swimming -canoeing -hiking -horseback riding -fishing: catfish, largemouth bass, bluegills, crappies rainbow trout stocked in winter -shore fishing	-1 unimproved launch -electric motor only -boat/motor rental at lodge	-telephone -convenience store at lake: groceries, bait, tackle, boat rental -restaurant -motel -nearest town is Nogales, 16 miles away -Pena Blanca Lodge telephone number is 281-2800
Information:	Coronado National Forest (602) 281-2296		

Located within the Coronado National Forest, Arivaca Lake is managed by the Arizona Game and Fish Department. It is primarily an angler's lake serving southern Arizona. A relatively small lake at 90 acres, Arivaca is best fished by boat although shore fishing is adequate along its three miles of shoreline. Set in oak-studded, grassy hills at 3700 foot elevation, day time summer temperatures are hot at 100-plus degrees. Camping is primitive at best, with essentially no facilities or conveniences. You must bring in all you need and please remember to pack it out also. The fishing can be quite good at Arivaca, if not for volume then for size. Three times this lake has held the state record for red ear sunfish. Just try catching a two-plus pound sunfish on ultra-light tackle. The 30-plus pound catfish can also give you a struggle. Access is via Interstate 19, 6 miles south of Tucson, turn west at the Arivaca Junction exit (State Highway 22) and travel 20 miles to the town of Arivaca. Most of this 20 miles is paved. The lake is 7 miles southeast of the town. Follow Forest Route 216 out of town to Forest Route 39, then just follow the signs.

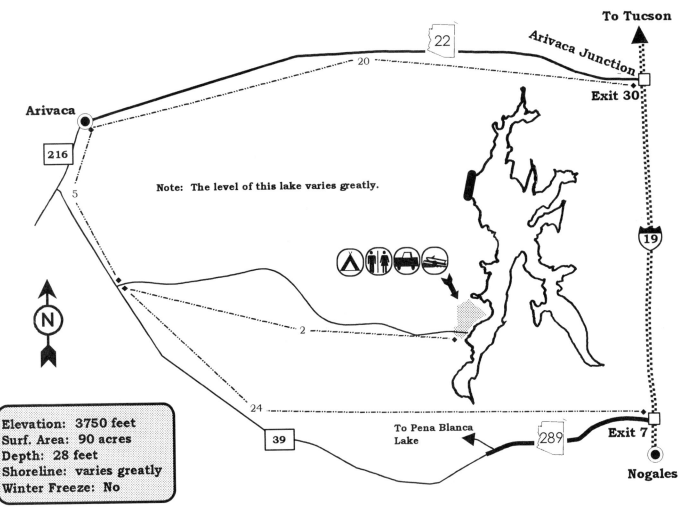

Note: The level of this lake varies greatly.

Elevation: 3750 feet
Surf. Area: 90 acres
Depth: 28 feet
Shoreline: varies greatly
Winter Freeze: No

CAMPING/RVING	RECREATION	BOATING	MISCELLANEOUS
Tent/Trailer/RVs -no facilities/conveniences -no fees -primitive toilets	-swimming -hiking -horseback riding -canoeing -fishing: largemouth bass catfish, sunfish, rainbow trout in winter -shore fishing -quail hunting -bull frogging	-electric motor only -primitive launch ramp	-nearest conveniences in town of Arivaca, seven miles northwest -nearest large city is Nogales
Information:	Arizona Game and Fish Department (602) 628-5376		

WILLOW LAKE (91A)

Willow Lake is located just north of Prescott and is inaccessible for public use. All the land surrounding the lake is private; therefore, access would necessitate trespassing - stay away from Willow Lake.

WHITE MOUNTAIN LAKE (91B)

A beautiful lake on the east side of Highway 77 just north of Show Low. This is a private lake to be used only by certain members of the local community of Silver Creek and the local country club. Again, White Mountain Lake is not for public use. And that's too bad, because it's a beauty.

GANADO LAKE (91C)

Near a town of the same name, Ganado Lake in northeastern Arizona has been drained. Try another spot where there is water.

CLEAR CREEK RESERVOIR (91D)

What we have here is a name change. If you're looking for Clear Creek Reservoir, you find that it is now call McHood Lake. Simple enough.

LOWER GOLDWATER LAKE (91E)

Located just south of Prescott, Lower Goldwater Lake is inaccessible. Just stick with Upper Goldwater Lake. The responsible authorities have determined that this body of water is "not for public use!" Simple enough, we'll just all stay away.

DRY LAKE (#1) (91F)

This is one of the many "Dry Lakes" of Arizona and is the body of water located just north of Heber, in the middle of Navajo County. In reviewing most state maps, you'll see the lake with no name beside it. Somewhere the label "Dry Lake" was affixed but what this really is is a body of water that is used by the local wood pulp mill for industrial uses. You'll be able to smell the lake from five miles away. There is just no recreation at or near this sewer smelling pond. Please disregard this body of water.

DRY LAKE (#2) (91G)

Dry Lake (#2), 50 acres plus or minus the rainy season and time of year. Located west of Point of Pines Lake, on the San Carlos Indian Reservation in east central Arizona. Dry Lake (#2) is a get-way-from-it lake usually devoid of humans other than the most private or hard-nosed trout fisherman. There is significant wildlife in the area, you'll enjoy the naturness. To access Dry Lake (#2), follow the directions to Point of Pines Lake and proceed southwest a few miles via the signage on Indian Service Road 1570.

TROUT LAKE (91H)

Trout Lake sits on the Navajo Nation at 7500 foot elevation. There are 20 surface acres and the lake is 15 feet deep. Reports are that Trout Lake will be stocked in 1993, the first time in several years. Trout Lake lies just north of Fort Defiance and just south of Sawmill on the west side of Indian Route 7. There are no facilities at the lake. It is recommended that you contact the appropriate departments on the Navajo Nation to get an update on Trout Lake. Department of Tourism-(602) 871-6673, Department of Parks and Recreation-(602) 871-6451.

This Red Lake (#2) is located 8 miles northeast of Williams, Arizona, just off Arizona Highway 64. This lake is currently dry and has no aquatic recreational value. There is a modest, private campground nearby, which has full RV hookups. If you desire to visit a "Red Lake" with water in it, there is a Red Lake (#1) on the Navajo Nation which sits directly on the Arizona/New Mexico Border. Look elsewhere in this book for Red Lake (#1).

PAINTED ROCK (92B)

Located northwest of Gila Bend, this lake was contained within the Arizona Painted Rock State Park. This is no longer a State Park and the responsibility for the lake and surrounding facilities are now under the jurisdiction of the Bureau of Land Management, in coordination with the Army Corps of Engineers, who are in charge of the dam. This change has resulted from the discovery, a few years ago, that agricultural runoff of pesticides and fertilizers combined with industrial metals have contaminated the lake. The park facilities on the lake are closed indefinitely. The 1993 heavy spring rains certainly have had an impact again on the area but specifics, be they good or bad, are not yet available. Please, just stay away. There is no recreation allowed at or on the lake. Questions can be forwarded to the Bureau of Land Management at (602) 780-8090, or the Army Corps of Engineers at (602) 683-6488.

BILL'S LAKE (92C)

Bill's Lake is a private lake which charges a fee for the trout and catfish taken out of the lake. Bill's Lake consists of five ponds covering eight acres. Twelve (12) RV hookups are located at the lake which charges $10 per night for full hookups. There is also a $50 weekly rate. Tent camping is available also. A small concession which sells snacks, bait, tackle, and rents fishing gear is located on site. They will also clean the fish for you. Trout are cleaned free with a $1 charge per catfish. The fee for fishing Bill's Lake is based on live weight of the fish; $2.80/pound for catfish, $3.20/pound for rainbow trout. No boats are allowed on Bill's Lake, strictly shore fishing. There is a picnic area with tables and grills; you can cook your "shore meal" right there. The elevation is 5600 feet, thus the weather in summer is pleasant to warmish. Bill's Lake is located 8 miles north of Show Low, just off Arizona Highway 77. Proceed north on Arizona Highway 77 from Show Low towards Holbrok and turn east on White Mountain Lake Road (approximately Mile Marker 351). The lake is 1/4 mile from Arizona Highway 77 on the north side of the road. The signs are adequate, you can't miss it. The telephone number is (602) 537-9589.

FRED'S LAKE (92D)

Fred's Lake is a private lake located in Pinetop, Arizona. Its primary purpose is to shore fish for rainbow trout for a fee. There is a picnic area with ramadas, tables, flush toilets, and drinking water. There is a restaurant on site which serves breakfast, lunch, and dinner. There is a concession at the lake that sells snacks and bait and also rents fishing gear. This two-acre pond is open year round except when snow is heavy. Again, the primary activity is shore fishing for the stocked rainbow trout. This is a great place to teach children how to fish. The facilities are "handicapped accessible." Fred's Lake lays claim to "the cleanest rest rooms" which might give you an idea of the quality of the facilities. The lake is located 1 mile south of Highway 260 on Penrod within the city of Pinetop. The telephone number is (602) 367-3474.

NASH TANK (92E)

Resting on the south central portion of the White Mountain Apache Indian Reservation at 5680 feet elevation, Nash Tank is a recluse's dream. The few willing to brave the roads south of White River/Fort Apache will be rewarded with solitude, channel catfish, and bass. The facilities are minimal to nonexistent at Nash Tank, but if you're "self-contained" you're just fine. The roads are particularly tough in wet weather. Before proceeding to Nash Tank, be sure you are cognizant of the Reservation's rules and regulations and that you have your recreation permits. They are obtainable in White River. (See section in this book on the "White Mountain Apache Reservation.")

MEADOWS LAKES (93A)

Located in Greer Arizona, Meadows Lakes is a private concession consisting of 3 ponds covering 11 acres. Trout, primarily rainbow, are catchable for a fee. You may retain the fish at $3.75 per pound or you can do "catch and release" on barbless hooks for $5 per hour. Fees may vary year to year. No state fishing license is required. There are no facilities at the lake, but you might consider a primitive picnic while you're there. There are various RV parks and camping facilities within the immediate area. No boats are allowed on the ponds, all fishing is from shore. Meadows Lakes is open seasonally from May 1 to October 1. Groups may reserve the lakes for their exclusive use by appointment. The hours of operation are 8 a.m. to ?. Fishing tackle is available at the lake. For further information, call (602) 735-7290.

LAKE OF THE WOODS (93B)

Lake of the Woods is a private lake of 12 acres and may be used by those staying at Hogan's Lake of the Woods Resort. There are 25 cabins capable of sleeping from 2 to 18 people. The cabins are fully equipped with nearly all conveniences of home, including a fire place. There are no camping/RVing facilities. Row boats and canoes can be rented. You can also fish from shore for the rainbow trout, bass, catfish, and bluegills. No state fishing license is required, since the lake is privately owned. On-site facilities include a playground, recreation hall, spa, sauna, laundry room, shuffleboard court, and horseshoe pits. Golf courses and ski area are minutes away. The resort is open year round and rates are seasonal. This lake is located "in town" so all conveniences and facilities are in easy reach. The resort is embedded in a pine forest at 7000 feet. The weather is consistent with the elevation. Reservations are recommended. Lake of the Woods is located just off Arizona Highway 260, in Lakeside, Arizona, 3 miles southeast of Show Low. The telephone number is 1-602-368-5353.

ROSE CANYON LAKE (93C)

A little guy at 7 acres, Rose Canyon Lake reside at 7000 foot elevation in the Santa Catalina Mountains on the Coronado National Forest adjacent to Tucson. At a minimum, the drive to Rose Canyon Lake is lovely; paved all the way. Beware though, the mountainous highway requires special attention and care. There is plenty of camping in the area surrounding Rose Canyon Lake. But the hot summer weekends are very, very busy. Nearly 100 developed campsites with tables, grills, and drinking water are accessible. A private concessionaire licensed by the Forest Service tends the camping and day-use facilities. There are fees. Given its size, no boats are allowed on the lake. Trout are frequently stocked so there's plenty of fishing. The lake is relatively deep, averaging 44 feet. You may have to get way down deep during the summer months. If you take a day trip to Rose Canyon Lake there is marginally ample parking (very busy on summer weekends). You'll have to trek a hundred yards to get to the shoreline. A fine picnic area is available for those who bring up their goodies. Access to Rose Canyon Lake is simple. In Tucson, find your way to the northeast side of town (a city map would be useful) and jump on Catalina Highway (A.K.A. General Hitchcock Road). Proceed up the hill for 18 miles to the lake. Again, it is paved all the way. The turn off is to the left as indicated by the signs. The lake is one mile off the main road. While you're up on the hill, you might venture another 10 miles to Summerhaven. This quaint, little town has a few shops and restaurants. Campers may even resupply there. For further information call the Coronado National Forest and (602) 670-4552.

SABINO LAKE (93D)

Located on the Coronado National Forest, Sabino Lake is just a few miles northeast of Tucson. This body of water is not really a lake at less than 2 feet deep. What we have here is just a small dam on Sabino Creek. There are no fish in Sabino Lake but the above ground wildlife are abundant - this is a great place for a hike if you're in the Tucson area. Sabino Lake is located just off Sabino Canyon Road which runs north and south in the northeast corner of Tucson. You pass the Coronado National Forest Visitor's Center on your right as you approach the "lake;" be sure to stop. For further information call (602) 670-4552.

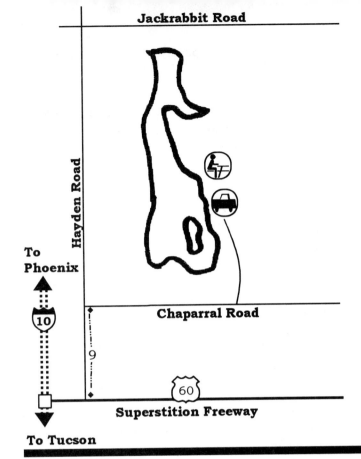

LOCATION: Northeast corner of Hayden and Chaparral Roads, Scottsdale.

SIZE: 10 acres, maximum depth 15 feet.

HOURS: Sunrise to 10:30 p.m.

DAILY BAG AND POSSESSION LIMIT: 4 catfish, 4 trout, 6 largemouth bass.

BOATING: Permitted until sunset only.

COMMENTS: Urban fishing license required. Park is available at the south end of the lake, accessed by Chaparral Road. Contains: channel catfish, flathead catfish, rainbow trout (in season), redear sunfish, bluegill, largemouth bass, and carp.

PARK RULES: Groups of three or more persons must obtain a permit to drink beer in the park. These permits are available at no charge from the City of Scottsdale Parks and Recreation Department Office or from roving recreation department staff. All other alcoholic beverages and glass containers are prohibited. Dogs must be on leashes at all times. Model boats may be operated only in areas that are designated for that purpose. For more information call 994-2353.

CANAL LAKE - Tempe

LOCATION: Canal Park, Tempe. College Avenue and McKellips Road, 1 mile north of the Salt River and 1/2 mile west of Scottsdale Road.

SIZE: 3 acres, maximum depth 6 feet.

HOURS: 6 a.m. to 10 p.m.

DAILY BAG AND POSSESSION LIMIT: 4 catfish, 4 trout, 6 largemouth bass. No limit on bluegill or redear sunfish.

BOATING: Not allowed.

COMMENTS: Urban fishing license required. Contains: channel catfish, rainbow trout (in season), redear sunfish, bluegill, largemouth bass, common and grass carp. Access to parking is from Marigold.

PARK RULES: Motor vehicles not allowed inside park. Swimming is prohibited. For more information call 994-2408.

KIWANIS LAKE - Tempe

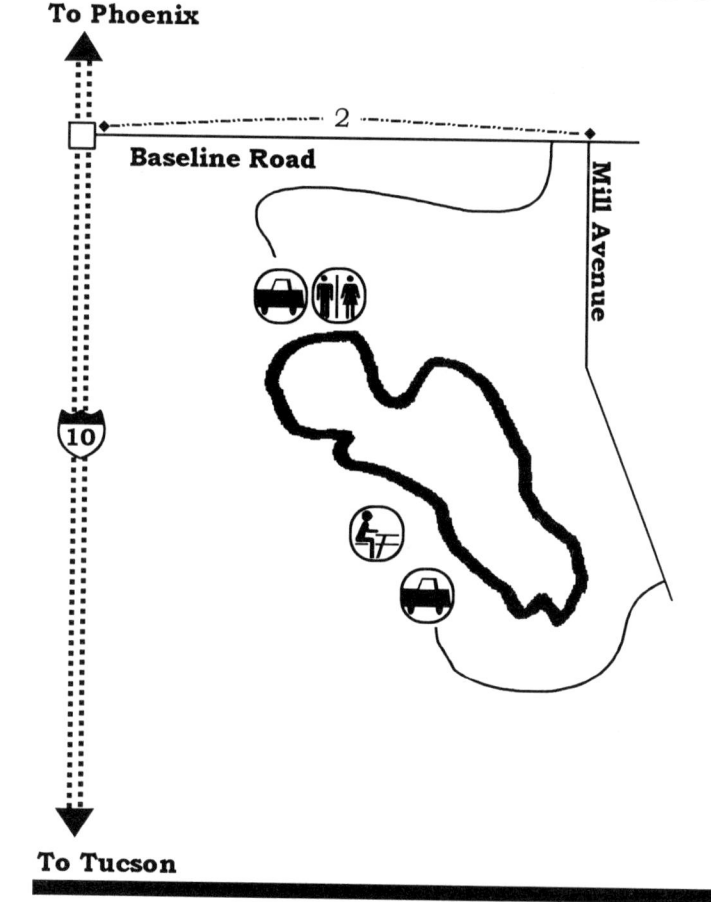

LOCATION: Kiwanis Park, Tempe. Baseline Road 1 block west of Mill Avenue.

SIZE: 13 acres, maximum depth 8 feet.

HOURS: 6 a.m. to 12 midnight.

DAILY BAG AND POSSESSION LIMIT: 4 catfish, 4 trout, 6 largemouth bass.

BOATING: City of Tempe boating permit required (call 731-8381). Boat ramp is provided.

COMMENTS: Urban fishing license required. Contains: channel catfish, rainbow trout (in season), redear sunfish, bluegill, largemouth bass, flathead catfish, common and grass carp. Access to parking is from Baseline Road.

PARK RULES: Motor vehicles not allowed inside park. Swimming is prohibited. For more information call 350-5200.

RIVERVIEW LAKE - Mesa

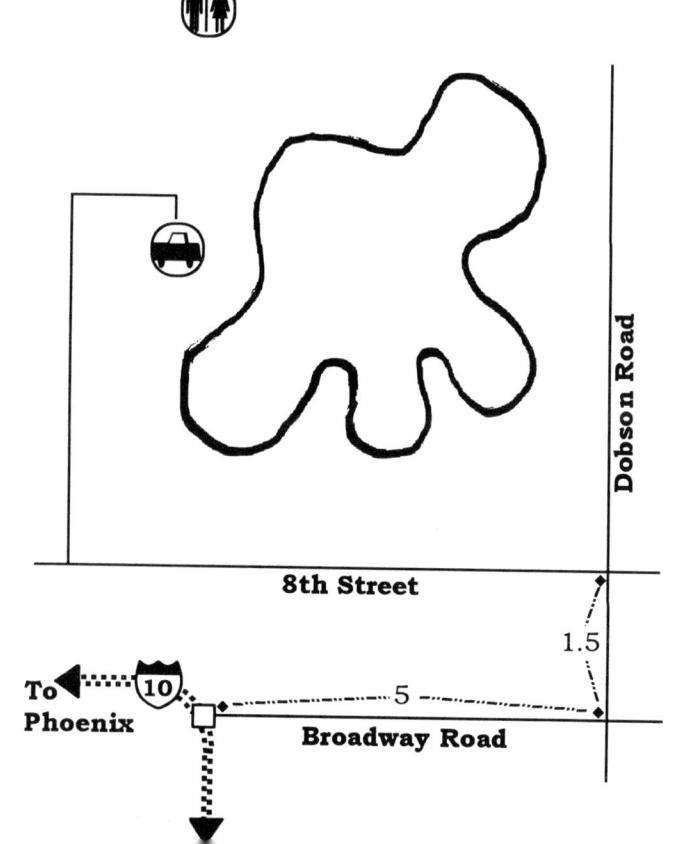

LOCATION: Riverview Park, Mesa. North Dobson Road at 8th Street.

SIZE: 3 acres, maximum depth 18 feet.

HOURS: Sunrise to 10 p.m.

DAILY BAG AND POSSESSION LIMIT: 4 catfish, 4 trout, 6 bass, No limit on redear sunfish, bluegill or carp.

BOATING: Not allowed.

COMMENTS: Urban fishing license required. Contains: channel catfish, rainbow trout (in season), redear sunfish, bluegill, largemouth bass, and carp.

PARK RULES: No _distilled_ alcoholic beverages permitted. Vehicles must remain in designated areas. Swimming or wading is prohibited. No pets allowed in park. For more information call 644-2351.

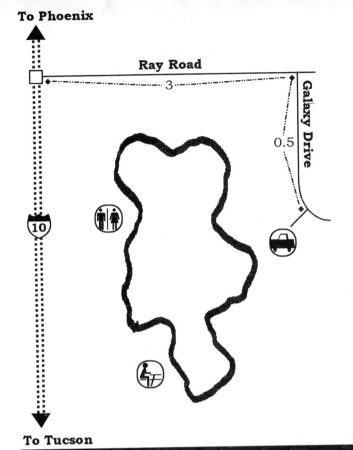

To Phoenix

Ray Road

3

0.5

Galaxy Drive

10

To Tucson

LOCATION: Desert Breeze Park in west Chandler, south of Ray Road on Galaxy Drive.

SIZE: 4 acres. Maximum depth 12 feet, average depth 10 feet.

HOURS: Sunrise to 10 p.m.

DAILY BAG AND POSSESSION LIMIT: 4 catfish, 4 trout, 6 bass. No limit on redear sunfish bluegill or carp.

BOATING: Boating permitted only between 6 a.m. and sunset. Boats not to exceed 14 feet in length. EXCEPTIONS: Rubber boats must be at least 6 feet in length and not exceed 14 feet. Canoes must have proper floatation and not exceed 17 feet in length. No rafts, inner tubes, inflatable mattresses, catamarans, or sail boards allowed. No motors (gas or electric).

COMMENTS: Urban fishing license required. Contains: channel catfish, rainbow trout (in season), largemouth bass, bluegill, redear sunfish, and carp.

PARK RULES: No swimming or wading permitted in Desert Breeze Park Lake. For more information call 786-2727.

ALVORD LAKE - Phoenix

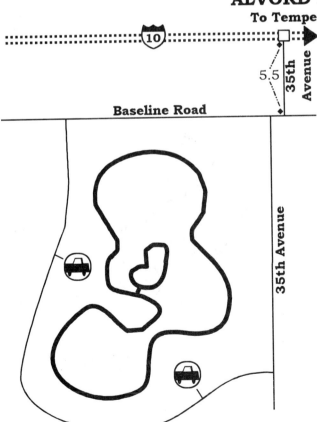

To Tempe

10

5.5

35th Avenue

Baseline Road

35th Avenue

LOCATION: Alvord Park in southwest Phoenix, at southwest corner of 35th Avenue and Baseline Road.

SIZE: 25 acres, largest of Arizona's designated urban fishing lakes.

HOURS: 5:30 a.m. to 10:30 p.m.

DAILY BAG AND POSSESSION LIMIT: 4 catfish, 4 trout, 6 bass. No limit on redear sunfish, bluegill or carp.

BOATING: No motors allowed. Fishing from a boat is prohibited. Boat launch is at southeast entrance.

COMMENTS: Urban fishing license required. Contains: channel catfish, rainbow trout (in season), largemouth bass, yellow bass, bluegill, tilapia, and carp.

PARK RULES: Glass containers prohibited. Alcoholic beverage permits required. For more information call 262-6111.

96

CORTEZ LAKE - Phoenix

To Tucson

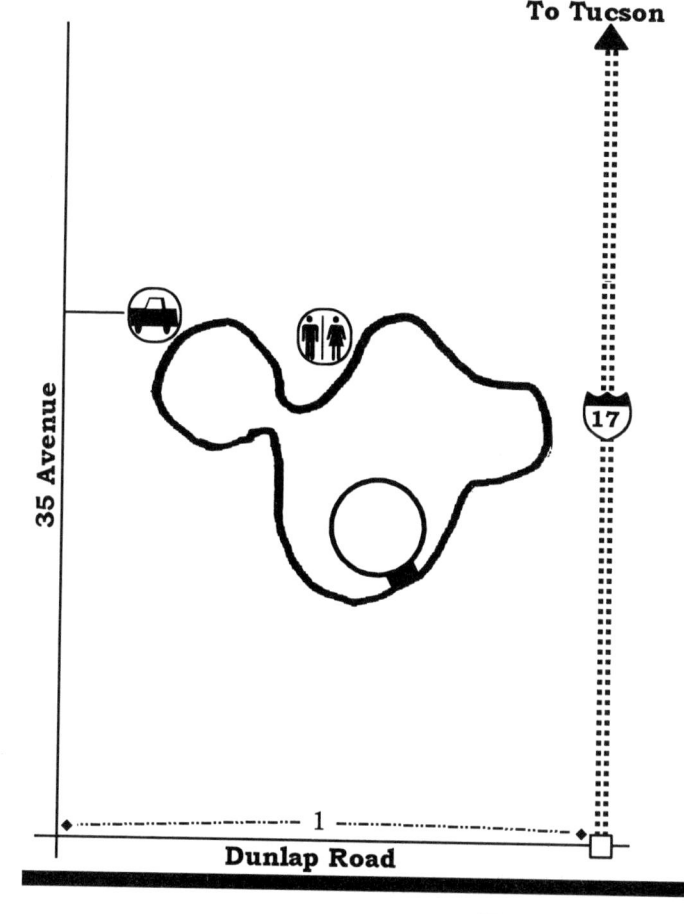

LOCATION: Cortez Park in northwest Phoenix, at northeast corner of 35th Avenue and Dunlap.

SIZE: 3 acres, maximum depth 10 feet. Lake renovation completed in 1989.

HOURS: 5:30 a.m. to 10:30 p.m.

DAILY BAG AND POSSESSION LIMIT: 4 catfish, 4 trout, 6 bass. No limit on redear sunfish, bluegill or carp.

BOATING: Private boats prohibited. Shore fishing only.

COMMENTS: Urban fishing license required. Contains: channel catfish, rainbow trout (in season), largemouth bass, bluegill, redear sunfish, and carp.

PARK RULES: Glass containers prohibited. Alcoholic beverage permits required. For more information call 262-6575.

ENCANTO LAKE - Phoenix

Thomas Road

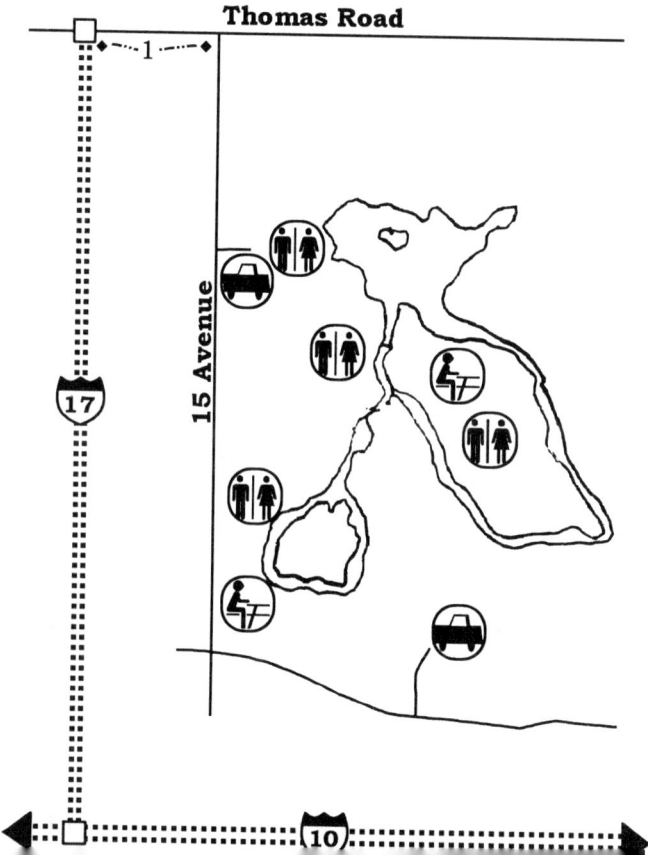

LOCATION: Encanto Park in central Phoenix, between 7th and 15th Avenue and north of Encanto Blvd.

SIZE: 7.5 acres, maximum depth 10 feet in main lake, 4 feet in channels.

HOURS: 5:30 a.m. to 12:30 a.m.

DAILY BAG AND POSSESSION LIMIT: 4 catfish, 4 trout, 6 bass. No limit on redear sunfish, bluegill or carp.

BOATING: Private boats prohibited. Shore fishing only.

COMMENTS: Urban fishing license required. Contains: channel catfish, rainbow trout (in season), largemouth bass, bluegill, redear sunfish, and carp.

PARK RULES: Glass containers prohibited. Alcoholic beverage permits required. For more information call 261-8993.

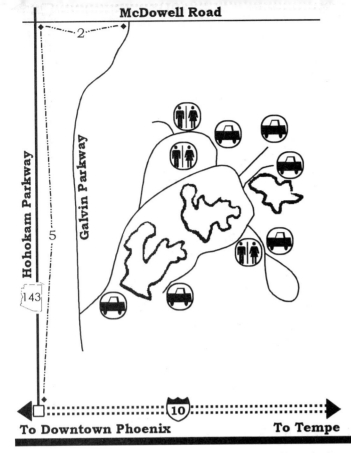

LOCATION: Papago Park in east Phoenix, south on Galvin Parkway from McDowell.

SIZE: Total of 6 acres (Pond 1 - 1 acre, Pond 2 - 2 acres, Pond 3 - 3 acres).

HOURS: 6 a.m. to 12 midnight.

DAILY BAG AND POSSESSION LIMIT: 1 bass (**13 INCH MINIMUM**), 4 catfish, 4 trout. No limit on redear sunfish, bluegill or carp.

BOATING: Not allowed.

COMMENTS: Urban fishing license required. Contains: channel catfish, flathead catfish, rainbow trout (in season), largemouth bass, bluegill, redear sunfish, and carp. Managed primarily to provide quality bass fishing opportunity for the urban angler. Receives 4 catfish stockings and 3 trout stockings per season.

PARK RULES: Glass containers prohibited. Alcoholic beverage permits required. For more information call 256-3220.

KENNEDY LAKE - Tucson

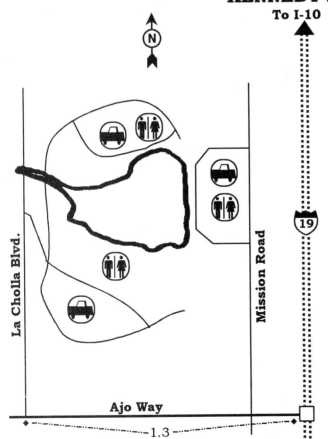

LOCATION: J. F. Kennedy Park, Mission and Ajo Roads, Tucson

SIZE: 10 acres, maximum depth 12 feet.

HOURS: Sunrise to 10:30 p.m.

DAILY BAG AND POSSESSION LIMIT: 4 catfish, 4 trout, 4 largemouth bass (**13 INCH MINIMUM**). No limit on bluegill.

BOATING: Rental boats available on weekends. Canoes up to 17 feet and boats 14 feet and under are permitted. Electric trolling motors up to 1 horsepower may be used. Gasoline motors prohibited.

COMMENTS: Urban fishing license required. Contains: channel catfish, rainbow trout (in season), redear sunfish, bluegill, largemouth bass, common and grass carp. Access to parking from Mission Road or La Cholla Boulevard.

PARK RULES: No campfires or open fires allowed along shoreline. Swimming or wading is prohibited. Dogs or other animals are not allowed in lake. No glass containers. For more information call 791-4873.

98

LAKESIDE LAKE - Tucson

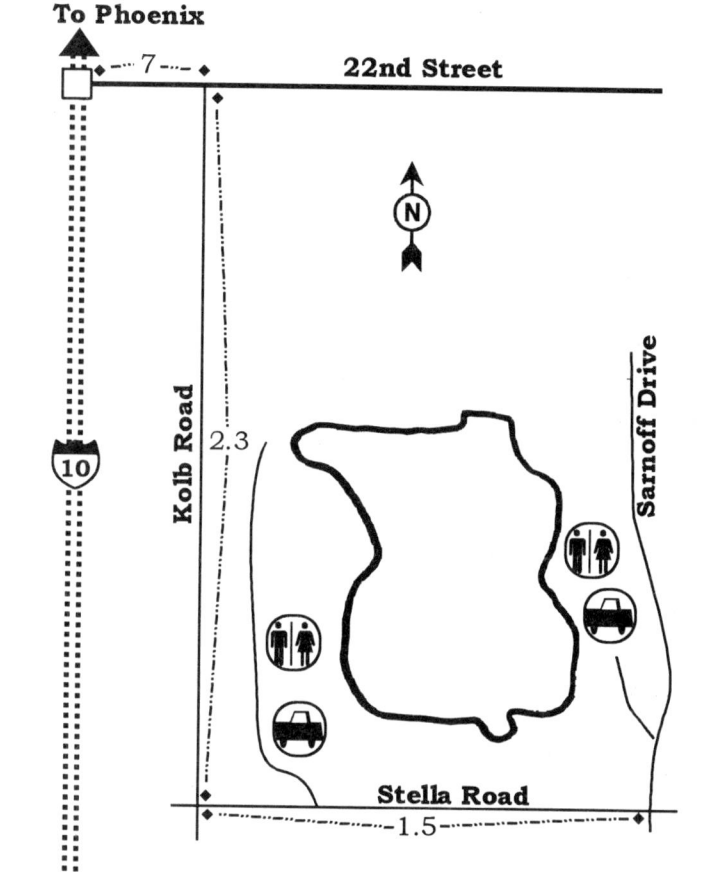

To Phoenix

22nd Street

Kolb Road

Sarnoff Drive

Stella Road

LOCATION: Lakeside Park, Stella and Sarnoff Roads, Tucson.

SIZE: 14 acres at full capacity, maximum depth 35 feet.

HOURS: Sunrise to 10:30 p.m.

DAILY BAG AND POSSESSION LIMIT: 4 catfish, 4 trout, 4 largemouth bass (**13 INCH MINIMUM**). No limit on bluegill or redear sunfish.

BOATING: Canoes up to 17 feet and boats 14 feet and under are permitted. Electric trolling motors up to 1 horsepower may be used. Gasoline motors prohibited.

COMMENTS: Urban fishing license required. Contains: channel catfish, rainbow trout (in season), redear sunfish, bluegill, and largemouth bass. Boats must be launched manually from western edge of lake. Eastern shore of lake is closed to entry. The 13-inch minimum-length size limit is to protect young bass that feed on small bluegill. (Predators help keep bluegill from overpopulating and stunting.) The goal is to provide good-sized bluegill and legal bass weighting 1 pound or more. Access to parking from Stella Road.

PARK RULES: No campfires or open fires allowed along shoreline. Swimming or wading is prohibited. Dogs or other animals are not allowed in lake. No glass containers. For more information call 791-4873.

SILVERBELL LAKE - Tucson

To Phoenix

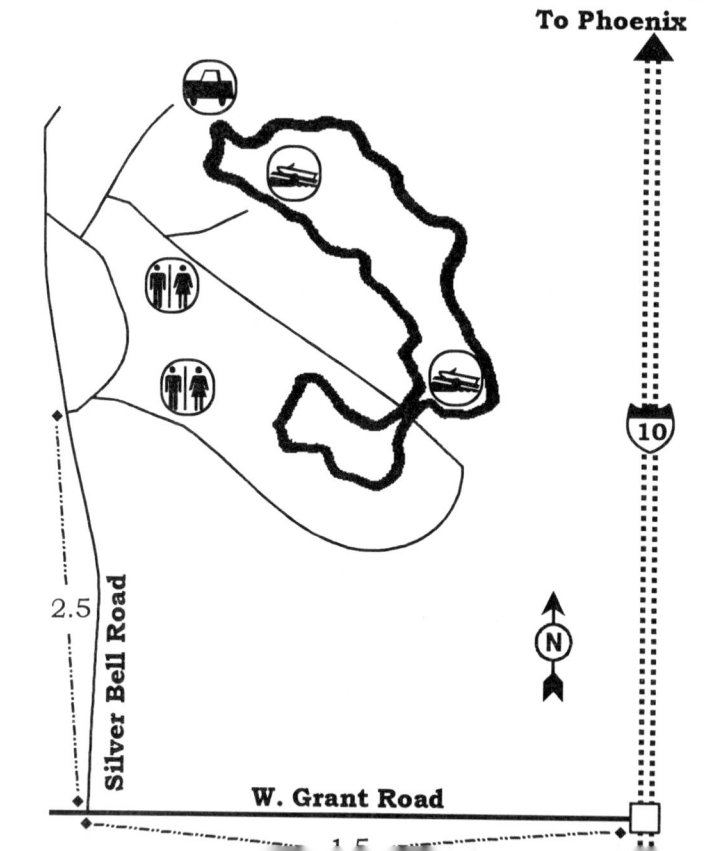

Silver Bell Road

W. Grant Road

LOCATION: Christopher Columbus Park, 4600 North Silverbell Road, between Camino del Cerro and Grant Roads, Tucson.

SIZE: 13 acres, maximum depth 6 feet.

HOURS: Sunrise to 10:30 p.m.

DAILY BAG AND POSSESSION LIMIT: 4 catfish, 4 trout, 4 largemouth bass (**13 INCH MINIMUM**). No limit on bluegill.

BOATING: Canoes up to 17 feet and boats 14 feet and under are permitted. Electric trolling motors up to 1 horsepower may be used. Gasoline motors prohibited.

COMMENTS: Urban fishing license required. Contains: channel catfish, rainbow trout (in season) redear sunfish, bluegill, largemouth bass, and carp. Access is from Silverbell Road.

☐ Arizona's number one Recreation Rule: **SAFETY 1st.**

☐ Arizona is a large state covering 113,900 square miles. There is much to see.

☐ Remember: **The shortest distance between 2 points is pretty boring.**

☐ Arizona's terrain varies significantly from its 70 feet above sea level near Yuma, to 12,633 feet (Humphries Peak) near Flagstaff. The wildlife, weather and flora change dramatically with variations in altitude.

☐ There are six National Forests within Arizona covering 11.2 million acres. They are:

Apache-Sitgreaves National Forest   Kaibab National Forest
Coconino National Forest   Prescott National Forest
Coronado National Forest   Tonto National Forest

☐ There are 20 Indian reservations within Arizona covering 19 million acres. These reservations are home to 14 tribes representing nearly 200,000 people.

☐ There are 15 counties in Arizona each with their distinct historical, climatic, geographical, and cultural atmospheres.

☐ The State of Arizona manages 13 percent of the state's acreage and professionally operates a State Park program. Call their headquarters in Phoenix at **(602) 542-4174** and they'll send you their State Parks booklet.

☐ A consolidated list of addresses and phone numbers of the federal, state, city, county, and tribal jurisdictions governing the recreational lands within Arizona is contained within the 4-times-a-year publication entitled Arizona Great Outdoors. This is a free periodical available throughout the state at many bait and tackle shops, sporting good stores, and park and recreational agencies. It is a very informative periodical servicing Arizona's outdoor enthusiasts. A subscription is also available for a modest fee. Call **(602) 945-6746** for subscription information.

☐ The Bureau of Land Management (BLM), under the U.S. Department of the Interior, manages 12.5 million acres of recreational lands within Arizona. A free camping and vacation planner is available from them by calling **1-800-47SUNNY**. The BLM is also an excellent source of maps and recreational information. Call **(602) 241-5547** and they'll send you some.

☐ If you're interested in fishing, whether a rookie or an expert, pick up a copy of Arizona's Fishing News at over 80 bait and tackle shops within the state. It is published monthly and it's free.

☐ There are in excess of 110,000 boats registered in Arizona.

☐ There are 829 species of fish, amphibians, birds, and mammals resident in Arizona. Many of them are unique to the region.

☐ If you're looking for fishing updates (what's biting, where) call the Arizona Republic's "Press Line" in Phoenix at **271-5656**, then code **3474 (FISH)**. The Arizona Game and Fish Department also operates a fishing hotline at **789-3701**. Both of these are Area Code 602 if you're not in the Phoenix metropolitan area.

FACTS, HINTS, AND RECOMMENDATIONS (Continued)

☐ Camping reservations for National Forest campgrounds (there are more than 140 within Arizona) can be made by calling **1-800-283-CAMP (2267).** There are also more than two dozen campgrounds for primitive camping. Reservations for group campgrounds need to be made with the ranger district in which the campground resides.

☐ National forest campgrounds at higher elevations, which close seasonally, can still be used by the public. The facilities are not maintained, there is no fee, and you must "pack it in - pack it out."

☐ Arizona's Urban Fishing program operates from 12 lakes scattered through Phoenix (4), Tucson (3), Tempe (2), Scottsdale (1), Mesa (1), and Chandler (1). Only a special "Urban Fishing License" is required for those 14 years old and above. Rainbow trout and channel catfish are stocked seasonally. Bluegill and largemouth bass are also contained within these lakes. An excellent brochure detailing the regulations and containing maps and details on each lake is available free at most bait and tackle shops or sporting goods retail stores within the above mentioned cities. This program offers an excellent opportunity to teach children how to fish or for those who elect to remain within these metropolitan areas. Further information can be obtained via the Arizona Game and Fish Department at **(602) 942-3000**.

☐ Christmas trees may be cut for your personal use in most National Forests. There is a specific season and a permit with a modest fee is required. Call any National Forest headquarters for details.

☐ A recent change in Arizona law now permits the use of two poles when fishing. You must be properly licensed to do so. Arizona also now has a "4-month non-resident license." There is also a "lifetime" license for those residents with long-range fishing plans.

☐ The Arizona Game and Fish Department conducts free "Boating Safety" classes throughout the state. Contact their headquarters at **(602) 942-3000** or one of there six regional offices throughout the state for dates and locations. This would be an excellent class for young adults.

☐ Fire wood for camp fires may be gathered (if dead and down) in any of the National Forests. This is typically true of Indian Reservations, but check local regulations. Cutting of fire wood throughout the state requires a permit and may be done only in designated areas. Check with local ranger districts, Indian Reservations, and State Parks for details. Remember: a permit is required for the cutting or removal of any forest products.

☐ The National Forest Service, which operates the six National Forests in Arizona, offers a variety of regional maps. They are superb. There are topographic, planimetric, forest visitor, and wilderness maps. They are all excellent and very inexpensive. Call the headquarters of any of the National Forests to obtain information on acquiring these maps. They may be ordered or picked up. Additionally, local maps of each ranger district within a National Forest are obtainable at the ranger district office at no charge. A polite phone call will also have them sent by mail at no charge.

☐ The Arizona Office of Tourism is another excellent source of recreational information. You may call their office in Phoenix at **(602) 542-TOUR** or stop in at any of the many locations throughout the state marked by the little blue signs "Tourist Information."

☐ If you want to obtain some "immortality" catch a striped bass greater than 6.0 ounces in one of Arizona's inland lakes and you'll hold the state record.

☐ "Operation Game Thief" is a state program intended to assist in compliance with the state's hunting, trapping, and fishing laws. If you observe any illegal "game and fish" violation or suspected violations, call **1-800-352-0700** to report it. You may remain anonymous. There is a reward system associated with this program. Violations on Indian Reservations should be reported to local tribal authorities within the specific jurisdictions.

☐ There is a "new wave" emerging called "non-consumption wildlife use." Activities such as bird watching and wild life photography head line this ecological leaning. Try it, you'll like it.

☐ For the mountain bike enthusiast, the area around Woods Canyon Lake is excellent for your purposes. Contact the Apache-Sitgreaves National Forest at **(602) 289-2471** for details.

☐ For mature or disabled Arizona travelers, an excellent book detailing those outdoor recreation areas best suited for their needs is available from the Arizona State Park system. This book, <u>Access Arizona</u>, details over 70 state parks, regional/community parks, in addition to national parks and monuments. This book is a superb choice for those looking for comprehensive detailed information written in a simple, usable form. Contact the Arizona State Park headquarters in Phoenix at **(602) 542-1996** for information on how to obtain this fine document.

A similar book is available free from the National Forest Service, titled, <u>Recreation Guide to Barrier Free Facilities, Southwestern Forests</u>; it is a 66-page booklet which directly addresses those camping and "day-use" facilities within Arizona and New Mexico's National Forests which contain facilities for those of us who are physically impaired. This booklet specifically details 43 recreation sites with handicapped facilities and also speaks to another 69 recreation sites and their accessibility. To obtain this booklet, contact the headquarters of any of Arizona's six National Forests.

☐ <u>Recreation Sites in Southwestern National Forests</u>, which details camping and other recreations sites in Arizona and New Mexico is available free from the Forest Service. This 70-page pamphlet is comprehensive and very useful. Call the headquarters of the National Forest in either of these two states and ask them to send you a copy.

☐ There are three periodicals which are available free to the public and are very informative to Arizona's sports people. The Arizona Fish and Game Department routinely publishes <u>Wildlife News</u> and it is available at many sporting good stores throughout the state. The <u>Outdoor Almanac</u> is published every other week and is available at any of the 14 POPULAR (Outdoor OutFitters for Less) stores located throughout the state. <u>Outdoor News</u> is published monthly and is also complimentary at many sporting goods stores in Arizona, or it may be had via subscription.

☐ The Desert Botanical Gardens in Phoenix operates a "Wildflower Hotline" during the spring months. It is updated weekly. You can find out what is blooming where by calling **(602) 481-8134**.

☐ If you're interested in being a campground host or maintenance volunteer for the National Forest Service, call any of the 11 National Forests in Arizona or New Mexico.

☐ No state license, tag, or permit is required to hunt or fish on any Indian Reservation in Arizona. However, A license, tag, or permit is required and issued by the reservation. Check with local reservation authorities.

☐ The Arizona Game and Fish Department publishes their <u>Wildlife News Letter</u> every other week. A useful tool for the sports minded. It is issued free of charge to Arizona addresses. Call **(602) 789-3214** to get on their distribution list. Again, there is no charge.

FACTS, HINTS, AND RECOMMENDATIONS (Continued)

☐ Firearms: Shooting is illegal in or within 1/4 mile of a residence, building, camp site, developed recreation site, occupied area or on or across a road or body of water. it is also illegal to discharge a firearm from a vehicle (land or water vehicle). Requirements for water fowl hunting are different. See Migrating Birds Requirements published by the Arizona Fish and Game Department.

☐ Arizona's Wildlife Views, a monthly magazine published by the State Arizona's Game and Fish Department, Information and Education Division is available at any of the Game and Fish Department offices or a variety of sporting good stores across the state. There is a fee for this publication or it may be had by subscription. Call **1-800-777-0015** for further information.

☐ If you're up on the "Rim Area" between Payson and Heber in the summer months, try your hand at gathering some raspberries in Leonard Canyon, just north of Chevelon Canyon Lake. You may even find some elderberries, gooseberries, or strawberries, but raspberries are predominant and plentiful.

☐ If you or an organization you're associated with is interested in the. "Adopt-a-Trail" program, a free handbook detailing the specifics can be obtained by calling **(602) 542-4662**.

☐ If you or an organization you're associated with is interested in the "Adopt-a-Ranch" program, you can call the Arizona Game and Fish Department at **(602) 789-3624** for further information.

☐ Remember, when your children are in or near the water, never let them out of your sight.

☐ Whether a rookie or a progressive expert, the book entitled Fishing Basics will enhance your angling skills. Call **(602) 795-8544** for information on where to obtain it.

☐ The State of Arizona is divided up into eighty (80) hunting management units. Each has its very specific boundaries and is managed relative to who, what, where, when, and how it may be hunted. Details are contained in the Game and Fish Department's Arizona Hunting Regulations brochure available at most retail sporting good stores or through the Game and Fish Department.

☐ Private lands are just that. You must have written or verbal permission from private property owners for use of their legally posted private lands for any purpose, including crossing the lands by foot or vehicle. Remember, when given permission to access private land you are a guest.

☐ The Canyon State Naturists routinely hold two events per month. Given Arizona's climate, nude recreating is going on somewhere in the state year round. Join in if you're so inclined. Membership in the club is preferred.

☐ If you're a "cycler" or "cyclist," there are some excellent publications/guides specific to your style of Arizona recreation. The Canyon Sate Cyclist, published monthly out of Tempe, can be subscribed to by calling **(602) 839-5796**. The Greater Arizona Bicycling Association, publishes Arizona Bicycling out of Tucson. You can subscribe by calling **(602) 885-8807**. Both of these periodicals can be acquired free at the Arizona Department of Tourism on Washington Street in Phoenix.

☐ If you follow the "Hints and Recommendations" contained within this section of the book, you'll have a leg up on most other outdoor recreators. Certainly, you'll be among the best informed.

The San Carlos Apache Indian Reservation sits in east central Arizona and covers greater than 1.5 million acres. The terrain varies from desert altitudes to midsection mountains of pine, juniper, and oak to altitudes of 8000 feet with ponderosa pine, spruce, fir, and aspen forests. The San Carlos Reservation is rugged and natural. It is predominantly a sportsman's domain with its hunting and fishing, but water skiers and pleasure boaters certainly take advantage of the reservation center piece, San Carlos Lake. There are 100-plus lakes, ponds, and tanks, many of which contain trout or warm water species. Facilities and conveniences on the reservation are limited. You'll enjoy yourself much more if you're fully stocked and self-contained. There are fully four seasons of recreation on the San Carlos Reservation and the weather is consistent with the varying altitudes. Summer months in the low lands are hot, hot, hot. The higher altitudes bring cool, fresh pleasure. Access to the various lakes can test your patience, but the quality of the outdoor life is superb. As the terrain varies so does the wildlife. These lands contain bear and mountain lion. Javelina and turkey are plentiful with an abundance of migratory fowl. Again, San Carlos Lake is the jewel of these lands. Its size serves all recreational water users. The San Carlos Apache Tribe has sovereign rights over these lakes and lands and manages them with an earnest concern for the natural environment. Permits and fees are required for any recreational activity on these lands and can be obtained on the reservation or in the surrounding towns. Special rules apply to the users of this reservation and are not restrictive as long as the environment is maintained. A brochure detailing rules and regulations/permits and fees is easily obtained in the surrounding communities where permits are sold. There is no charge for the brochure. There is some excellent adventure to be had on the San Carlos Reservation, but it is asked that you maintain the natural lands.

NOTE: Permit types and fees may change annually.
Please refer to current publication of San Carlos Apache Tribe "Hunting, Fishing, And Outdoor Recreation Commissioner Orders For Non-Tribal Member." This document is available wherever permits are sold.

RECREATION PERMITS AND FEES:

FEES: Individual recreation permit - $5/day per person.

Family recreation permit - $10/day.

The family permit applies to all members of one immediate family (mother, father, and children under 18 years old).

A recreation permit allows the holder to camp, hike, picnic, tour, and generally recreate on the Reservation.

WATERCRAFT PERMITS AND FEES:

Required for anyone (each individual) using any watercraft to include but not limited to any boat, canoe, sailboat, or sailboard.

Note:
☐   Recreation, fishing, and water skiing permits are sold and required separately.

FEES: Daily boating permit - $3.
Annual boating permit - $30.

SAN CARLOS APACHE INDIAN RESERVATION (Continued)

WATER SKIING AND JET SKIING PERMITS AND FEES:

FEES: Daily water skiing and jet skiing permits - $10/person.
Annual water skiing and jet skiing permits - $75/person.

Notes:

☐ All operators and passengers of a boat being used for water skiing must have a water skiing permit.

☐ No water skiing or jet skiing allowed within 400 feet of shore except as detailed in the "Commission Orders."

FISHING PERMITS AND FEES:

FEES: Daily fishing permit - $7.
Annual fishing permit - $75.
Trotline permit - $12/day (includes the privilege of boating).
Daily combination boating/fishing permit - $10.
Annual combination boating/fishing permit - $100.

Notes:

☐ Fishing permits for the Black and Salt Rivers are sold separately.

☐ Live bate may not be possessed or used on Reservation waters except San Carlos and Talkalai Lakes.

☐ A fishing permit is required for all those 12 years or older for taking aquatic wildlife on the San Carlos Reservation.

☐ Fishing permits and trotline permits also allow the holder to camp for the period covered by the permit.

☐ Special bag limits apply - see "Commission Orders" for details.

PERMITS ARE AVAILABLE FROM:

Noline's Country Store
P.O. Box 566
Peridot, AZ 85542
(602) 475-2334

San Carlos Lake Store
HCR 1, Box 24
Peridot, AZ 85542
(602) 475-2756

Tiger Mart
1740 East Ash Street
Globe, AZ 85501
(602) 425-2640

O'Leary's Market
Globe/Miami Highway
Miami, AZ 85501
(602) 425-2540

Tempe Marine
629 West Broadway Road
Mesa, AZ 85202
(602) 844-0165

Circle K (Jack Horn)
1951 East Ash Street
Globe, AZ 85501
(602) 425-5942

Pinky's Bait and Tackle
P.O. Box 1
Pima, AZ 85543
(602) 428-5611

Bob Keen's Store
P.O. Box 295
Fort Thomas, AZ 85536
(602) 485-2261

Outdoor recreation on the 1.6-million-acre White Mountain Indian Reservation is among the best on the continent. Residing in east central Arizona, the elevation is generally at 5000 feet and above. The lakes freeze over in winter and access is difficult due to snow accumulation, but the warmer months bring every bit of beauty into focus. The meadows, lakes, streams, and mountains covered with forests and wild flowers are fantastic. Summer weather is warmish days and cool evenings with frequent thunderstorms in the late afternoons and evenings. Wildlife abounds, from black bear, elk, and deer , to uncountable small ground animals and fowl. As in any natural setting, the normal insects abound also. In general, the area is remote and rugged, but the professional landlord has done a fine job in creating and maintaining access roads. There are 25 primary lakes (18 mentioned within this book) plus 400 or more streams many of which abound with trout, the primary catch of the day. Reservation authorities do a fine job coordinating the stocking. With over 1000 campsites, you can locate yourself as you please. Services and conveniences are accessible along Arizona Highway 260, on the northern edge of the reservation. The White Mountain Apache Tribe has sovereign rights over this fabulous wilderness and manage it with professionalism and strict concerns for the natural environment. Permits and fees are required for any recreational activity on these lands and are easily obtained. Special rules apply while on reservation land, and they are easily understood. A comprehensive pamphlet describing the rules and regulations pertaining to these lands is available at any location selling permits (see below). It's free. There are four seasons of excellent outdoor recreational adventure to be had in these "White Mountains." It is asked that you do all you can to maintain these natural lands.

PERMITS / FEES:

FISHING

				QUALITY WATERS	
Adults:	Yearly Permit	$80.00	Special Fishing	Hurricane Lake (Daily)	$15.00
	Summer Permit	$50.00	Permits:	Christmas Tree Lake (Daily)	$15.00
	(May 28 through September 6)			Bootleg Lake (Daily)	$5.00
	Daily Permit	$5.00		Tonto Lake (Daily)	$5.00
Juvenile:	Yearly Permit	$35.00			
	Summer Permit	$25.00		PERMITS ARE REQUIRED OF	
	(May 28 through September 6)			ANYONE FISHING IN THESE	
	Daily Permit	$2.50		AREAS INCLUDING	
				JUVENILES	

CAMPING

		BOATING PERMITS	
Daily Permit (Per Family)	$6.00	(Valid for lake use only)	
		Yearly Boat Permit	$10.00
		Daily Boat Permit	$2.00

GROUP CAMPING

		MISCELLANEOUS PERMITS	
(Good for 3 nights only)		Daily Winter Use (per family) includes Snowmobile, Cross Country Skiing	$5.00
Up to 25 people	$60.00		
26 to 50 people	$120.00	Outdoor Recreation (per family) includes Picnic, Hiking	$5.00
51 to 75 people	$180.00		

ONE NIGHT GROUP PERMITS 1/2 OF ABOVE. GROUP PERMITS ARE FOR CHURCH AND SCOUTS ONLY

PERMIT DEALERS:

OPEN YEAR ROUND

Game and Fish Dept.	Whiteriver	(602) 338-4385
Pinetop Sporting Goods	Pinetop	(602) 367-5050
Hon Dah Service Station	South of Pinetop	(602) 369-4311
Sunrise Services Station	Sunrise Lake	(602) 735-7335
Salt River Canyon Inn	Salt River Canyon	(602) 367-5126
Tempe Marine	Mesa	(602) 844-0165
Woody's Exxon (Open 24 Hours)	Show Low	(602) 537-4667
Bob's Bargain Barn	Tucson	(602) 325-3409

OPEN DURING THE SUMMER MONTHS ONLY
(Memorial Day through Labor Day)

Horseshoe Lake Boatdock	Horseshoe Lake	No Phone
Reservation Lake Boatdock	Reservation Lake	No Phone
Sunrise Lake Marina	Sunrise Lake	No Phone
Hawley Lake Store	Hawley Lake	(602) 335-7511

NAVAJO NATION

The Navajo Nation sprawls over 16 million acres and crosses into Utah to the north and New Mexico to the west. Most recreation takes place within the Chuska Mountains, along the border with New Mexico. This range is rugged country with pine-covered peaks complete with aspen-ringed meadows and modest lakes. Bear, turkey, deer, and small game are common in this stark natural setting. Of the 18 primary lakes on the reservation, 7 of Arizona's are mentioned within this book. Given its location to population centers, the Navajo Nation's lakes receive relatively little fishing pressure or recreational use. This country offers an unhurried pace on the lands of some fine and gentle people. Recreation is open year round on the Navajo Nation. Access is generally simple and easy just by heading north from I-40 in northeastern Arizona. The tribal headquarters is located in Window Rock, Arizona. Special permits and fees are required for hunting, fishing, camping, back country use, and boating. This sovereign nation maintains special rules and regulations for the use of its natural resources. Permits, fees and details of the area's regulations are obtainable as described below.

FISHING/SMALL GAME AND BOATING PERMITS

Season non-Navajo Fishing	$26.00	One-day Fishing	$5.00
Season non-Navajo Small Game	$24.00	Three-day Fishing	$10.00
Season-non Navajo Fishing and Small Game	$34.00	Second Rod Validation	$5.00
		Game Bird Validation	$5.00

All persons 12 year of age and older must possess a Navajo Nation permit to fish in Navajo waters, Season permits valid from January 1 through December 31

Boating Permit $15.00 annually

Navajo Nation Fish and Wildlife Department (602) 871-6451

Permits are available from:

CSWTA, Inc. Environ. Consult
P.O. Box 790
Tuba City, AZ 86045

Navajo Fish and Wildlife
P.O. Box 1480
Window Rock, AZ 86515

Kayenta T. P
P.O. Box 175
Kayenta, AZ 86033

Red Barn Trading Post
P.O. Box 245
Sanders, AZ 86512-0245

Lake Store Wheatfields
P.O. Box 2309
Window Rock, AZ 86515

Wal-Mart Store
700 Mikes Pike Blvd.
Winslow, AZ 86047

CAMPING HIKING AND BACK COUNTRY PERMITS

Camping: $2/person/night

Hiking and Back Country Use:
$5/person
$10 for 2 to 10 people
$20/groups of 11 or more

Permits are available from:
Navajo Nation Parks and Recreation Department
P.O. Box 308
Window Rock, Arizona 86515
(602) 871-4941

Camping permits are also available at some camping locations

For additional information contact:
Navajo Tourism Department
P.O. Box 663
Window Rock, Arizona 86515
(602) 871-7381

The Arizona State Park system touts more than 20 State Parks, of which nearly one half are water based. There are state parks located on the Colorado and Verde Rivers, in addition to the five inland lake-based units. Arizona lake-based state parks include Alamo, Lyman, Patagonia, Fool Hollow, Roper, and Dankworth Pond. You may review these individually in this book under those names. Other than Dankworth Pond, which is a day-use only facility located adjacent to Roper Lake State Park, the other five lake-based parks offer a full compliment of facilities and conveniences. Recreational opportunities at these lake-based state parks include picnicking, swimming, power boating, fishing, water skiing, jet skiing, sailing, sail boarding, canoeing, hiking, rock hounding, boat camping, tent/trailer camping, RVing, bird watching, and of course napping. Each lake-based park has its own peculiarities, so please check each park individually for specifics.

The facilities and conveniences of the Arizona State Park system are among the finest within Arizona. The parks are well equipped and have very courteous and helpful staff. The lake-based parks are located within the southern 2/3rds of the state and are at elevations ranging from 1250 to 6000 feet. The terrain and climates are consistent with these elevations. Arizona's state parks are open year round. The lakes within these parks are operated as both warm and/or cold water fisheries. The non-aquatic wildlife surrounding these lakes is plentiful and varied.

The Arizona State Park System also operates nearly a dozen other facilities which include desert, historical, and educational parks.

There are fees associated with using the Arizona State Park System. As of the printing of this book, they are as follows:

	Day Use	Camping	Camping with Hookups (Electric and Water)	Group Camping
Roper Lake State Park	$3.00	$7.00	$10.00	No
Dankworth Pond	$3.00	N/A	N/A	N/A
Patagonia Lake State Park	$5.00	$7.00	$12.00	Yes
Alamo Lake State Park	$3.00	$7.00	$10.00	Yes
Lyman Lake State Park	$3.00	$7.00	$10.00	Yes
Fool Hollow Park	$3.00	$7.00	$12.00	No

☐ Rates are per vehicle, per day
☐ Boat launching is included in above fees
☐ Group camping reservations recommended
☐ Reservations not accepted for individual camping
☐ Annual day use fee is $40
  (access to all Arizona Parks)

NOTE: **The Arizona State Park System distributes four fine outdoor/recreation guides as follows:**

- **Arizona Wildlife Viewing Guide**
- **Arizona's River and Streams Guide**
- **Access Arizona (dedicated to disables and mature travelers)**
- **Arizona Trails Guide**

There is a fee for each book. Call the Arizona State Park system for availability (602) 542-4174.

NATIONAL FORESTS

The National Forest Service, under the U.S. Department of Agriculture is responsible for managing 11 million acres or 15 percent of Arizona's land. The National Forest Service is separate and distinct from the National Park Services and Bureau of Land Management, both under the U.S. Department of Interior. These 11 million acres cover most of Arizona's forested land. There are six National Forests within Arizona. Not all National Forests within Arizona are contiguous. Some have as many as 12 divisions, each geographically separate. Each National Forest is managed separately and has between three and six "Ranger Districts" who in turn manage their own immediate lands and recreation sites. Within each of these National Forests are "wilderness areas," totaling 36. There is also one "primitive area." These "wilderness areas" are defined as "....an area where the earth and its community of life are untrammeled by man, where man himself is a visitor who does not remain." The Forest Service is chartered to manage the wilderness areas ".... as a resource in which naturalness is perpetuated."

Essentially all of the developed Forest Service recreation areas are outside of wilderness areas. As you can see from the chart on the next page, there are nearly 300 developed recreation sites within Arizona's 6 National Forests and you can camp at more than 170 of them. Of those 300, you can access a stream, river or lake for water recreation at more than half of them. Many of these National Forests' recreation sites are now partially "accessible," thus serving those mature and physically impaired travelers.

The National Forests within Arizona are marked by a wide range of landscapes, ranging from alpine peaks to colorful mesas to dramatic canyons to rolling deserts.

In addition to finding solitude, you may also participate in any of the following on Forest Service lands (excluding wilderness areas, primitive areas, and local regulations): horseback riding, rock hounding, hunting, fishing, rock climbing, trapping, tobogganing, sledding, skiing, cross-country skiing, snowmobiling, picnicking, camping, water skiing, jet skiing, mountain biking, hiking, photography, wind surfing, sailing, rafting, canoeing, swimming, bird watching, boating, boat camping, ATV/ACTing, and napping. As you can see, there is wide range of recreational opportunities on the National Forests within Arizona.

The following narrative is intended to highlight some of the regulations and hints for recreating in Forest Service land but should not be considered comprehensive. Details are obtainable from each ranger district within each National Forest.

CAMPING:

There are in excess of 3300 developed camp sites (individual and group) within the nationa forests contained within Arizona. In general, you can camp nearly anywhere within a National Forest, but again there are general and local regulations. Developed camp sites with drinking water require a fee ranging from $4 to $12 per night/site. The $12/night is for RV hookups. Private concessions are licensed by the Forest Service and operate facilities to include marinas, lodges, cabins, stores, campgrounds, RV parks, and restaurants. You may contact them directly for information on their services. There are numerous group campgrounds which can accommodate up to 100 people each. These group camp sites require reservations. Reservations for individual campsites can be made by calling 1-800-283-CAMP. There is a fee charged for the reservation service in addition to the site fee. Group campground reservations are generally made through the local ranger district, but some of the six National Forests use the same system as for individual camp sites. Call the (800) number first to see if they make reservations for the particular group campground you've selected.

WATER RECREATION:

Use of the lakes, streams, or rivers contained within the National Forests is managed by the State of Arizona Game and Fish Department. To hunt, trap, fish, or boat on any of the National Forest waters requires licensing by the state.

WILDERNESS AREA:

No fee or permit is required to access the National Forest Wilderness Areas. There are no developed facilities within wilderness areas. The primary rules for wilderness area use are: Absolutely no vehicular traffic (motorized or not) allowed. Pets must be on a leash at all times. Pack out all you carry in. (Leave no trace of your presence.) Disturb nothing, remove nothing. The specific ranger district responsible for a particular wilderness area should always be consulted for any special considerations.

FEES:

Other than the camping fees discussed above, there are generally no fees charged for "day-use" facilities.

SEASON OF USE:

Seasonal use of National Forest recreation sites vary between each other and from year to year. Weather, road or site repair and agency funding can alter both opening and closing dates. Always check with the local ranger district for exact dates.

FULL ACCESS:

Full access to all public lands and facilities, and equal opportunity to use them are guaranteed to all persons regardless of race, color, national origin, age, sex, religion, physical handicap, or marital status. If you feel you have been denied any benefits on the grounds, write directly to the Secretary of Agriculture, Washington, DC. 20250.

National Forest Headquarters' Telephone #	# of Ranger Districts	Acres	Elevation Range	# Day-Use Sites	# Sites with Camping	# of Developed Camp sites	# With Access to Lake, Stream, or River
Apache-Sitgreaves 1-602-333-4301	6	2 million	5,000 - 11,500	19	38	1010	46
Coconino 1-602-556-7400	6	1.8 million	3,500 - 12,600	16	23	520	26
Coronado 1-602-670-6438	5	1.7 million	3,000 - 10,700	24	31	565	16
Kaibab 1-602-635-2681	4	1.5 million	3,000 - 10,400	22	9	370	4
Prescott 1-602-771-4700	3	1.2 million	3,000 - 8,000	11	17	235	9
Tonto 1-602-225-5200	6	2.9 million	1,300 - 7,900	23	55	660	56

BOAT MOTOR RESTRICTIONS

There are various restrictions on the size of boat motor which may be used on any particular lake in Arizona. Below are listed those lakes which have no motor restrictions and those that are limited to eight or ten horse power. All other lakes contained within this book are limited to a single electric trolling motor. There are two lakes which allow no motorized watercraft at all. See below. Consult local authorities if questions arise.

A. No motor restrictions (any horse power):

Alamo Lake	Horseshoe Lake	McHood Lake	San Carlos Lake
Apache Lake	Long Lake	Mormon Lake	Saguaro Lake
Bartlett Lake	Lower Lake Mary	Patagonia Lake	Soldier Annex
Canyon Lake	Lyman Lake	Pleasant Lake	Upper Lake Mary
Cholla Lake	Many Farms Lake	Roosevelt Lake	Watson Lake

B. Motor restrictions to a maximum of eight horse power:

Ashurst Lake	Chevelon Canyon	Kinnikinick Lake	Rainbow Lake
Big Lake	Lake	Luna Lake	Show Low Lake
Blue Ridge Reservoir	Crescent Lake	Mexican Hay Lake	Willow Springs Lake
Cataract Lake	Fool Hollow Lake	Parker Canyon Lake	
	Kaibab Lake		

C. Motor restrictions to a maximum of ten horse power:

Sunrise Lake

D. Watercraft are prohibited on Rose Canyon Lake, and Snow Flat Lake.

E. Watercraft are prohibited from entering the following waters during the dates designated.

1. The posted portion of Luna Lake from April 1 through July 31.
2. The posted portions of Alamo Lake from December 1 to the end of waterfowl season.
3. The posted portions of the Tonto Arm of Roosevelt Lake from November 15 through February 15.
4. The posted portions of Becker Lake from April 1 through July 31.

The fish listed below are common in these waters. Because water conditions change rapidly from season to season or within a year, please contact the responsible agency when planning your fishing trip. This list is an alphabetized list and the order in which they appear has nothing to do with the likelihood that you will catch that specific fish. For further information or details, contact the main office of the Arizona Game and Fish Department at (602) 942-3000. You may also contact any of the six regional Arizona Game and Fish Departments located throughout the state by looking them up in your local telephone directory. For real-time fishing information, you may call either of the two hotlines suggested in the "Facts, Hints, and Recommendations" section of this book.

Apache Trout -- Christmas Tree, Hurricane

Bluegill -- (sunfish) Apache, Arivaca, Bartlett, Lake Pleasant, Many Farms, Roper, Saguaro

Carp -- Apache, Bartlett, Canyon, Horseshoe, Lake Pleasant, Roosevelt, Saguaro, San Carlos

Crappie -- Bartlett, Lake Pleasant, Patagonia, Pena Blanca, Roosevelt, Roper, San Carlos

Catfish -- Alamo, Bartlett, Cholla, Cooley, Fool Hollow, George's, Horseshoe, Lyman, Many Farms, McHood Park Lake, Nash Tank, Parker Canyon, Pena Blanca, Patagonia, Red Lake, Roosevelt, Round Rock Reservoir, San Carlos, Seneca, Show Low, Talkalai, Whipple

Grayling -- Lee Valley Lake

Largemouth Bass -- Alamo, Apache, Arivaca, Bartlett, Canyon, Cataract, Cholla, Cooley, Fool Hollow, George's Lake, Horseshoe, Long, Lower Lake Mary, Lyman, Many Farms, McHood Park, Parker Canyon, Patagonia, Pena Blanca, Red, Roosevelt, Roper, Saguaro, San Carlos, Scott's Reservoir, Show Low, Talkalai, Upper Goldwater Lake, Whipple, Woodland, Woods Canyon

Northern Pike -- Lower Lake Mary, Stoneman, Upper Lake Mary

Perch -- Lyman, Stoneman

Smallmouth Bass -- Apache, Bootleg Lake, Roosevelt, Show Low

Trout -- A-1 Lake, Ackre, Antelope, Apache, Ashurst, Bear Canyon, Becker, Big Lake, Black Canyon, Blue Ridge Reservoir, Bog Tank, Bootleg, Chaparral, Chevelon Canyon, Concho, Crescent, Cyclone, Dog Town Reservoir, Drift Fence, Hawley/Earl Park Lakes, Horseshoe Cienega, Hulsey, J.D. Dam Lake, Kaibab, Kinnikinick, Knoll, Lake Sierra Blanca, Lee Valley Lake, Little Hell's Canyon Lake, Long, Luna, Lyman, Marshall, McHood Park Lake, Mexican Hay, Nelson Reservoir, Pacheta, Parker Canyon, Patagonia, Pena Blanca, Point of Pines, Reservation, Riggs Flat, Roper, Scott's Reservoir, Seneca, Show Low, Shush Be Tou, Shush Be Zahze, Sunrise, Tonto, Trout, Tsaile, Tunnel/Bunch & River Reservoir, Wheatfields, White Horse, Willows Springs, Woodland Reservoir, Woods Canyon,

Walleye -- Apache, Canyon, Lower Lake Mary, Show Low, Upper Lake Mary

Arizona Interstate Mileage

	Bisbee	Casa Grande	Coolidge	Cottonwood	Douglas	Flagstaff	Florence	Globe	Holbrook	Mesa	Miami	Nogales	Page	Payson	Phoenix	Prescott	Safford	St. Johns	Sedona	Show Low	Sierra Vista	Springerville	Tombstone	Tuba City	Tucson	Wickenburg	Williams	Winkelman	Winslow	Yuma
Bisbee	◆	161	161	311	24	351	163	200	335	201	206	89	482	276	205	307	121	332	324	287	33	334	24	426	93	263	383	165	368	331
Casa Grande	161	◆	21	150	185	191	34	89	207	32	82	131	322	117	45	147	165	220	164	175	148	217	138	266	68	103	203	95	201	172
Coolidge	161	21	◆	157	185	198	9	68	204	41	61	131	330	119	52	154	144	201	171	156	147	196	137	281	67	110	228	71	208	193
Cottonwood	311	150	157	◆	335	48	166	172	139	121	175	280	179	72	105	41	250	196	19	163	296	218	286	127	216	101	80	196	105	287
Douglas	24	185	185	335	◆	374	188	200	333	226	231	113	507	282	229	331	123	321	349	285	57	328	48	455	118	287	406	189	367	355
Flagstaff	351	191	198	48	374	◆	207	173	91	161	194	321	132	91	146	87	250	149	28	139	337	182	327	80	257	150	32	209	58	316
Florence	163	34	9	166	188	207	◆	56	191	49	48	134	337	127	61	163	133	188	180	143	150	185	140	285	70	119	238	58	208	204
Globe	200	89	68	172	200	173	56	◆	135	72	7	171	365	82	87	189	77	132	142	87	187	130	177	254	107	145	205	36	168	269
Holbrook	335	207	204	139	333	91	191	135	◆	175	142	303	212	98	221	174	212	58	120	48	320	84	310	162	240	279	123	170	33	404
Mesa	201	32	41	121	226	161	49	72	175	◆	65	169	293	78	15	117	149	204	135	159	188	202	178	236	108	73	193	75	189	197
Miami	206	82	61	175	231	194	48	7	142	65	◆	177	358	83	80	182	84	139	193	94	193	137	183	225	113	138	228	43	175	262
Nogales	89	131	131	280	113	321	134	171	303	169	177	◆	453	247	175	277	154	301	294	255	65	299	71	396	64	233	353	135	336	302
Page	482	322	330	179	507	132	337	365	212	292	358	453	◆	233	278	231	421	269	160	259	469	295	459	77	389	288	164	358	179	448
Payson	276	117	119	72	282	91	127	82	98	78	83	247	223	◆	93	178	159	135	119	90	263	136	253	171	183	151	123	118	91	275
Phoenix	205	45	52	105	229	146	61	87	221	15	80	175	278	93	◆	102	164	219	119	174	191	217	181	221	111	58	169	90	204	182
Prescott	307	147	154	41	331	87	163	189	174	117	182	277	231	178	102	◆	266	236	60	226	293	273	283	162	213	61	657	192	145	216
Safford	131	165	144	250	123	250	133	77	212	149	84	154	421	159	164	266	◆	198	283	164	117	205	108	329	126	222	282	112	245	364
St. Johns	332	220	201	196	321	149	188	132	58	204	139	301	269	135	219	236	198	◆	177	45	317	26	309	222	237	277	181	167	91	401
Sedona	324	164	171	19	349	28	180	142	120	135	193	294	160	119	119	60	283	177	◆	175	310	220	300	108	230	120	60	204	86	301
Show Low	287	175	156	163	285	139	143	87	48	159	94	255	259	980	174	226	164	45	175	◆	274	43	264	219	192	232	171	122	81	346
Sierra Vista	33	148	147	296	57	337	150	187	320	188	193	65	469	263	191	293	117	317	310	274	◆	317	33	415	80	249	368	150	353	318
Springerville	334	217	196	218	328	182	185	130	84	202	137	299	295	136	217	273	205	26	220	43	317	◆	310	254	235	275	206	166	116	399
Tombstone	24	138	137	286	48	327	140	177	310	178	183	71	459	253	181	283	108	309	300	264	33	310	◆	405	70	239	350	141	343	307
Tuba City	426	266	281	127	455	80	285	254	162	236	225	396	77	171	221	162	329	222	108	219	415	254	405	◆	335	222	112	290	129	403
Tucson	93	68	67	216	118	257	70	107	240	108	113	64	389	183	111	213	26	237	230	192	80	235	70	335	◆	169	280	71	273	238
Wickenburg	263	103	110	101	287	150	119	145	279	73	138	233	288	151	58	61	222	277	120	232	249	275	239	222	169	◆	128	148	208	172
Williams	383	203	228	80	406	32	238	205	123	193	228	353	164	123	169	67	282	181	60	171	368	206	350	112	280	128	◆	241	90	283
Winkelman	165	95	71	196	189	209	58	36	170	75	43	135	258	118	90	192	112	167	204	122	150	166	141	290	71	148	241	◆	201	268
Winslow	368	201	208	105	367	58	208	168	33	189	175	336	179	91	204	145	245	91	86	81	353	116	343	129	273	208	90	201	◆	376
Yuma	331	172	193	287	355	316	204	269	404	197	262	302	448	275	182	216	364	401	301	346	318	399	307	403	238	172	283	268	376	◆

Mileage information compiled by the Travel and Facilities Branch of the Arizona Department of Transportation and Planning.